Transformers for Machine Learning

Chapman & Hall/CRC Machine Learning & Pattern Recognition

For more information on this series please visit: https://www.routledge.com/Chapman--Hall CRC-Machine-Learning--Pattern-Recognition/book-series/CRCMACLEAPAT

Transformers for Machine Learning

A Deep Dive

Uday Kamath
Kenneth L. Graham
Wael Emara

CRC Press
Taylor & Francis Group
Boca Raton London New York

CRC Press is an imprint of the
Taylor & Francis Group, an **informa** business
A CHAPMAN & HALL BOOK

First edition published 2022
by CRC Press
6000 Broken Sound Parkway NW, Suite 300, Boca Raton, FL 33487-2742

and by CRC Press
4 Park Square, Milton Park, Abingdon, Oxon, OX14 4RN

CRC Press is an imprint of Taylor & Francis Group, LLC

Library of Congress Cataloging-in-Publication Data

Names: Kamath, Uday, author.
Title: Transformers for machine learning : a deep dive / Uday Kamath, Kenneth L. Graham, Wael Emara.
Description: First edition. | Boca Raton : CRC Press, 2022. | Includes bibliographical references and index.
Identifiers: LCCN 2021059529 | ISBN 9780367771652 (hardback) | ISBN 9780367767341 (paperback) | ISBN 9781003170082 (ebook)
Subjects: LCSH: Neural networks (Computer science). | Computational intelligence. | Machine learning.
Classification: LCC QA76.87 .K354 2022 | DDC 006.3/2--dc23/eng/20220218
LC record available at https://lccn.loc.gov/2021059529

ISBN: 978-0-367-77165-2 (hbk)
ISBN: 978-0-367-76734-1 (pbk)
ISBN: 978-1-003-17008-2 (ebk)

DOI: 10.1201/9781003170082

Typeset in Latin Modern font
by KnowledgeWorks Global Ltd.

Publisher's note: This book has been prepared from camera-ready copy provided by the authors.

To all the researchers and frontline COVID workers for their extraordinary service.
– Uday Kamath, Kenneth L. Graham, and Wael Emara

To my parents Krishna and Bharathi, my wife Pratibha, the kids Aaroh and Brandy, my family and friends for their support.
–Uday Kamath

To my wife Alyson, to my mother, my in-laws, my family and friends, thank you for the support and your willingness to sacrifice your time with me.
–Kenneth L. Graham

To my wife Noha, my parents Ali and Zainab, my sister Wesam, my extended family and friends, thank you all for being there for me all the time.
–Wael Emara

Contents

Foreword

Renowned AI pioneer and Nobel laureate Herbert Simon underscored "attention" as the most valuable resource of the information economy, as necessary to allocate attention efficiently among the overabundance of information resources. Having written the foundational paper on meaning-aware AI and recently having served as MIT-Princeton-USAF-AFRL AI Faculty-SME, I had the privilege of publishing by invitation in the same journal's special issue of ASQ, and of being the Malcolm Baldrige National Quality Award administrator, as well as being ranked along with Dr. Simon in the same global academic citation impact studies.

Given the above background, I am thrilled to share with you the most thorough and up-to-date compendium of research, practices, case studies, and applications available today that can provide the best ROI on the latest AI technological advances on transformers inspired by the paper, "Attention is All You Need." Since Google introduced transformer architecture in 2017, transformers have provided exponential improvements in context-focused realization toward meaning-aware AI as deep (neural network) learning models based upon attention mechanisms such as dot-product attention and multi-head attention. Resulting advances in enhanced parallel processing of sequential data have made efficient context sensitive and hence more "meaningful" for ever-larger datasets and much more feasible than earlier.

Covering the latest advances in neural network architectures related to transformers spanning applications such as Natural Language Processing (NLP), speech recognition, time series analysis, and computer vision and domain-specific models spanning science, medicine, and finance, the book aims to meet the theoretical, research, application, and practical needs across academia and industry for multiple audiences including postgraduate students and researchers, undergraduate students, industry practitioners, and professionals. The book rounds off its theory-driven applied and practical coverage with hands-on case studies with focus on AI explainability, an increasingly important theme in practice imposed by greater focus on issues such as ethical AI and trustable AI.

– Dr. Yogesh Malhotra
Founding Chairman and CEO
U.S. Venture Capital and Private Equity Firm
Global Risk Management Network LLC
scientist
www.yogeshmalhotra.com

Preface

WHY THIS BOOK?

Since 2012 deep learning architectures have started to dominate the machine learning field. However, most of the breakthroughs were in computer vision applications. The main driver of that success was convolutional neural network (CNN) architecture. The efficiency and parallelization of CNN have allowed computer vision architectures to pre-train on enormous data which proved to be a key factor in their success. For years afterward natural language processing (NLP) applications did not see much impact from the new deep learning revolution. Traditional sequence modeling architectures, such as recurrent neural networks (RNNs) and long short-term memory (LSTM), have been used for NLP applications. The sequential nature of such architectures has limited the possibilities to train on the same scale of data that showed value for computer vision.

In 2017 Google introduced the transformer architecture to process sequential data with much more parallelization. Such architecture allowed efficient training on much larger datasets than was possible before. This allowed transformers to revolutionize the NLP field the same way CNN had to computer vision.

Transformers are now becoming the core part of many neural architectures employed in a wide range of applications such as NLP, speech recognition, time series, and computer vision. OpenAI uses transformers in their GPT2/GPT3, which has state-of-the-art performances levels in various NLP tasks. DeepMind's AlphaStar program, which defeated a top professional Starcraft player, also uses transformer architecture. Transformers have gone through many adaptations and alterations, resulting in newer techniques and methods. There is no single book that captures the basics and various changes to the transformers in one place.

This book acts as a unique resource for providing data scientists and researchers (academic and industry) with

- A comprehensive reference book for detailed explanations for every algorithm and technique related to transformers.

- Over 60 transformer architectures covered in a comprehensive manner.

- A book for understanding how to apply the transformer techniques in different NLP applications, speech, time series, and computer vision.

- Practical tips and tricks for each architecture and how to use it in the real world.

- Hands-on case studies providing practical insights to real-world scenarios in diverse topics such as machine translation, topic mining, zero-shot multilingual classification, sentiment analysis, automatic speech recognition, and text classification/categorization are covered in sufficient detail from the task, process, and analysis perspective, all ready to run in Google Colab.

WHO IS THIS BOOK WRITTEN FOR?

The theoretical explanations of the state-of-the-art transformer architectures will appeal to postgraduate students and researchers (academic and industry) as it will provide a single-entry point with deep discussions of a quickly moving field. The practical hands-on case studies and code will appeal to undergraduate students, practitioners, and professionals as it allows for quick experimentation and lowers the barrier to entry into the field.

Transformers are already a cornerstone for NLP deep learning architectures. They are also rapidly employed in other applications such as computer vision and audio. Any course on neural networks, deep learning, or artificial intelligence must delve into discussing transformers as a key state-of-the-art architecture. The book can act as a reference for readers, to brush up on specific pieces of their understanding, or as a way to explore the uses of the transformer for specific challenges. We aim for the book to be a resource to refer back to multiple times, to gain insight and use as readers are faced with different challenges or when lacking understanding.

WHAT THIS BOOK COVERS

This book takes an in-depth approach to presenting the fundamentals of transformers through mathematical theory and practical use cases.

A brief description of each chapter is given below.

1. Chapter 1 will introduce readers to transformers from the timeline, history, and its impact on the academic and industrial world. We will then lay out a complete roadmap based on the taxonomy and how each chapter renders from the theory, practice, and application perspective. The chapter then proceeds with a comprehensive discussion on practical aspects such as resources, tools, books, and courses that will be employed in other chapters.

2. Chapter 2 starts by introducing the sequence-to-sequence models and their limitations. The chapter then lays out various building blocks of transformers such as attention, multi-headed attention, positional encodings, residual connections, and encoder-decoder frameworks in a step-by-step manner. All these functional units get detailed treatment from a theoretical and practical perspectives for the readers to get a complete handle on the topic. Finally, a real-world case study using transformers for machine translation tasks showing the operative aspects concludes the chapter.

3. The advent of BERT has revolutionized the field of natural language processing (NLP) and helped to get close to human-level performance in many conventionally challenging tasks. Chapter 3 introduces the details of the BERT architecture and how it is pre-trained and fine-tuned for classical NLP tasks such as single/pair text classification, token tagging, and question answering. The chapter also discusses the field of BERTology, which is research related to the inner workings of BERT and how it processes and analyzes text and information. Finally, the chapter introduces some deep learning architectures that modify BERT for more efficiency (e.g., RoBERTa) and other types of NLP applications (e.g., NLP for tabular data—TaBERT). The chapter concludes with real-world case studies on using BERT for sentiment classification and topic modeling applications.

4. Multilingual transfer learning is an area where transformer architectures have significantly impacted the field of machine learning. Chapter 4 introduces an overview of transformer-based

multilingual architectures and how cross-lingual transfer learning is pre-trained and fine-tuned for NLP tasks. The chapter also provides an overview of the state-of-the-art benchmarks used for multilingual NLP. The chapter further provides some insights into the research and techniques identifying the factors affecting cross-lingual and zero-shot transfer learning in NLP. Finally, a real-world case study of using multilingual universal sentence encoders for zero-shot cross-lingual sentiment classification is presented.

5. In Chapter 5 we discuss various modifications made to the standard transformer architecture to tackle longer sequences with limited memory, to build transformer models that are faster and of higher quality, and that perform better on text generation and summarization. We also discuss the key differences between the model architectures and approaches that are centered around key ideas such as knowledge distillation and making computations more efficient by reducing attention mechanism complexity. This chapter includes a case study that uses a pre-trained transformer model for sentiment classification, including a look at the contents of the model's multi-head attention mechanisms.

6. Since BERT, many flavors of pre-trained models have been made available across different domains, providing models that can be fine-tuned to domain-specific data across science, medicine, and finance. In addition, language-specific pre-trained models offer increasingly competitive results on downstream language specific tasks. In Chapter 6, we discuss the pre-trained models that are available, showing their benefits and applications to specific domains such as computer vision, speech, time series, and text. This chapter includes a case study that compares the performance of three transformer-based automatic speech recognition models.

7. There is a need to understand the models from an explainability standpoint in many critical applications and given the black-box nature of transformers-based models. In Chapter 7, we will cover the traits of the models that address explainability, related areas that impact explainability, the taxonomy of explainable methods applied to the transformer-based and attention-based systems, and finally, a detailed case study in the electronic health record systems using transformers with different explainable techniques to become more practical.

Authors

Uday Kamath has spent more than two decades developing analytics products and combines this experience with learning in statistics, optimization, machine learning, bioinformatics, and evolutionary computing. He has contributed to many journals, conferences, and books, is the author of *XAI: An Introduction to Interpretable XAI, Deep Learning for NLP and Speech Recognition, Mastering Java Machine Learning, and Machine Learning: End-to-End Guide for Java Developers.* He held many senior roles: chief analytics officer for Digital Reasoning, advisor for Falkonry, and chief data scientist for BAE Systems Applied Intelligence. Dr. Kamath has many patents and has built commercial products using AI in domains such as compliance, cybersecurity, financial crime, and bioinformatics. He currently works as the chief analytics officer for Smarsh. He is responsible for data science, research of analytical products employing deep learning, transformers, explainable AI, and modern techniques in speech and text for the financial domain and healthcare.

Kenneth L. Graham has two decades experience solving quantitative problems in multiple domains, including Monte Carlo simulation, NLP, anomaly detection, cybersecurity, and behavioral profiling. For the past ten years, he has focused on building scalable solutions in NLP for government and industry, including entity coreference resolution, text classification, active learning, automatic speech recognition, and temporal normalization. He currently works at AppFolio as a senior machine learning engineer. Dr. Graham has five patents for his work in natural language processing, seven research publications, and a PhD in condensed matter physics.

Wael Emara has two decades of experience in academia and industry. He has a PhD in computer engineering and computer science with emphasis on machine learning and artificial intelligence. His technical background and research spans signal and image processing, computer vision, medical imaging, social media analytics, machine learning, and natural language processing. Dr. Emara has contributed to many peer-reviewed publications in various machine learning topics and he is active in the technical community in the greater New York area. He currently works as a principal data scientist at Smarsh, Inc. for Digital Reasoning where he is doing research on state-of-the-art artificial intelligence NLP systems.

Contributors

Krishna Choppella
BAE Systems AI
Toronto, Canada

Mitch Naylor
Smarsh, Inc.
Nashville, Tennessee

Vedant Vajre
Stone Bridge High School
Ashburn, Virginia

## CHAPTER 1

Deep Learning and Transformers: An Introduction

TRANSFORMERS are deep learning models that have achieved state-of-the-art performance in several fields such as natural language processing, computer vision, and speech recognition. Indeed, the massive surge of recently proposed transformer model variants has meant researchers and practitioners alike find it challenging to keep pace. In this chapter, we provide a brief history of diverse research directly or indirectly connected to the innovation of transformers. Next, we discuss a taxonomy based on changes in the architecture for efficiency in computation, memory, applications, etc., which can help navigate the complex innovation space. Finally, we provide resources in tools, libraries, books, and online courses that the readers can benefit from in their pursuit.

1.1 DEEP LEARNING: A HISTORIC PERSPECTIVE

In the early 1940s, S. McCulloch and W. Pitts, using a simple electrical circuit called a "threshold logic unit", simulated intelligent behavior by emulating how the brain works [179]. The simple model had the first neuron with inputs and outputs that would generate an output 0 when the "weighted sum" was below a threshold and 1 otherwise, which later became the basis of all the neural architectures. The weights were not learned but adjusted. In his book *The Organization of Behaviour* (1949), Donald Hebb laid the foundation of complex neural processing

DOI: 10.1201/9781003170082-1

by proposing how neural pathways can have multiple neurons firing and strengthening over time [108]. Frank Rosenblatt, in his seminal work, extended the McCulloch–Pitts neuron, referring to it as the "Mark I Perceptron"; given the inputs, it generated outputs using linear thresholding logic [212].

The weights in the perceptron were "learned" by repeatedly passing the inputs and reducing the difference between the predicted output and the desired output, thus giving birth to the basic neural learning algorithm. Marvin Minsky and Seymour Papert later published the book *Perceptrons* which revealed the limitations of perceptrons in learning the simple exclusive-or function (XOR) and thus prompting the so-called The First AI Winter [186].

John Hopfield introduced "Hopfield Networks", one of the first recurrent neural networks (RNNs) that serve as a content-addressable memory system [117].

In 1986, David Rumelhart, Geoff Hinton, and Ronald Williams published the seminal work "Learning representations by back-propagating errors" [217]. Their work confirms how a multi-layered neural network using many "hidden" layers can overcome the weakness of perceptrons in learning complex patterns with relatively simple training procedures. The building blocks for this work had been laid down by various research over the years by S. Linnainmaa, P. Werbos, K. Fukushima, D. Parker, and Y. LeCun [164, 267, 91, 196, 149].

LeCun et al., through their research and implementation, led to the first widespread application of neural networks to recognize the handwritten digits used by the U.S. Postal Service [150]. This work is a critical milestone in deep learning history, proving the utility of convolution operations and weight sharing in learning the features in computer vision.

Backpropagation, the key optimization technique, encountered a number of issues such as vanishing gradients, exploding gradients, and the inability to learn long-term information, to name a few [115]. Hochreiter and Schmidhuber, in their work, "Long short-term memory (LSTM)" architecture, demonstrated how issues with long-term dependencies could overcome shortcomings of backpropagation over time [116].

Hinton et al. published a breakthrough paper in 2006 titled "A fast learning algorithm for deep belief nets"; it was one of the reasons for the resurgence of deep learning [113]. The research highlighted the effectiveness of layer-by-layer training using unsupervised methods followed by supervised "fine-tuning" to achieve state-of-the-art results in character recognition. Bengio et al., in their seminal work following this, offered deep insights into why deep learning networks with multiple layers can hierarchically learn features as compared to shallow neural networks [27]. In their research, Bengio and LeCun emphasized the advantages of deep learning through architectures such as convolutional neural networks (CNNs), restricted Boltzmann machines (RBMs), and deep belief networks (DBNs), and through techniques such as unsupervised pre-training with fine-tuning, thus inspiring the next wave of deep learning [28]. Fei-Fei Li, head of the artificial intelligence lab at Stanford University, along with other researchers, launched ImageNet, which resulted in the most extensive collection of images and, for the first time, highlighted the usefulness of data in learning essential tasks such as object recognition, classification, and clustering [70]. Improvements in computer hardware, primarily through GPUs, increasing the throughput by almost 10× every five years, and the existence of a large amount of data to learn from resulted in a paradigm shift in the field. Instead of hand-engineered features that were the primary focus for many sophisticated applications, by learning from a large volume of training data, where the necessary features emerge, the deep learning network became the foundation for many state-of-the-art techniques.

Mikolov et al. and Graves proposed language models using RNNs and long short-term memory, which later became the building blocks for many natural language processing (NLP) architectures [184, 97]. The research paper by Collobert and Weston was instrumental in demonstrating many concepts such as pre-trained word embeddings, CNNs for text, and sharing of the embedding matrix for multi-task learning [60]. Mikolov et al. further improved the efficiency of training the word embeddings proposed by Bengio et al. by eliminating the hidden layer and formulating an approximate objective for learning giving rise to "word2vec", an efficient large-scale implementation of word embeddings [185, 183]. Sutskever's research, which proposed a Hessian-free optimizer to train RNNs efficiently on long-term dependencies, was a breakthrough in reviving the usage of RNNs, especially in NLP [237]. Sutskever et al. introduced sequence-to-sequence learning as a generic neural framework comprised of an encoder neural network processing inputs as a sequence and a decoder neural network predicting the outputs based on the input sequence states and the current output states [238]. As a result, the sequence-to-sequence framework became the core architecture for a wide range of NLP tasks such as constituency parsing, named entity recognition (NER), machine translation, question-answering, and summarization, to name a few. Furthermore, even Google started replacing its monolithic phrase-based machine translation models with sequence-to-sequence neural machine translation models [272]. To overcome the bottleneck issues with the sequence-to-sequence framework, seminal work by Bahdanau et al. proposed the attention mechanism, which plays a crucial role in transformers and their variants [17].

1.2 TRANSFORMERS AND TAXONOMY

The transformer architecture [254] was introduced in 2017, in the paper *Attention Is All You Need*, for sequence-to-sequence problems. It was an alternative to using recurrent or convolutional layers. Since its introduction, there's been a wide variety of research into various ways to improve upon the standard transformer. Two surveys [163, 243] have categorized transformer-related papers. Transformer research has focused on three things: architecture modification, pre-training methods, and applications. In this book, we'll spend time on a subset of architecture modifications, pre-training methods of large language models, like BERT [71], and a few applications.

1.2.1 Modified Transformer Architecture

Modified transformer architectures can be split into two broad categories [163]: changes to the internal arrangement of the transformer block and changes to the layers that a transformer block is made of. A summary of the types of transformer modifications are shown in Table 1.1

1.2.1.1 *Transformer block changes*

Thus far, modifications to the transformer block have fallen into five categories [163]:

- Decreasing memory footprint and compute

- Adding connections between transformer blocks

- Adaptive computation time (e.g., allow early stopping during training)

- Recurrence or hierarchical structure

- Changing the architecture more drastically (e.g., neural architecture search)

TABLE 1.1 Types of modifications to the transformer block

Modification	Transformer
Lightweight transformers	
	Lite Transformer [274]
	Funnel Transformer [66]
	DeLighT [180]
Cross-block connectivity	
	Realformer [107]
	Transparent Attention [19]
Adaptive computation time	
	Universal Transformer [69]
	Conditional Computation Transformer [18]
	DeeBERT [276]
Recurrent	
	Transformer-XL [67]
	Compressive Transformer [204]
	Memformer [287]
Hierarchical	
	HIBERT [296]
	Hi-Transformer [270]
Different architectures	
	Macaron Transformer [174]
	Sandwich Transformer [201]
	Differentiable Architecture Search [299]

In this book, we'll focus on several architecture modifications that allow a transformer to process longer sequences and/or lower the computational complexity of the attention mechanism. We show a partial list of modified transformers in Table 1.1.

1.2.1.2 Transformer sublayer changes

In Chapter 2, we'll take a detailed look at the structure of a transformer block, covering its four components so we can later discuss ways in which researchers have modified them. In general, there are four parts to a transformer block [254]: positional encodings, multi-head attention, residual connections with layer normalization [13], and a position-wise feedforward network. Changes to transformer sublayers have focused on

TABLE 1.2 Types of modifications to the multi-head attention module

Modification	Transformer
Low-rank	
	Performer [53] Nystromformer [277] Synthesizer [241]
Attention with prior	
	Gaussian Transformer [102] Realformer [107] Synthesizer [241] Longformer [25]
Improved multi-head attention	
	Talking-heads Attention [227] Multi-Scale Transformer [234]
Complexity reduction	
	Longformer [25] Reformer [142] Big Bird [292] Performer [53] Routing Transformer [214]
Prototype queries	
	Clustered Attention [256] Informer [302]
Clustered key-value memory	
	Set Transformer [151] Memory Compressed Transformer [167] Linformer [259]

these four types of components, most of which has focused on changing aspects of the multi-head attention [163, 243]. Table 1.2 shows a selected list of transformer variants that have modified multi-head attention mechanisms.

Multi-head attention Much effort has been directed at the multi-head attention mechanism; studying its quadratic computational complexity, ways to address said complexity, and how it might be changed for specific kinds of problems. Most of this work falls into two broad categories: reducing the computational complexity of the attention mechanism, or changing the attention mechanism so it can learn more things.

As discussed in refs [163, 243], there are many ways to address the complexity of the attention mechanism. There are low-rank approximations, like Linformer [259] and Performer [53]. There are several ways to sparsify the attention mechanism, some of which effectively reduce the complexity of the attention mechanism to be linear in the sequence length. For example Longformer [25] and BigBird [292] add sparsity by fixing the positions to which a given token can attend. Some other transformers, like Reformer [142], introduce a learnable sparsity by sorting or clustering the input tokens. There are others still which reduce the size of the attention matrix [163].

There is also a variety of work that has tried to improve the multi-head attention mechanism [163]. For instance, attention heads have been allowed to "communicate" with each other and/or share information [158, 227, 65, 226], learn the optimal span to attend over [235], and use different attention spans in different attention heads [103]. This list is not exhaustive. We discuss several such methods in Chapter 5.

Positional encodings Positional encodings [254] are a way of encoding sequence order into the transformer. They also comprise another avenue for modifying the components of a transformer block. Thus far, four kinds of positional encodings have been used [163]: absolute positional encodings (like those of the standard transformer), relative positional encodings (such as in Transformer-XL), hybrid encodings that have absolute and relative position information, and implicit encodings that provide information about sequence order in other ways. This is shown in Table 1.3. We discuss the absolute positional encodings used in the standard transformer in Chapter 2 and the relative encodings used in Transformer-XL in Chapter 5.

TABLE 1.3 Changes to positional encodings

Modification	Transformer
Absolute position	Original Transformer [254]
Relative position	Transformer-XL [67]
Absolute/relative hybrid	Roformer [232]
Other representations	R-Transformer [262]

Residual connections and position-wise feedforward networks
Some work has included changes to the residual blocks that come after
the multi-head attention mechanism and after the position-wise feedforward network, including the position of the layer normalization, swapping layer normalization with something else, removal of layer normalization entirely [163], or the introduction or reversible residual layers to
conserve memory (used in Reformer) [142]. Reformer will be discussed in
Chapter 5. Other work has studied ways to change the position-wise feed-
forward network, including changing the activation function, increasing
its representational capacity, or removing the feedforward network.

1.2.2 Pre-training Methods and Applications

A large body of work has focused on how a transformer can be
pre-trained. There are encoder-only models, such as BERT [71], decoder-
only models like the famed generative pre-trained transformer models
GPT-3 [32], and encoder-decoder models like T5 [205] and ByT5 [280].
BERT is discussed in detail in Chapter 3, T5 in Chapter 5, and ByT5
in Chapter 6.

There have been many application and domain-specific transformers made for specific data domains (e.g., financial or medical text) and
specific kinds of data (e.g., images or video). We discuss several such
applications in Chapter 6.

1.3 RESOURCES

In this section, we will discuss some resources that can be useful for
researchers and practitioners.

1.3.1 Libraries and Implementations

Here are some useful libraries, tools, and implementations (Table 1.4):

TABLE 1.4 Libraries and Tools

Organization	Language and Framework	API	Pre-trained
AllenNLP	Python and PyTorch	Yes	Yes
HuggingFace	Jax, PyTorch, and TensorFlow	Yes	Yes
Google Brain	TensorFlow	Yes	
GluonNLP	MXNet	Yes	Yes

1.3.2   Books

Some of the books that we found useful are:

- Transfer Learning for Natural Language Processing by Paul Azunre [12]

- Transformers for Natural Language Processing by Denis Rothman [213]

- Deep Learning Algorithms: Transformers, gans, encoders, rnns, cnns, and more by Ricardo A. Calix [35]

- Python Transformers By Huggingface Hands On by Joshua K. Cage [33]

- Deep Learning for NLP and Speech Recognition by Uday Kamath, John Liu, and James Whitaker [248]

1.3.3   Courses, Tutorials, and Lectures

Some of the very relevant online courses and tutorials:

- The Annotated Transformer by Alexander Rush et al. `http://nlp.seas.harvard.edu/2018/04/03/attention.html`

- HuggingFace course on transformers `https://huggingface.co/course`

- DeepLearning.AI course on sequence models `https://www.coursera.org/learn/nlp-sequence-models`

- DeepLearning.AI course on transformers and BERT `https://www.coursera.org/learn/attention-models-in-nlp`

- Stanford CS224N: NLP with Deep Learning by Christopher Manning `http://web.stanford.edu/class/cs224n/`

- UC Berkeley's Applied Natural Language Processing by David Bamman `https://people.ischool.berkeley.edu/~dbamman/info256.html`

- Advanced NLP with spaCy by Ines Montani `https://course.spacy.io/en/`

- Deep Learning for Coders with fastai and PyTorch by Sylvain Gugger and Jeremy Howard `https://course.fast.ai/`

- Jay Alammar's visual explanation of transformers and related architectures `https://jalammar.github.io/`

1.3.4 Case Studies and Details

At the end of Chapters 2–7, we include a case study that allows the reader to see how one or more of the models and methods discussed in the chapter can be applied, or how they stack up against one another when applied to the same problem. The aim is for the case study to provide a small starting point in working with transformer models from which one can branch out further. Each case study has been chosen to run within approximately one hour on GPUs at least as powerful as the NVIDIA K80 (Google Colaboratory provides these for free). Case studies are also available in the Github repository which accompanies this book: `https://github.com/CRCTransformers/deepdive-book`.

## CHAPTER 2

Transformers: Basics and Introduction

M ANY natural language processing and speech recognition techniques need the ability to handle large sequences as inputs and transform them to specific outputs. Traditional approaches, such as recurrent neural networks (RNN) have several shortcomings that prohibit real-world solutions. Transformers have become the fundamental design piece overcoming most of these limitations, and they have state-of-the-art results. This chapter starts by introducing the sequence-to-sequence models and their limitations. The chapter then lays out various building blocks of transformers such as attention, multi-head attention, positional encodings, residual connections, and encoder-decoder frameworks in a step-by-step manner. All these functional units get detailed treatment from a theoretical and practical perspective for the reader to get a complete handle on the topic. Finally, a real-world case study concludes the chapter by showing the operative aspects, using well-known libraries and datasets.

2.1 ENCODER-DECODER ARCHITECTURE

Many NLP problems, such as machine translation, question answering, and text summarization, to name a few, use pairs of sequences as inputs to train the model. Generally, the sequences are of variable lengths. The use of an encoder-decoder architecture, as shown in Fig. 2.1 is a common practice to solve the problem. The encoder component takes a variable-length sequence and converts it into a fixed-length output-state. The

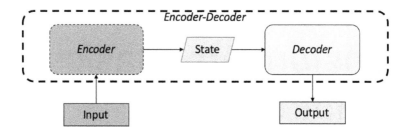

Figure 2.1 Encoder-Decoder architecture.

decoder component takes a fixed-length state and converts it back into a variable-length output.

2.2 SEQUENCE-TO-SEQUENCE

Machine translation and many other NLP problems produced promising results using sequence-to-sequence architecture (abbreviated as seq2seq) with a recurrent neural network (e.g., RNN) based encoder and decoder [238, 51]. Fig. 2.2 shows an example of machine translation where a French sentence, *J'aime le thé.*, and it's English equivalent, *I love tea.* form the sentence pair as an example of input for the training. The tokens <eos> and <bos> are special ways to handle the end and beginning of the sentence, respectively. As shown in Fig. 2.2 the final hidden state of the encoder acts as the input for the decoder.

2.2.1 Encoder

The input sentence is tokenized into words and words are mapped into feature vectors which are the inputs for the encoder. Suppose that the input sequence is represented by $x_1, \cdots, x_T$ such that token x_t in the input text sequence is the tth token. Embedding mappings transform the input tokens $x_1, \ldots, x_T$ to $\mathbf{x}_1, \cdots, \mathbf{x}_T$ vectors. A unidirectional RNN at any time t with a previous hidden state $\mathbf{h}_{t-1}$ and input $\mathbf{x}_t$ generates a new hidden state

$$\mathbf{h}_t = f(\mathbf{h}_{t-1}, \mathbf{x}_t) \tag{2.1}$$

The above equation can be more concretely written as

$$\mathbf{h}_t = \tanh(\mathbf{W}^{(hh)}\mathbf{h}_{t-1} + \mathbf{W}^{(hx)}\mathbf{x}_t) \tag{2.2}$$

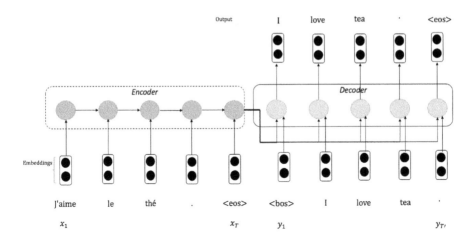

Figure 2.2 RNN-based sequence-to-sequence for machine translation.

The state $\mathbf{h}_t$, known as the **context variable** or the **context vector**, encodes the information of the entire input sequence and is given by:

$$\mathbf{c} = m(\mathbf{h}_1, \cdots, \mathbf{h}_T) \tag{2.3}$$

where m is the mapping function and in the simplest case maps the context variable to the last hidden state

$$\mathbf{c} = m(\mathbf{h}_1, \cdots, \mathbf{h}_T) = \mathbf{h}_T \tag{2.4}$$

Adding more complexity to the architecture, the RNN can be bidirectional and thus the hidden state would not only depend on the previous hidden state $\mathbf{h}_{t-1}$ and input $\mathbf{x}_t$, but also on the next state $\mathbf{h}_{t+1}$.

2.2.2 Decoder

The decoder has the output of the encoder, the context variable $\mathbf{c}$, and the given output sequence $y_1, \ldots, y'_T$ to generate the decoded outputs. In Sutskever et al., the context variable from the encoder—the final hidden state—initiates the decoder, whereas in Cho et al. the context variable is passed to every time step.

Similar to the encoder, decoder hidden state at any time t' is given by

$$\mathbf{s}_{t'} = g(\mathbf{s}_{t-1}, \mathbf{y}_{t'-1}, \mathbf{c}) \tag{2.5}$$

The hidden state of the decoder flows to an output layer and the conditional distribution of the next token at t' is given by

$$P(\mathbf{y}_{t'}|\mathbf{y}_{t'-1},\cdots,y_1,\mathbf{c}) = \text{softmax}(\mathbf{s}_{t-1},\mathbf{y}_{t'-1},\mathbf{c}) \qquad (2.6)$$

2.2.3 Training

The decoder predicts a probability distribution for the output tokens at each time step, and the softmax gives the distribution over the words. Thus, the encoder and decoder are jointly trained, and the cross-entropy loss is used for optimization and is given by

$$\max_{\theta} \frac{1}{N} \sum_{n=1}^{N} \log p_\theta(\mathbf{y}^{(n)}|\mathbf{x}^{(n)}) \qquad (2.7)$$

The process of concatenating the <bos> and the original output sequence, excluding the final token, as the input to the decoder during the training is called **teacher forcing**. The teacher forcing helps in addressing the slow convergence and instability problems when training RNNs.

2.2.4 Issues with RNN-Based Encoder-Decoder

As described in the above section, complete information about the source sentence is compressed and encoded in one context variable used by the decoder component. As the input size increases, there will be a loss of information while compressing the input. The words in a sentence can also have complex structure and long-distance associations based on the language. Capturing this in a compressed way in a single vector also leads to inefficiencies. On the other hand, each time step's hidden variables on the encoder side are available and carry information to be used by the decoder network. Each time step in the decoder can be influenced differently by the hidden variables in the encoder. RNNs also have issues with vanishing and explosive gradients [115]. One of the computational issues with RNNs is that the recurrence or dependence on previous time steps makes the architecture very difficult to parallelize.

2.3 ATTENTION MECHANISM

2.3.1 Background

The attention mechanism involves selectively focusing on specific elements while filtering out the less relevant ones. The human optic nerve receives information in the order of billion bits per second, while the brain's capacity to process is far less. Visual attention, a form of attention, involves orienting to and sustaining focus on a stimulus such as a person or inanimate object or a specific task, thus enabling the brain's efficient processing. Therefore, the attention mechanism has allowed humans to focus on only a fraction of information of interest, thus enabling optimum resource usage, leading to better survival and growth.

The "father of American psychology", William James, created a two-component framework to explain the visual attention mechanism [133]. In this framework, the spotlight of attention uses both *nonvolitional* (involuntary) and *volitional* (voluntary) cues to bias the sensory input. The *nonvolitional* cue is involuntary and is based on the saliency and noticeability of targets in the environment. In contrast, the *volitional* cue is based on the subject's voluntary effort to focus on the target deliberately. For example, drawing attention to specific objects by coloring them differently or attending to a crying baby are nonvolitional cues. In contrast, attending to specific text for answering question or solving specific problems are volitional cues.

In the context of attention mechanisms in deep learning, volitional cues map to queries, keys to nonvolitional cues, and sensory inputs to value. Every sensory input (value) maps to the nonvolitional cue (key) of that sensory input. Attention mechanisms can be thus considered as a process of biasing selection over values (sensory inputs) via attention pooling, using the queries (volitional cues) and keys (nonvolitional cues) as shown in Fig. 2.3.

The attention mechanism is designed in a way to overcome the issues described with RNN-based encoder-decoder architecture.

As shown in Fig. 2.3, an **attention** mechanism can be considered as a memory with keys and values and a layer which, when someone queries it, generates an output from value whose keys map the input [17].

To formalize, let us consider the memory unit consisting of n key-value pairs $(\mathbf{k}_1, \mathbf{v}_1), \ldots, (\mathbf{k}_n, \mathbf{v}_n)$ with $\mathbf{k}_i \in \mathbb{R}^{d_k}$ and $\mathbf{v}_i \in \mathbb{R}^{d_v}$. The attention layer receives an input as query $\mathbf{q} \in \mathbb{R}^{d_q}$ and returns an output $\mathbf{o} \in \mathbb{R}^{d_v}$ with same shape as the value $\mathbf{v}$.

The attention layer measures the similarity between the query and the key using a score function α which returns scores $a_1, \ldots, a_n$ for keys $\mathbf{k}_1, \ldots, \mathbf{k}_n$ given by

$$a_i = \alpha(\mathbf{q}, \mathbf{k}_i) \tag{2.8}$$

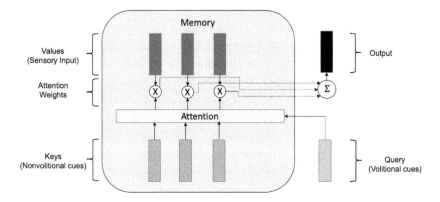

Figure 2.3 Attention mechanism showing query, keys, values, and output vector interactions.

Attention weights are computed as a softmax function on the scores

$$\mathbf{b} = \text{softmax}(\mathbf{a}) \tag{2.9}$$

Each element of $\mathbf{b}$ is

$$b_i = \frac{\exp(a_i)}{\sum_j \exp(a_j)} \tag{2.10}$$

The output is the weighted sum of the attention weights and the values

$$\mathbf{o} = \sum_{i=1}^{n} b_i \mathbf{v}_i \tag{2.11}$$

Fig. 2.4 captures the interactions between various vectors and scalars from input query to output.

2.3.2 Types of Score-Based Attention

As discussed, the score function, $\alpha(\mathbf{q}, \mathbf{k})$, can take various forms, which has given rise to a number of attention mechanisms, each having its advantage.

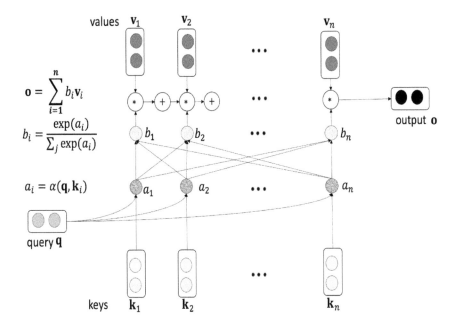

values $\mathbf{v}_1$ $\quad$ $\mathbf{v}_2$ $\qquad$ $\mathbf{v}_n$

$$\mathbf{o} = \sum_{i=1}^{n} b_i \mathbf{v}_i$$

output $\mathbf{o}$

$$b_i = \frac{\exp(a_i)}{\sum_j \exp(a_i)}$$

b_1 $\qquad$ b_2 $\qquad$ b_n

$$a_i = \alpha(\mathbf{q}, \mathbf{k}_i)$$

a_1 $\qquad$ a_2 $\qquad$ a_n

query $\mathbf{q}$

keys $\mathbf{k}_1$ $\quad$ $\mathbf{k}_2$ $\qquad$ $\mathbf{k}_n$

Figure 2.4 Attention mechanism showing query, keys, values, and output vector interactions.

2.3.2.1 Dot product (multiplicative)

The dot product-based scoring function is the simplest one and has no parameters to tune [176].

$$\alpha(\mathbf{q}, \mathbf{k}) = \mathbf{q} \cdot \mathbf{k} \qquad (2.12)$$

2.3.2.2 Scaled dot product or multiplicative

The scaled dot product-based scoring function divides the dot product by $\sqrt{d_k}$ to remove the influence of dimension d_k [254]. According to Vaswani et al., as the dimension increases, the dot products grow larger, which pushes the softmax function into regions with extreme gradients.

$$\alpha(\mathbf{q}, \mathbf{k}) = \frac{\mathbf{q} \cdot \mathbf{k}}{\sqrt{d_k}} \qquad (2.13)$$

2.3.2.3 Linear, MLP, or Additive

Luong et al. also experimented by projecting the query and keys to a hidden layer of dimension h, learning the weights $(\mathbf{W}_k, \mathbf{W}_q)$, and using

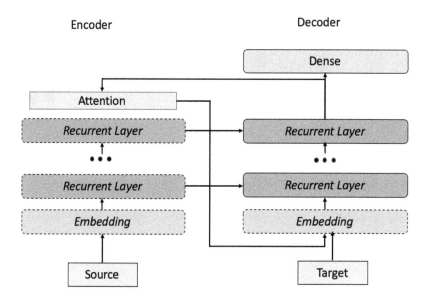

Figure 2.5 Encoder-decoder with attention layer.

a sigmoid function to combine them with the values, as given by

$$\alpha(\mathbf{q}, \mathbf{k}) = \mathbf{v}^{\mathrm{T}} \tanh(\mathbf{W}_k \mathbf{k} + \mathbf{W}_q \mathbf{q}) \tag{2.14}$$

Scaled dot product, or dot product-based scoring, are faster and more memory efficient than additive attention mechanisms.

2.3.3 Attention-Based Sequence-to-Sequence

The general changes to an encoder-decoder with the addition of an attention layer and the mapping to query, keys, and values are shown in Fig. 2.5 and are

1. The output of the last encoder states are used as keys $\mathbf{k}$ and values $\mathbf{v}$

2. The output of the last decoder state, at time $t-1$ is used as query $\mathbf{q}$

3. The output from the attention layer $\mathbf{o}$, the context variable, is used for the next decoder state t

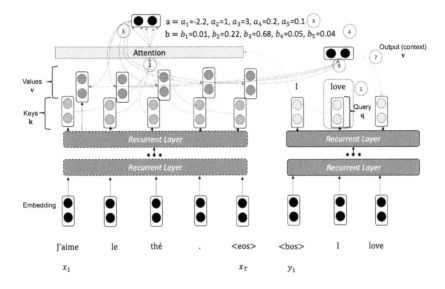

Figure 2.6 Sequence-to-sequence, at a given time t, when the decoder has generated *love* at $t-1$ and the token *tea* will be generated as the output.

To understand the flow in more details, let us consider the French translation example where the keys and values are the encoder states for the tokens $\{J'aime, le, thé, .\}$ and the decoder at time $t-1$ has generated the tokens $I, love$. As shown in Fig. 2.6, the decoder output at time $t-1$, *love*, flows into attention layer as a query, which combines with the keys and generates the unnormalized scores $\mathbf{a} = \alpha(\mathbf{q}, \mathbf{k})$, which then get normalized to give the attention weights $\mathbf{b}$. These attention weights further combine with the values (encoder outputs) to give the context variable or the output vector $\mathbf{o}$. The output then combines with the previous decoder state to generate the next token *tea* at time t.

2.4 TRANSFORMER

As shown in Fig. 2.7, the primary transformer structure proposed by Vaswani et al. is based on the encoder-decoder architecture described before. The transformer combines the advantages of convolutional neural networks (CNN) to parallelize the computations and recurrent neural networks (RNN) to capture long-range, variable-length sequential information. There are many systemic changes proposed in the transformer architecture, and in the next few subsections, we will go through each of them in sufficient detail.

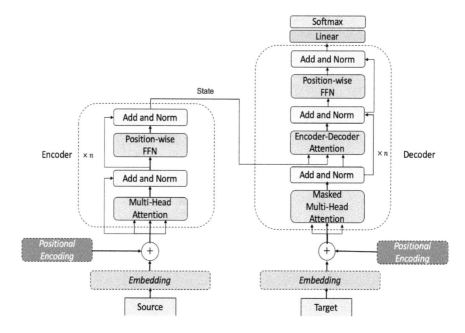

Figure 2.7 Transformer architecture.

2.4.1 Source and Target Representation

Both source and target words are tokenized and the tokens go through word embedding and positional encoding to give position encoded representation for all sentences.

2.4.1.1 Word embedding

Standard word embedding lookup for tokens in a sentence can convert a sentence of length l, to a matrix $\mathbf{W}$ of dimension (l, d), i.e., $\mathbf{W} \in \mathbb{R}^{l \times d}$.

2.4.1.2 Positional encoding

Word order and positions play a crucial role in most of the NLP tasks. By taking one word at a time, recurrent neural networks essentially incorporate word order. In transformer architecture, to gain speed and parallelism, recurrent neural networks are replaced by multi-head attention layers, which we will cover later in detail. Thus it becomes necessary to explicitly pass the information about the word order to the model layer as one way of capturing it. This encoding of word order information is

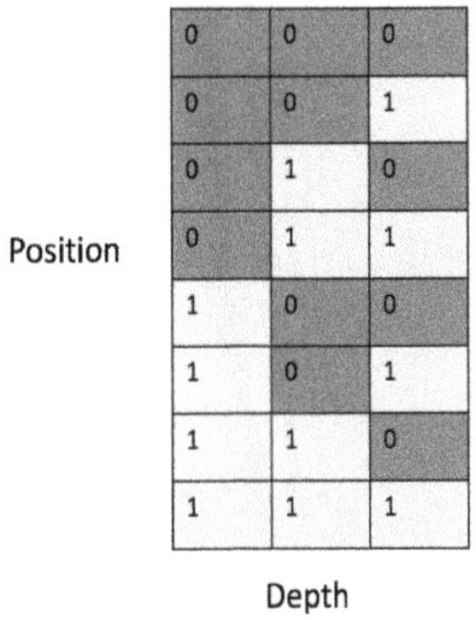

0	0	0
0	0	1
0	1	0
0	1	1
1	0	0
1	0	1
1	1	0
1	1	1

Position

Depth

Figure 2.8 Positional encoding for 8 positions with dimensionality 3.

known as positional encoding. One can derive various requirements for effective positional encodings. They are

1. Unique encoding value for each time-step (word in the sentence).

2. Consistent distance between two time-steps across sentences of various lengths.

3. Encoding results are generalized independent of the length of the sentence.

4. The encoding is deterministic.

One trivial way of accomplishing all the requirements for positional encoding is to use binary representation. Fig. 2.8 highlights how with a vector of size or depth 3, we can generate 8 positional encodings using binary values that meet all the requirements given above. The representation of each bit as grey (0) and white (1) shows how each position is different and has a constant difference. Using binary values is very costly from a memory perspective.

If the length of the sentence is given by l and the embedding dimension/depth is given by d, positional encoding $\mathbf{P}$ is a 2-d matrix of same dimension, i.e., $\mathbf{P} \in \mathbb{R}^{l \times d}$. Every position can be represented with equation in terms of i which is along the l and j which is along the d dimension as

$$\mathbf{P}_{i,2j} = \sin(i/1000^{2j/d}) \tag{2.15}$$

$$\mathbf{P}_{i,2j+1} = \cos(i/1000^{2j/d}) \tag{2.16}$$

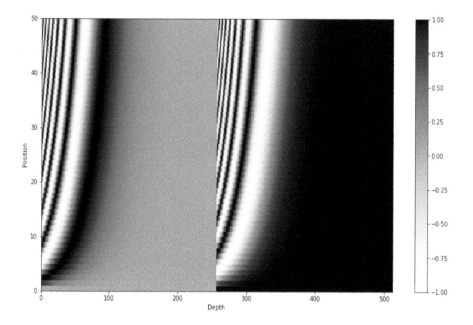

Figure 2.9 Positional encoding for 50 positions with dimensionality 512.

$for\ i = 0, \cdots, l-1, j = 0, \cdots, \lfloor (d-1)/2 \rfloor$. The function definition above indicates that the frequencies are decreasing along the vector dimension and forms a geometric progression from 2π to $10000 \cdot 2\pi$ on the wavelengths. For $d = 512$ dimensions for maximum positional length $l = 50$, the positional encoding visualization is shown in Fig. 2.9.

As shown in Fig. 2.7, the two matrices, i.e., the word embeddings $\mathbf{W}$ and the positional encoding $\mathbf{P}$ are added to generate the input representation $\mathbf{X} = \mathbf{W} + \mathbf{P} \in \mathbb{R}^{l \times d}$.

2.4.2 Attention Layers

The basic building block in transformers, in both encoders and decoders, is the self-attention. It has small variations based on how and where it is used in the encoder and the decoder side. In the next subsections we gradually build the attention layers starting from the self-attention.

2.4.2.1 Self-attention

To understand multi-head attention, it is imperative to break-down the computations and understand the single head portion of it known as

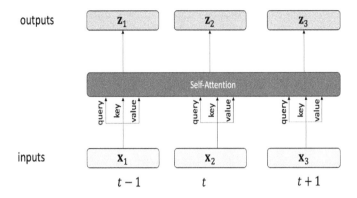

Figure 2.10 Self-attention inputs mapped to query, keys, and values and generated output for each input.

self-attention. Fig. 2.10 shows how the input vectors, $\mathbf{x}_i$, are converted to the output vectors, $\mathbf{z}_i$, through the self-attention layer. Each input vector, $\mathbf{x}_i$, generates three different vectors: the query, key, and value, $(\mathbf{q}_i, \mathbf{k}_i, \mathbf{v}_i,)$. The query, key, and value vectors are obtained by projecting the input vector, $\mathbf{x}_i$, at time i on the learnable weight matrices $\mathbf{W}_q, \mathbf{W}_k$, and $\mathbf{W}_v$ to get $\mathbf{q}_i$, $\mathbf{k}_i$, and $\mathbf{v}_i$, respectively. These query/key/value weight matrices are randomly initialized and the weights are jointly learned from the training process. For the first attention layer of the encoder and decoder, the inputs are the summation of the word embeddings and positional encodings.

Similar to the attention discussion in section 2.3 where we discussed the query, key, and values, and how they impact the final attention scores, the self-attention has all three vectors generated for every input and the following are their key roles:

1. The role of the query vector of token i, $\mathbf{q}_i$, is to combine with every other key vectors $\sum_{j=0}^{l} \mathbf{q}_i \mathbf{k}_j{}^T$ to influence the weights for its own output, $\mathbf{z}_i$.

2. The role of the key vector of token i, $\mathbf{k}_i$, is to be matched with every other query vectors to get similarity with query and to influence the output through query-key product scoring.

3. The role of the value vector of token i, $\mathbf{v}_i$, is extracting information by combining with the output of the query-key scores to get the output vector $\mathbf{z}_i$.

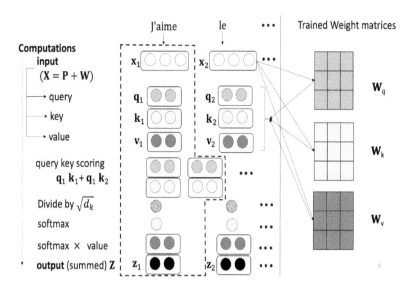

Figure 2.11 The dotted lines show the complete flow of computation for one input through a self-attention layer.

The logical flow of all the computations carried out for each token i from input to output is demonstrated in Fig. 2.11.

Instead of a vector computation for each token i, input matrix $\mathbf{X} \in \mathbb{R}^{l \times d}$ where l is the maximum length of the sentence and d is the dimension of the inputs, combines with each of the query, key, and value matrices as a single computation given by

$$attention(\mathbf{Q}, \mathbf{K}, \mathbf{V}) = \text{softmax}\left(\frac{\mathbf{Q}\mathbf{K}^{\mathrm{T}}}{\sqrt{d_k}}\right)\mathbf{V} \qquad (2.17)$$

2.4.2.2 Multi-head attention

Instead of a single self-attention head, there can be h parallel self-attention heads; this is known as multi-head attention. In the original transformer paper, the authors used $h = 8$ heads. Multi-head attention provides different subspace representations instead of just a single representation for the inputs, which helps capture different aspects of the same inputs. It also helps the model expand the focus to different positions. Each head can learn something different, for example, in machine translation, it may be about learning grammar, tense, conjugation, etc.

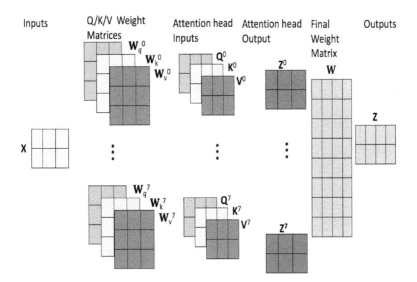

Figure 2.12 Multi-head attention.

Multi-head attention have multiple sets of query/key/value weight matrices, each resulting in different query/key/value matrices for the inputs, finally generating output matrices z_i. These output matrices from each head are concatenated and multiplied with an additional weight matrix, $\mathbf{W}_O$, to get a single final matrix, $\mathbf{Z}$, with vectors z_i as output for each input x_i. The parallel input to output transformations for all the heads is depicted in Fig. 2.12.

$$head_i = attention(\mathbf{W}_q{}^i\mathbf{Q}, \mathbf{W}_k{}^i\mathbf{K}, \mathbf{W}_v{}^i\mathbf{V}) \tag{2.18}$$

$$multihead(\mathbf{Q}, \mathbf{K}, \mathbf{V}) = \mathbf{W}_O\, concat(head_1, \ldots, head_h) \tag{2.19}$$

2.4.2.3 Masked multi-head attention

We want the decoder to learn from the encoder sequence and a particular decoder sequence, which has been already seen by the model, to predict the next word/character. Thus, for the first layer of the decoder, similar to the sequence-to-sequence architecture, only previous target tokens need to be present and others to be masked. This special alteration results in the masked multi-head attention. This is implemented by having a masking weight matrix $\mathbf{M}$ that has $-\infty$ for future tokens and 0 for previous tokens. This computation is inserted after the scaling of the multiplication of $\mathbf{Q}$ and $\mathbf{K}^T$ and before the softmax so that the softmax results in the actual scaled values for previous tokens and the value 0 for future tokens.

$$maskedAttention(\mathbf{Q}, \mathbf{K}, \mathbf{V}) = \text{softmax}\left(\frac{\mathbf{QK}^{\mathrm{T}} + \mathbf{M}}{\sqrt{d_k}}\right)\mathbf{V} \qquad (2.20)$$

2.4.2.4 Encoder-decoder multi-head attention

In the decoder side there is a need to learn the attention relationship between the entire source input and the target output at a given time. Therefore, the query vectors from the target sequence (before a given time) and the keys and values from the entire input sequence of the encoder are passed to the self-attention layer in the decoder as shown in Fig. 2.7.

2.4.3 Residuals and Layer Normalization

Similar to ResNets, the inputs, $\mathbf{X}$, are short circuited to the output, $\mathbf{Z}$, and both are added and passed through layer normalization $addAndNorm(\mathbf{X} + \mathbf{Z})[105]$. Layer normalization ensures each layer to have 0 mean and a unit (1) variance.

For each hidden unit, h_i, we can compute

$$h_i = \frac{g}{\sigma}(h_i - \mu) \qquad (2.21)$$

where g is the gain variable (can be set to 1), μ is the mean given by $\frac{1}{H}\sum_{i=1}^{H} h_i$ and σ is the standard deviation given by $\sqrt{\frac{1}{H}(h_i - \mu)^2}$.

Layer normalization reduces the **covariance shift**, i.e., the gradient dependencies between each layer, and therefore speeds up the convergence as fewer iterations are needed [13]. This is related to batch normalization, where batch normalization happens at one hidden unit level and a 0 mean and a unit (1) variance is achieved on that one batch [130]. Advantage of layer normalization is that it works independent of the batch size, i.e., can give a single example, small batch or a large batch.

2.4.4 Positionwise Feed-forward Networks

Both encoder and decoder contain a fully connected feed-forward network after the attention sub layers. For each position, similar linear transformations with a ReLU activation in between is performed.

$$FFN(\mathbf{x}) = \max(0, \mathbf{x}\mathbf{W}_1 + b_1)\mathbf{W}_2 + b_2 \qquad (2.22)$$

Every position goes through the same transformations and they are different only at the layer level.

2.4.5 Encoder

The encoder block in the transformer consists of n blocks of {*multiheadAttention, addAndNorm, FFN, addAndNorm*} as shown in Fig. 2.7. Every layer of multi-head attention in the encoder side attends to the input or the source, i.e., attention between inputs and inputs. Tenney et al. show that each layer of transformer in the encoder side performs a different NLP task in classical sense such as part-of-speech, constituents, dependencies, entity resolution, etc. [244].

2.4.6 Decoder

The decoder block in the transformer consists of n blocks of {*maskedMultiheadAttention, addAndNorm, encoderDecoderAttention, addAndNorm, FFN, addAndNorm*} as shown in Fig. 2.7. The first layer of multi-head attention in the decoder side attends to the target, i.e., attention between masked outputs with themselves. The encoder-decoder attention layer creates attention between the source and the target.

2.5 CASE STUDY: MACHINE TRANSLATION

2.5.1 Goal

This section will go through a real-world use case of sequence to sequence in the NLP domain—machine translation between English and French sentences. We will apply attention-based and transformer-based techniques to understand, compare, and contrast between the two architectures.

2.5.2 Data, Tools, and Libraries

The English-French parallel corpus from `https://www.manythings.org/anki/` is used for the machine translation. For necessary data wrangling and visualization, we use standard Python libraries like Pandas, NumPy, and Matplotlib. We use TorchText and spaCy for basic text processing such as tokenization. Attention-based and Transformer-based sequence-to-sequence are implemented using the PyTorch library.

2.5.3 Experiments, Results, and Analysis

2.5.3.1 Exploratory data analysis

Basic data preprocessing like converting sentences to ASCII and filtering out the pairs that are too long is performed as a text normalization step. Then we tokenize the sentences, convert the words to token IDs, and append <bos> and <eos> IDs to the beginning and end of the token ID sequences. Padding the variable-length sequences to the maximum observed length in the batch using the <pad> token ensures a fixed-size tensor for training and evaluation.

The total of $135,842$ language pairs after filtering reduce to $131,951$ and we further split it into 80% training, 10% validation and 10% test data, i.e., $105,460$, $13,308$, and $13,183$ respectively.

Figs. 2.13 and 2.14 show the distribution plots as histograms for English/French and joint distribution. Most of the sentences in the parallel corpus are between 4 and 8 tokens/words length.

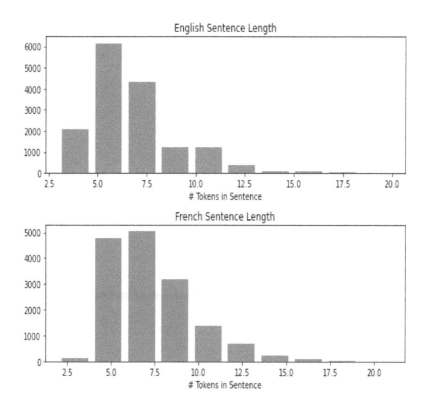

Figure 2.13 Sentence length distribution for English and French sentences.

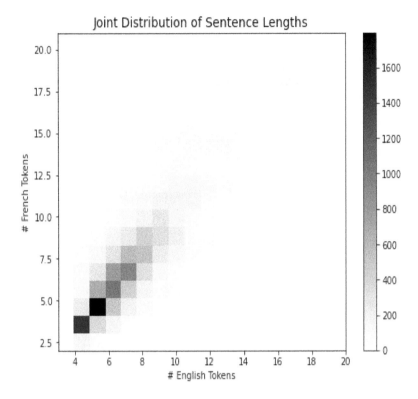

Figure 2.14 Joint distribution for English and French sentences based on length.

The top 20 words for English and French are shown in Fig. 2.15. The frequency and distribution shows some common words as expected such as "the-le", "is-est", etc. It also highlights certain contractions such as "don" for "don't" and how the underlying tokenizer (spaCy) performs preprocessing. Iteratively improving and analyzing the data helps in the overall model results.

Bahdanau attention-based sequence-to-sequence and transformer-based will be used to train/validate on the data and the best model from both will be evaluated on the test set.

2.5.3.2 Attention

The encoder model class **BahdanauEncoder** as given in the Listing 2.1 uses a bidirectional gated recurrent unit (GRU) to encode sentences in the source language.

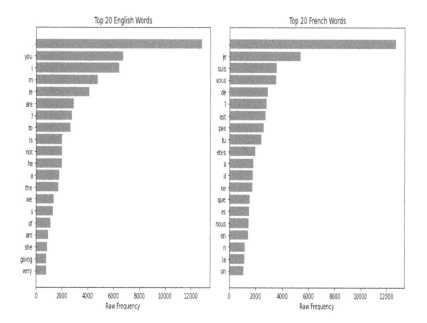

Figure 2.15 Top 20 words from English and French sentences.

```
class BahdanauEncoder(nn.Module):
    def __init__(self, input_dim, embedding_dim,
        encoder_hidden_dim,
                decoder_hidden_dim, dropout_p):
        super().__init__()
        self.input_dim = input_dim
        self.embedding_dim = embedding_dim
        self.encoder_hidden_dim = encoder_hidden_dim
        self.decoder_hidden_dim = decoder_hidden_dim
        self.dropout_p = dropout_p

        self.embedding = nn.Embedding(input_dim, embedding_dim)
        self.gru = nn.GRU(embedding_dim, encoder_hidden_dim,
            bidirectional=True)
        self.linear = nn.Linear(encoder_hidden_dim * 2,
            decoder_hidden_dim)
        self.dropout = nn.Dropout(dropout_p)

    def forward(self, x):
        embedded = self.dropout(self.embedding(x))
        outputs, hidden = self.gru(embedded)
```

```
hidden = torch.tanh(self.linear(
    torch.cat((hidden[-2, :, :], hidden[-1, :, :]),
        dim=1)
))
return outputs, hidden
```

Listing 2.1 Bahdanau encoder

The encoder model class **BahdanauAttentionQKV** as given in the Listing 2.2 calculates the attention weights using query and key tensors.

```
class BahdanauAttentionQKV(nn.Module):
    def __init__(self, hidden_size, query_size=None,
                key_size=None, dropout_p=0.15):
        super().__init__()
        self.hidden_size = hidden_size
        self.query_size = hidden_size if query_size is None
            else query_size

        # assume bidirectional encoder, but can specify
            otherwise
        self.key_size = 2*hidden_size if key_size is None else
            key_size

        self.query_layer = nn.Linear(self.query_size,
            hidden_size)
        self.key_layer = nn.Linear(self.key_size, hidden_size)
        self.energy_layer = nn.Linear(hidden_size, 1)
        self.dropout = nn.Dropout(dropout_p)

    def forward(self, hidden, encoder_outputs, src_mask=None):
        # (B, H)
        query_out = self.query_layer(hidden)
        # (Src, B, 2*H) --> (Src, B, H)
        key_out = self.key_layer(encoder_outputs)
        # (B, H) + (Src, B, H) = (Src, B, H)
        energy_input = torch.tanh(query_out + key_out)
        # (Src, B, H) --> (Src, B, 1) --> (Src, B)
        energies = self.energy_layer(energy_input).squeeze(2)
        # if a mask is provided, remove masked tokens from
            softmax calc
        if src_mask is not None:
            energies.data.masked_fill_(src_mask == 0,
                float("-inf"))
        # softmax over the length dimension
```

```
weights = F.softmax(energies, dim=0)
# return as (B, Src) as expected by later
    multiplication
return weights.transpose(0, 1)
```

Listing 2.2 Bahdanau attention layer

The decoder model class **BahdanauDecoder** as given in the Listing 2.3 uses the hidden, encoder outputs and the attention weights to generate the next token.

```
class BahdanauDecoder(nn.Module):
    def __init__(self, output_dim, embedding_dim,
      encoder_hidden_dim,
            decoder_hidden_dim, attention, dropout_p):
        super().__init__()

        self.embedding_dim = embedding_dim
        self.output_dim = output_dim
        self.encoder_hidden_dim = encoder_hidden_dim
        self.decoder_hidden_dim = decoder_hidden_dim
        self.dropout_p = dropout_p

        self.embedding = nn.Embedding(output_dim, embedding_dim)
        self.attention = attention # allowing for custom attention
        self.gru = nn.GRU((encoder_hidden_dim * 2) +
            embedding_dim,
        decoder_hidden_dim)
        self.out = nn.Linear((encoder_hidden_dim * 2) +
            embedding_dim + decoder_hidden_dim,
        output_dim)
        self.dropout = nn.Dropout(dropout_p)

    def forward(self, input, hidden, encoder_outputs,
      src_mask=None):
        # (B) --> (1, B)
        input = input.unsqueeze(0)
        embedded = self.dropout(self.embedding(input))
        attentions = self.attention(hidden, encoder_outputs,
            src_mask)
        # (B, S) --> (B, 1, S)
        a = attentions.unsqueeze(1)
        # (S, B, 2*Enc) --> (B, S, 2*Enc)
        encoder_outputs = encoder_outputs.transpose(0, 1)
        # weighted encoder representation
```

```
# (B, 1, S) @ (B, S, 2*Enc) = (B, 1, 2*Enc)
weighted = torch.bmm(a, encoder_outputs)
# (B, 1, 2*Enc) --> (1, B, 2*Enc)
weighted = weighted.transpose(0, 1)
# concat (1, B, Emb) and (1, B, 2*Enc)
# results in (1, B, Emb + 2*Enc)
rnn_input = torch.cat((embedded, weighted), dim=2)
output, hidden = self.gru(rnn_input, hidden.unsqueeze(0))

assert (output == hidden).all()

# get rid of empty leading dimensions
embedded = embedded.squeeze(0)
output = output.squeeze(0)
weighted = weighted.squeeze(0)

# concatenate the pieces above
# (B, Dec), (B, 2*Enc), and (B, Emb)
# result is (B, Dec + 2*Enc + Emb)
linear_input = torch.cat((output, weighted, embedded),
    dim=1)

# (B, Dec + 2*Enc + Emb) --> (B, O)
output = self.out(linear_input)
return output, hidden.squeeze(0), attentions
```

Listing 2.3 Bahdanau decoder

Listing 2.4 gives the overall structure of the sequence-to-sequence. The encoder and decoder has embedding fixed dimension of 256 and hidden layer size of 256. Regularization is done by adding a dropout of 0.15 for both encoders and decoders and the norms of the gradients are clipped at 10.

```
enc = BahdanauEncoder(input_dim=len(en_vocab),
                embedding_dim=ENCODER_EMBEDDING_DIM,
                ncoder_hidden_dim=ENCODER_HIDDEN_SIZE,
                decoder_hidden_dim=DECODER_HIDDEN_SIZE,
                dropout_p=0.15)

attn = BahdanauAttentionQKV(DECODER_HIDDEN_SIZE)

dec = BahdanauDecoder(output_dim=len(fr_vocab),
                embedding_dim=DECODER_EMBEDDING_DIM,
                encoder_hidden_dim=ENCODER_HIDDEN_SIZE,
```

```
                              decoder_hidden_dim=DECODER_HIDDEN_SIZE,
                              attention=attn,
                              dropout_p=0.15)
        seq2seq = BahdanauSeq2Seq(enc, dec, device)
```

Listing 2.4 Seq2seq with encoder, attention and decoder

Listing 2.5 shows the model training with both encoder and decoder using AdamW variant of Adam which is an improvement where the weight decay is decoupled from the optimization [172]. The learning rate is manually grid searched and fixed at 0.0001 for both encoder and decoder.

```
enc_optim = torch.optim.AdamW(seq2seq.encoder.parameters(),
    lr=1e-4)
dec_optim = torch.optim.AdamW(seq2seq.decoder.parameters(),
    lr=1e-4)
optims = MultipleOptimizer(enc_optim, dec_optim)

best_valid_loss = float("inf")
for epoch in tqdm(range(N_EPOCHS), leave=False,
    desc="Epoch"):
    train_loss = train(seq2seq, train_iter, optims, loss_fn,
        device, clip=CLIP)
    valid_loss = evaluate(seq2seq, valid_iter, loss_fn,
        device)

    if valid_loss < best_valid_loss:
        best_valid_loss = valid_loss
        torch.save(seq2seq.state_dict(), model_path)
```

Listing 2.5 Training for Bahdanau attention-based network

Perplexity is an intrinsic evaluation method often used for measuring the performance of tasks such as language modeling and machine translation [42]. In Fig. 2.16, we show plots of perplexity and training/validation loss for the attention model, measured per epoch during the training process. It is interesting to note that the validation loss starts flattening out around epoch 14 and training loss further reduces, thus indicating overfitting. The best model for both approaches are chosen based on the best fit on the validation data.

To understand how the attention mechanism operates during the translation process, we plot a few examples of the decoded attention outputs highlighting where the decoder is attending as shown in Fig. 2.17.

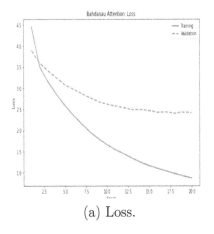

(a) Loss.

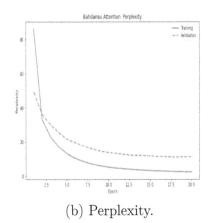

(b) Perplexity.

Figure 2.16 Attention-based seq2seq loss and perplexity on training and validation sets.

The outputs help visualizing and diagnosing issues in the data and the model. For example, Fig. 2.17(a) shows how English word "going" pays attention to "je" and "vais" and similarly how the "store" word pays attention to "au", "magasin", "." and "<eos>".

2.5.3.3 Transformer

The Listing 2.6 shows transformer model wrapping the PyTorch transformer block.

```
class TransformerModel(nn.Module):
    def __init__(self, input_dim, output_dim, d_model,
        num_attention_heads,
                num_encoder_layers, num_decoder_layers,
                    dim_feedforward,
                max_seq_length, pos_dropout,
                    transformer_dropout):
        super().__init__()
        self.d_model = d_model
        self.embed_src = nn.Embedding(input_dim, d_model)
        self.embed_tgt = nn.Embedding(output_dim, d_model)
        self.pos_enc = PositionalEncoding(d_model, pos_dropout,
            max_seq_length)

        self.transformer = nn.Transformer(d_model,
            num_attention_heads, num_encoder_layers,
        num_decoder_layers, dim_feedforward, transformer_dropout)
```

```
    self.output = nn.Linear(d_model, output_dim)

def forward(self, src, tgt,
            src_mask=None,
            tgt_mask=None,
            src_key_padding_mask=None,
            tgt_key_padding_mask=None,
            memory_key_padding_mask=None):

    src_embedded = self.embed_src(src) * np.sqrt(self.d_model)
    tgt_embedded = self.embed_tgt(tgt) * np.sqrt(self.d_model)

    src_embedded = self.pos_enc(src_embedded)
    tgt_embedded = self.pos_enc(tgt_embedded)

    output = self.transformer(src_embedded,
    tgt_embedded,
    tgt_mask=tgt_mask,
    src_key_padding_mask=src_key_padding_mask,
    tgt_key_padding_mask=tgt_key_padding_mask,
    memory_key_padding_mask=memory_key_padding_mask)

    return self.output(output)
```

Listing 2.6 Transformer model

```
transformer = TransformerModel(input_dim=len(en_vocab),
                               output_dim=len(fr_vocab),
                               d_model=256,
                               num_attention_heads=8,
                               num_encoder_layers=6,
                               num_decoder_layers=6,
                               dim_feedforward=2048,
                               max_seq_length=32,
                               pos_dropout=0.15,
                               transformer_dropout=0.3)

transformer = transformer.to(device)
```

Listing 2.7 Transformer model with attention heads, encoding and decoding

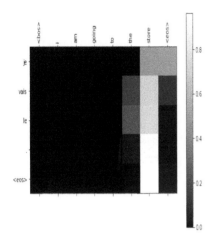

(a) Example showing the English word "going" pays attention to "je" and "vais".

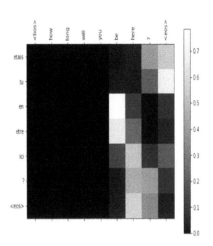

(b) Example showing the English word "be" pays attention to "en" and "etre".

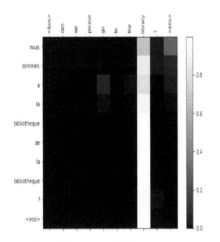

(c) English word "library" pays attention to multiple words.

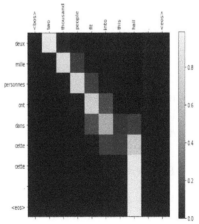

(d) The words "two" and "deux" are matched.

Figure 2.17 Attention examples and plots.

2.5.3.4 *Results and analysis*

Fig. 2.18 are the plots for perplexity and training/validation loss for the transformer model measured per epoch during the training process.

The validation loss plateau's at a value less than 2 in epoch 20, comparing to the value around 2.5 in the attention mechanism. Also, the perplexity of attention is almost double of the transformer model in the validation set.

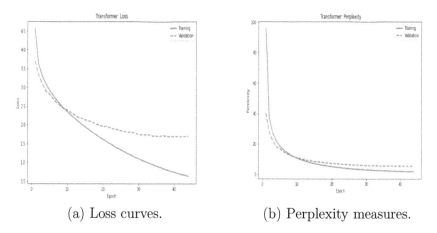

(a) Loss curves.   (b) Perplexity measures.

Figure 2.18 Transformer loss and perplexity on training and validation sets.

Fig. 2.19 shows comparative performance of attention-based and transformer-based models on the same test dataset. Perplexity of transformers is almost three times less than that of attention proving the benefits of the architecture in the real-world translation problem.

2.5.3.5 *Explainability*

We can use the gradient values for the input sequence to illustrate each generated token's dependence on each input token. We start by performing a forward pass on embedded inputs. We then take the token with the highest logit value (in the same way as greedy decoding earlier), and perform a backward pass from the highest logit value. This populates the gradients back through the model to embedded inputs, showing the resulting distribution. Finally, we repeat this process for each generated token and visualize the resulting matrix.

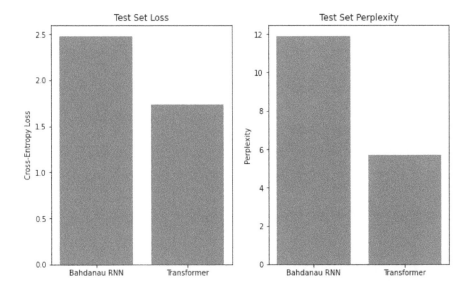

Figure 2.19 Loss and perplexity on the test set.

Fig. 2.20 shows RNN vs. Transformer for the translation and it can be seen that the RNN pairs the formal/plural "serez" with the informal/singular "tu" while transformer matches "seras tu".

Fig. 2.21 shows another RNN vs. Transformer for the translation and it can be seen that the RNN doesn't capture the "snowing" portion of the sentence and produces a different phrasing of "my house".

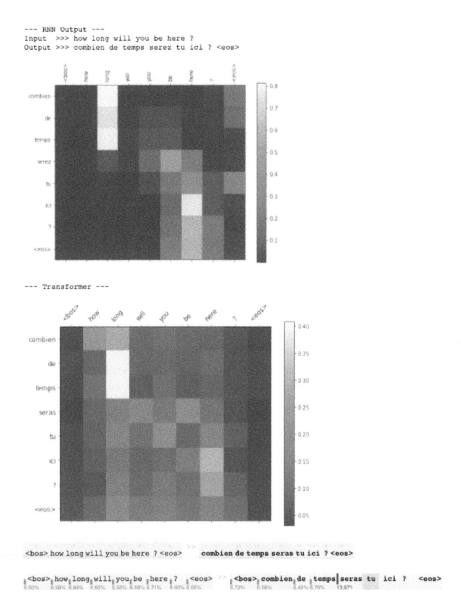

Figure 2.20 Explaining translations for—How long you will be here?

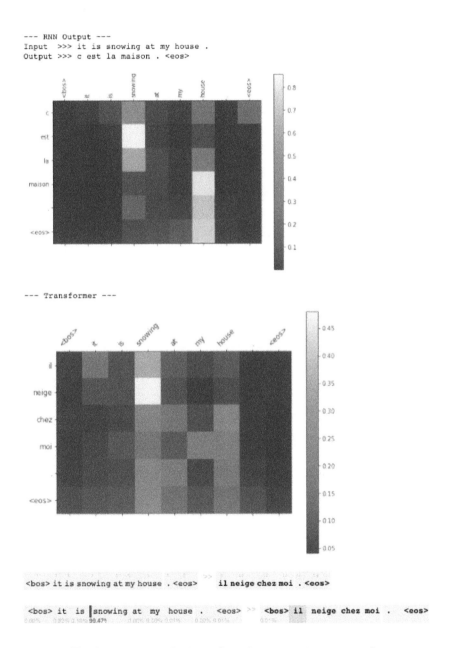

```
--- RNN Output ---
Input  >>> it is snowing at my house .
Output >>> c est la maison . <eos>
```

```
--- Transformer ---
```

Figure 2.21 Explaining translations for—It is snowing at my house.

## CHAPTER 3

Bidirectional Encoder Representations from Transformers (BERT)

T HE advent of Bidirectional Encoder Representations from Transformer (BERT) [72] is considered the onset of a revolution in the field of Natural Language Processing (NLP). BERT uses unlabeled text to pre-train deep bidirectional contextual representations. This resulted in rich pre-trained language models that can be fine-tuned with a simple additional output layer and a reasonably sized labeled dataset to produce state-of-the-art performance in a broad range of NLP tasks. These developments lowered the barrier of entry for the wide adoption of these powerful pre-trained models. It is now common practice in the artificial intelligence field to share pre-trained models and fine-tune them with minimal cost as opposed to the old paradigm of designing task-specific architectures. In this chapter, we cover BERT's basic design concepts, developments, and applications.

3.1 BERT

3.1.1 Architecture

Core layers One of the major contributions of BERT is the simplicity of design and the diversity of covered downstream tasks. BERT's architecture consists of multi-layers of the bidirectional transformer encoder [253]. The capacity of the BERT architecture is characterized by (i) the

DOI: 10.1201/9781003170082-3

number of transformer layers L, (ii) the size of hidden representations H, and the number of bidirectional self-attention heads A.

Input and output representations Given the simplicity of the BERT's core architecture, just a stack of bidirectional transformer encoders, the ingenuity of BERT lies in the design of input and output representations that can be used to train many downstream NLP tasks with the same architecture. To that end, BERT's input is designed to distinctly represent NLP downstream tasks involving a single or a pair of sentences using the same input representation design. Most major NLP downstream tasks can be covered using a single sentence (e.g., text classification, sequence tagging, summarization, etc.) or paired sentences (e.g., question answering, natural language inference, etc.).

For any input sequence, BERT prefixes a special [CLS] token. The hidden vector of this token in the last BERT layer will be used as an aggregate representation for the entire input sequence and usually used for classification tasks. For NLP tasks with paired sentences, BERT concatenates the sentences into one sequence with a separator token [SEP] in between, which serves as one way BERT uses to distinguish the two sentences. BERT also uses a learned segment embedding to indicate to which sentence a token belongs. BERT employs WordPiece [272] to tokenize and embed input sequences. Finally, BERT uses position embedding layer to encode the order of tokens within the input. The input to BERT is the sum of the aforementioned token embedding, segment embedding, and positional embedding for each token as illustrated in Fig. 3.1.

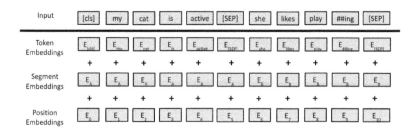

Figure 3.1 BERT input configuration [71].

3.1.2 Pre-Training

Masked Language Model (MLM)   The idea is to randomly mask-out a percentage of the input sequence tokens, replacing them with the special [MASK] token. During pre-training, the modified input sequence is run through BERT and the output representations of the masked tokens are then fed into a softmax layer over the WordPiece vocabulary as practiced in standard language models pre-training. The bidirectional attention of the transformer encoder forces the [MASK] prediction task to use the context provided by the other non-masked tokens in the sequence. BERT is pre-trained with a 15% mask-out rate. This simple MLM task has a downside where a mismatch is created between pre-training and fine-tuning tasks as the special [MASK] token does not appear during fine-tuning. To overcome this issue, every token in the 15% masked-out tokens is subjected to the following heuristic:

- With a probability of 80%, the token is replaced with the special [MASK] token.

- With a probability of 10%, the token is replaced with a random token.

- With a probability of 10%, the token is left unchanged.

The occasional insertion of random tokens (i.e., noise) pushes BERT to be less biased towards the masked token, especially when the masked token is left unchanged, in its bidirectional context attention. The MLM task uses cross-entropy loss only over the masked tokens and ignores the prediction of all non-masked ones.

Next Sentence Prediction (NSP)   Many downstream NLP tasks require understanding the relationship between two sentences, such as Question Answering (QA) and Natural Language Inference (NLI). Standard language models do not pick up this type of knowledge. This motivates the NSP task, where BERT is fed pairs of sentences and pre-trained to predict if the second sentence should follow the first one in a continuous context. As discussed earlier, the first sentence is prefixed with the [CLS] token, then the two sentences are delimited by the special token [SEP]. During NSP task pre-training, the model is given sentence pairs where 50% of the time the second sentence comes after the first sentence and the other 50% the second sentence is a random sentence from the full training corpus. The self-attention of Transformer layers encourages

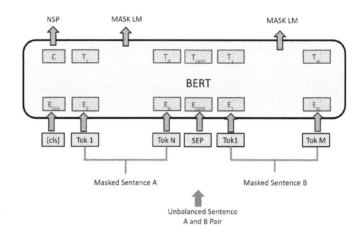

Figure 3.2 BERT pre-training architecture [71].

the BERT representation of [CLS] token to encode both input sentences. Therefore, NSP pre-training is performed by adding a single layer MLP with softmax atop the [CLS] token representation to predict the binary NSP label. BERT pre-training involves combined training with both MLM and NSP tasks by optimizing the model parameters over their combined loss function. Fig. 3.2 illustrates BERT's pre-training tasks.

3.1.3 Fine-Tuning

With BERT simple and yet versatile design, fine-tuning a pre-trained model for many downstream tasks is a straightforward task that involves simply plugging in the proper inputs and outputs and fine-tuning all the model's parameters end-to-end. As discussed earlier many NLP tasks can be modeled using two sentences input to BERT. For tasks like Question Answering (QA) and Natural Language Inference (NLI), the input to BERT is a concatenated question-answer sentence pair and the hypothesis-premise sentence pair, respectively. Other tasks with single input sentence, such as text classification and sequence tagging (e.g., POS, NER), the input to BERT is modeled again as concatenated sentences but with one of them empty. For token level tasks (e.g., QA, POS, and NER), BERT output tokens representations are fed into an output layer for token tagging. Fig. 3.3 provides an illustration for the BERT fine-tuning for token level tasks. For tasks like text classification and NLI, the output representation of the special token [CLS] is used

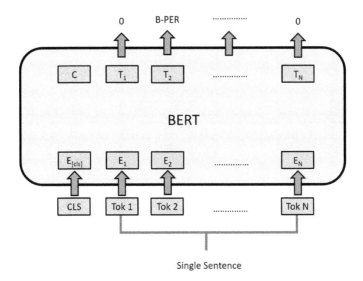

Figure 3.3 BERT fine-tuning architecture for token tagging tasks (e.g., POS, NER, and QA) [71].

as input to an output layer to produce a label. Figs. 3.4 and 3.5 depict BERT fine-tuning architectures for single sequence and paired-sequences classification tasks.

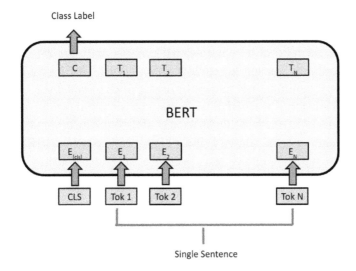

Figure 3.4 BERT fine-tuning architecture for single sequence classification tasks [71].

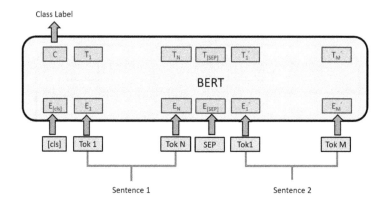

Figure 3.5 BERT fine-tuning architecture for paired-sequence classification tasks (e.g., NLI) [71].

3.2 BERT VARIANTS

3.2.1 Robustly Optimized BERT Pre-training Approach (RoBERTa)

RoBERTa [170] is a Robustly Optimized BERT Pre-training Approach that improves on the original BERT model in terms of pre-training tasks, training hyperparameters, and pre-training data. As discussed earlier, BERT uses two pre-training tasks, Masked Language Model (MLM) and Next Sentence Prediction (NSP). For the MLM task, BERT randomly masks token during the data pre-processing stage. Therefore, the masks stay static throughout the entire model training process. RoBERTa on the other hand follows a dynamic masking strategy where masked tokens are randomly chosen for each training epoch. RoBERTa also drops the NSP pre-training task and only uses the dynamic MLM task. Another contribution for RoBERTa is the size of input sequences, where full sentences of at most 512 tokens, are sampled contiguously from one or more documents. If the end of a document is reached before getting the required input sequence size, sentence sampling continues with the next document after adding an extra separator token.

On the hyperparameters front, RoBERTa showed that using large mini-batches with increased learning rates during pre-training improves the perplexity of the dynamic MLM task as well as the downstream task performance. RoBERTa is also pre-trained on an order of magnitude more data than BERT, the pre-training data consists of 160 GB including Books Corpus, English Wikipedia, and CommonCrawl News dataset

(63 million articles, 76 GB), Web text corpus (38 GB) and Stories from Common Crawl (31 GB).

To summarize, using the same basic architecture as BERT, RoBERTa has shown that the following design changes significantly improves RoBERTa performance over BERT.

1. Pre-training the model for longer time

2. Using bigger batches

3. Using more training data

4. Removing the NSP pre-training task

5. Training on longer sequences

6. Dynamically changing the masking pattern applied to the training data.

3.3 APPLICATIONS

3.3.1 TaBERT

TaBERT [289] is the first model to have been pre-trained on both natural language sentences and tabular data formats. These representations are advantageous for problems involving cooperative reasoning over natural language sentences and tables. Semantic parsing over databases is a sample example, in which a natural language inquiry (e.g., "Which nation has the largest GDP?") is translated to a program executable over database (DB) tables. This is the first technique of pre-training that spans structured and unstructured domains, and it opens up new possibilities for semantic parsing, where one of the primary issues has been comprehending the structure of a database table and how it fits with a query. TaBERT was trained on a corpus of 26 million tables and the English phrases that accompany them. Historically, language models have been trained only on free-form natural language text. While these models are excellent for jobs that need reasoning only in free-form natural language, they are insufficient for activities such as database-based question answering, which involves reasoning in both free-form language and database tables.

Two commonly used benchmarks for database-based question answering were utilized: a traditional supervised text-to-SQL job over structured data from the Spider dataset and a weakly supervised parsing task over a semi-structured dataset from the WikiTableQuestions dataset. Weakly supervised learning is substantially more difficult than supervised learning, since the parser lacks access to the labeled question and must instead explore a very vast search space of queries. TaBERT is a Natural Language Processing (NLP) model built on top of the BERT model that accepts natural language queries and tables as input. TaBERT acquires contextual representations for sentences as well as the constituents of the DB table in this manner. These representations may then be utilized to generate real database instructions in other neural networks. TaBERT's representations may then be fine-tuned further using the training data for that job.

TaBERT is trained via content snapshots, in which the model only encodes the bits of a table that are most relevant to a query. Due to the enormous amount of rows in certain database tables, encoding them is a computationally intensive and inefficient procedure. By encoding just the portion of material that is most relevant to the utterance, content snapshots enable TaBERT to handle with enormous tables. For instance, the phrase "In which city did Piotr finish first last time?" (sample extracted from the WikiTableQuestions dataset) may be accompanied with a table including information on the year, venue, position, and event. A snapshot of content will take a subset of three rows. This subset will not include all of the table's data, but it is sufficient for the model to understand that, for example, the venue column comprises cities. TaBERT describes table structure using a mix of traditional horizontal self-attention, which captures the dependence between cells in specific rows, and vertical self-attention, which catches the information flow between cells in different rows. The ultimate outputs of layers of such horizontal and vertical self-attention are distributed representations of utterance tokens and table columns, which may be utilized to calculate the database query by downstream semantic parsers.

3.3.2 BERTopic

Topic modeling is one of the challenging topics in NLP. The advances in BERT and its variants motivate the NLP community to leverage BERT in topic modeling. Grootendorst [101] introduced an elegant idea, BERTopic, to extract interpretable topics in documents using BERT and transformers embeddings. Hence, takes advantage of the state-of-the-art pre-trained transformers model. The method starts by creating the embeddings of the documents of interest using BERT models. Since documents can be very large and BERT models have limit on the token size, the documents are preprocessed before extracting the embeddings. Preprocessing divides the document to smaller paragraphs or sentences that are smaller than the token size for the transformer model. Then, clustering is performed on the document embeddings to cluster all the documents with similar topics together. It is worth noting that dimensionality reduction for the embeddings is recommended before performing the clustering. Dimensionality reduction algorithms such as t-Distributed Stochastic Neighbor Embedding (t-SNE) or Uniform Manifold Approximation and Projection (UMAP) can be used to lower the dimensions. The topics are then derived from the clustered documents using the novel class-based metric introduced by Grootendorst in [101]. Class-Based Term Frequency-Inverse Document Frequency (c-TF-IDF) is modification of the classic Term Frequency-Inverse Document Frequency (TF-IDF) in which all documents in a certain category is considered as a single document then compute TF-IDF. Therefore, the TF-IDF in this case would represent the importance of words in a topic, not in a document. The Class-Based Term Frequency-Inverse Document Frequency (c-TF-IDF) is computed as

$$c - TF - IDF_i = \frac{t_i}{w_i} \times \log \frac{m}{\sum_j^n t_j} \tag{3.1}$$

where the frequency of each word t is extracted for each class i and normalized by the total number of words and this is weighted by the normalized number of documents per the total frequency of the word t across all the classes n. In other words, instead of computing the relative importance of a word in a document as compared to the other documents, the metric in (3.1) computed the relative importance of a word in a class (i.e., topic) as compared to the other topics.

3.4 BERT INSIGHTS

3.4.1 BERT Sentence Representation

Due to self-attention in the Transformer encoder, the BERT representation of the special token [CLS] encodes both the two sentences from the input. Hence, the output layer of the MLP classifier takes X as the input, where X is the output of the MLP hidden layer whose input is the encoded [CLS] token. Because a pre-trained model is not fine-tuned on any downstream tasks yet. In this case, the hidden state of [CLS] is not a good sentence representation. If later you fine-tune the model, you may use [CLS] as well.

BERT sentence representation can also be obtained by pooling the individual token representations. However, the last layer is too close to the target functions (i.e., masked language model and next sentence prediction) during pre-training, therefore may be biased to those targets.

3.4.2 BERTology

The great push BERT has provided to the NLP field triggered much research into understanding how it works and the type of knowledge it extracts through massive pre-training. BERTology aims to answer some of the questions about why BERT performs well on so many NLP tasks. Some of the topics addressed by BERTology include the type of knowledge learned by BERT and where it is represented. In general there three types of knowledge BERT acquires: Syntactic knowledge, Semantic knowledge, World knowledge.

BERT representations of syntactic knowledge are hierarchical rather than linear, i.e., they include a syntactic tree structure in addition to the word order information. Additionally, BERT embeddings store information about speech segments, grammatical chunks, and roles. BERT's understanding of syntax, on the other hand, is incomplete, since probing classifiers were unable to retrieve the labels of distant parent nodes in the syntactic tree. In terms of how syntactic information is represented, it seems that self-attention weights do not directly encode syntactic structure, but they may be changed to reflect it. When executing the cloze task, BERT takes subject-predicate agreement into consideration. Additionally, it was shown that BERT does not "understand" negation and is indifferent to input that is faulty.

Regarding aspects of semantic knowledge, BERT has shown some knowledge for semantic roles. Also BERT encodes information about entity types, relations, semantic roles, and proto-roles. However, it was found that BERT struggles with representations of numbers. Research probing into BERT's world knowledge capabilities showed that, for some relation types, vanilla BERT is competitive with methods relying on knowledge bases. However, BERT cannot reason based on its world knowledge. Essentially BERT can "guess" the affordances and properties of many objects, but does not have the information about their interactions (e.g., it "knows" that people can walk into houses, and that houses are big, but it cannot infer that houses are bigger than people.)

Additionally, BERTology is concerned with the localization of linguistic information inside the BERT architecture, either at the self-attention heads or at the layer level. It was shown that the majority of self-attention heads do not encode any non-trivial linguistic information directly, since fewer than half of them exhibited the "heterogeneous" pattern2. The vertical pattern was stored in a large portion of the model (attention to [CLS], [SEP], and punctuation tokens). Additionally, certain BERT heads seem to specialize in particular sorts of syntactic relations, with heads paying much more attention to words in specific syntactic places than a random baseline. Other studies discovered that no one head contains the whole syntactic tree. Additionally, attention weights are illustrative of subject-verb agreement and reflexive anaphora. Additionally, it was shown that even when attention heads specialize in monitoring semantic relations, they do not always help BERT perform well on related tasks.

For layer-level knowledge localization, provided that the first layer of BERT gets representations in the form of a mix of token, segment, and positional embeddings as input. It comes to reason that the bottom levels contain the most linear information about word order. It was shown that the knowledge of linear word order decreases around layer 4 in the BERT-base. This is followed by an enhanced understanding of the hierarchical structure of sentences. Numerous studies have shown that the middle BERT layers contain the most syntactic information and that the last BERT levels include the most task-specific information. Additionally, it was shown that, although the majority of syntactic information may be localized in a few levels, semantic information is distributed across the model, which explains why some non-trivial cases are initially handled wrong then successfully at higher layers.

3.5 CASE STUDY: TOPIC MODELING WITH TRANSFORMERS

3.5.1 Goal

In this chapter, we looked at several applications of the Transformer architecture. In this case study, we see how to use pre-trained (or fine-tuned) Transformer models to do topic modeling. If one is exploring a new dataset, this method could be used during exploratory data analysis.

3.5.2 Data, Tools, and Libraries

```
pip install -U datasets bertopic
```

Listing 3.1 Python environment setup

We will use pre-trained transformers to explore the Yelp reviews dataset (from`https://huggingface.co/datasets/yelp_review_full`) and see what kind of topics are in the reviews. We'll generate sentence embeddings with the sentence-transformers library (see `https://github.com/UKPLab/sentence-transformers`). which provides models pre-trained for specific tasks, such as semantic search. Lastly, we're going to use BERTopic [101] (see `https://github.com/MaartenGr/BERTopic`) for topic modeling and Huggingface Datasets for loading the data. We can install these as shown in Listing. 3.1.

3.5.2.1 Data

```
from datasets import load_dataset

N = 10_000
dataset = load_dataset("yelp_review_full", split=f"train[:{N}]")
```
Listing 3.2 Load dataset

We begin by loading the Yelp Review Full dataset via Huggingface Datasets in Listing 3.2. There are $650,000$ reviews in the dataset. To keep the runtime of this case study within reason, we'll only process the first $10,000$ reviews. To process more reviews, simply change the value of N in Listing 3.2.

3.5.2.2 Compute embeddings

```
from sentence_transformers import SentenceTransformer
import numpy as np

# SentenceTransformer automatically checks if a GPU is
    available
embeddings_model = SentenceTransformer("all-mpnet-base-v2")

batch_size = 64

def embed(batch):
  batch["embedding"] =
      embeddings_model.encode(batch["text"])
  return batch
```

```
dataset = dataset.map(embed, batch_size=batch_size,
    batched=True)
dataset.set_format(type='numpy', columns=['embedding'],
    output_all_columns=True)
```

Listing 3.3 Compute embeddings

We'll generate embeddings using the "all-mpnet-base-v2" model from sentence-transformers in Listing 3.3. It's built to perform well on semantic search when embedding sentences and longer spans of text.

3.5.3 Experiments, Results, and Analysis

3.5.3.1 Building topics

```
from bertopic import BERTopic

topic_model = BERTopic(n_gram_range=(1, 3))
topics, probs = topic_model.fit_transform(
    dataset["text"],
    np.array(dataset["embedding"]))

print(f"Number of topics: {len(topic_model.get_topics())}")
```

Listing 3.4 Compute topics

Now that we've computed the embeddings for the specified subset of Yelp reviews, we can proceed with the topic modeling in Listing 3.4.

3.5.3.2 Topic size distribution

```
topic_sizes = topic_model.get_topic_freq()
topic_sizes
```

Listing 3.5 Sampling the topics

Now that we have computed a topic distribution, we need to see what kind of reviews are in each topic. Let's start by looking at the distribution of topic sizes.

The commands in Listing 3.5 will output a summary table of the sizes of the topics. Note that the size of a topic is the number of reviews that contain that topic. The table is shown in Fig. 3.6.

	Topic	Count	Name
0	-1	2588	-1_food_good_place_were
1	0	349	0_italian_pasta_sauce_it was
2	1	313	1_our_she_we_us
3	2	312	2_pittsburgh_in pittsburgh_sandwich_bar
4	3	278	3_pizza_the pizza_crust_cheese
...	...	...	...
145	144	11	144_brixx_pizza_gluten free_gluten
146	145	11	145_cream_ice cream_ice_klavons
147	146	10	146_thai_pad_thai house_pad thai
148	147	10	147_massage_spa_the spa_massages
149	148	10	148_store_the produce_pick save_produce

Figure 3.6 Table showing sizes and names of largest and smallest topics.

Note the topic with id of −1. This corresponds to the unassigned cluster output by the HDBSCAN algorithm. The unassigned cluster is composed of all the things that could not be assigned to one of the other clusters. It can *generally* be ignored, but if it were too large, it would be a sign that our choice of parameters are probably not good for our data. One can look at the contents of the unassigned cluster to verify that it contains words that are not relevant.

3.5.3.3 *Visualization of topics*

```
topic_model.visualize_barchart(top_n_topics=10,
                                n_words=5, width=1000, height=800)
```

Listing 3.6 Visualizing the 10 largest topics

BERTopic includes several ways to visualize different aspects of the topic distribution. In Listing 3.6 we sample the 10 largest topics, which are shown in Fig. 3.7.

```
topic_model.visualize_heatmap(top_n_topics=20, n_clusters=5)
```

Listing 3.7 Visualizing the cosine similarity of the 20 largest topics

BERTopic can also show a heatmap of the cosine similarities of the topic embeddings, using the $visualize_heatmap$ method, as shown in Listing. 3.7. The heatmap is shown in Fig. 3.8 and it shows the degree of overlap between the embedding vectors of each pair of topics.

Topic Word Scores

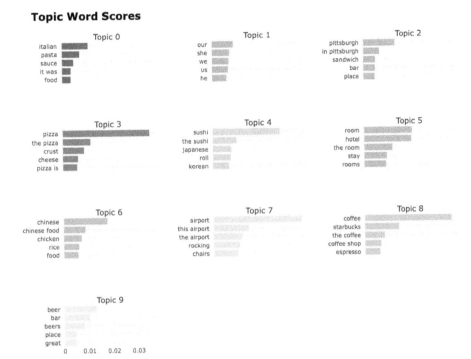

Figure 3.7 The 10 largest topics.

3.5.3.4 Content of topics

```
def dump_topic_and_docs(text, topic_id):
    print(f"{text} size: {topic_sizes['Count'][topic_id +
        1]}\n")
    n = len(topic_sizes) - 1

    if topic_id != -1:
        reviews = topic_model.get_representative_docs(topic_id)

        for review in reviews:
            print(review, "\n")

    return topic_model.get_topic(topic_id)[:10]
```

Listing 3.8 Print the topic size and representative words

Similarity Matrix

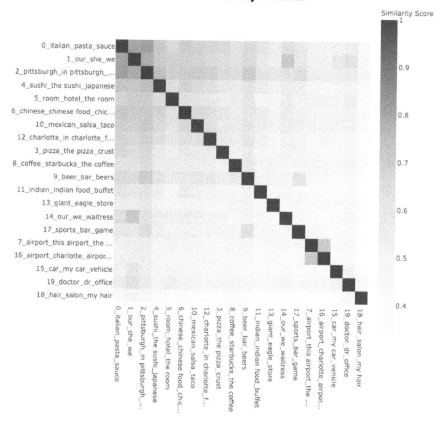

Figure 3.8 Heatmap of the cosine similarity of the 20 largest topics.

Now we'll look at a sample of topics. We looked at the 10 largest topics in Fig. 3.7, so here we'll look at the largest and smallest topics, the topic with median size, and the contents of the unassigned cluster. Listing 3.8 shows a simple helper function we can use to print the size of a topic and the 10 words most relevant to the topic.

```
>>> dump_topic_and_docs("Unassigned cluster", -1)

Unassigned cluster size: 2588

[('food', 0.0028285252847909887),
 ('good', 0.0027913860678148716),
 ('place', 0.0027706150477682947),
```

```
('were', 0.0026233026252016375),
('here', 0.0025870065464529087),
('had', 0.002496872164775201),
('great', 0.0024961777546672285),
('it was', 0.002469218043237805),
('there', 0.0024523636574226805),
('service', 0.0024482400423906816)]
```

Listing 3.9 Unassigned cluster

First, we'll look at the unassigned cluster, which has topic id –1, to verify that we can safely ignore its contents. It's in Listing 3.9.

As we can see, the content of the unassigned cluster contains words that do not strongly belong to any topic. The largest, smallest, and median topics are shown in Listings 3.10, 3.11, and 3.12, respectively.

```
>>> dump_topic_and_docs("Largest topic", 0)
Largest topic size: 349

**** Representative reviews ****
This place makes me cringe! I've dined here with large groups
    of friends when we needed to have a big table and they all
    wanted to be bursting full of cheap food and that is really
    the only excuse to go to this place. \n\nOne reviewer
    mentioned the 90's music and the goofy food art on the
    walls. I could not agree more that this is so funny. Whoa
    and talk about noisy. This place is deafening inside on a
    Friday or Saturday night, worse than a cafeteria. I think
    that everyone with a City-Pass crams in there in search of
    the best two-for-one deal on a massive mound of macaroni
    slathered in dreadful red sauce and salty cheese. \n\nI
    actually ordered a salad as my main the last time that I
    dined there because I know how universally disappointing
    the pasta dishes were and they actually screwed up a salad.
    I am not sure what on earth it was supposed to be, but they
    called it a chopped salad and it had a little M next to it
    in the menu as if it were a specialty of the house. I asked
    for grilled chicken on top and received a dried out piece
    of leather sitting above a mess of lettuce, beans, nuts,
    cheese and peppers. Just plain salty and awful. Everything
    was either from a can or a jar. \n\nI do agree with others
    who have said that the service is very fast and friendly.
    They kept the beer and wine flowing at our table at every
    visit. I think that is why so many of my friends just
```

shovel this stuff down. \n\nAh well, Arrivederci (no more) Mama Ricotta

I met up with friends for a birthday gathering at Frankie's. It was my first time and, while I usually don't go out of my way for Italian, I was very impressed with Frankie's. I felt like I stepped back in time. The ambiance and decor seemed elegant from the 50s era, yet the friendliness of the server and the atmosphere was casual. \n\nThe menu contained everything you'd expect on an Italian restaurant menu and everything from the bread to the appetizer to the entree to the wine tasted delicious. Frankie's is definitely a place you can take friends and family to impress them, but not spend a fortune doing so.

When you think of a nice Italian restaurant, you don't think it would come in a strip mall, but Mama Ricotta's bucks the trend. Not only does the atmosphere & decor give the impression of a nicer Italian place, the food is pretty good.\n\nWhile you may be thinking that this is a dinner only place, this is actually a really popular lunch place. There is usually a line during lunch, but it moves pretty quickly, especially if the outside seating is open. While the food can be a tad on the pricey side, I have yet to have a meal I haven't been happy with. They have plenty of selections for all Italian lovers so don't expect just the obvious options. \n\nI'd suggest this place as more of a dinner place, mainly because of the prices along with the portion sizes. If you lunch it here, it may be a long afternoon at work trying to stay awake. And with their wine selection, making this a date destination isn't a bad idea either.

```
[('italian', 0.010707434311063687),
 ('pasta', 0.007218630048706305),
 ('sauce', 0.004690392541116093),
 ('it was', 0.003576349729937027),
 ('food', 0.0035416017180294685),
 ('restaurant', 0.0034094836517629345),
 ('salad', 0.003321322452779836),
 ('olive', 0.0032739980714160824),
 ('bread', 0.0032417620081978916),
 ('italian food', 0.0031995754647714428)]
```

Listing 3.10 Largest topic: Italian food restaurants

```
>>> dump_topic_and_docs("Smallest topic", n-1)
Smallest topic size: 10

**** Representative reviews ****
There is no doubt that the ambiance is better than many other
    optical's shops but the prices are very high. \n\nWe saw
    the same product in Carolina's mall in sears Optical's at a
    way lower price point. I am definitely disappointed.

Meh. I hate how this store is laid out, and everything is
    tackily displayed. I also hate how they gouge you for
    printer ink. Huge store, not much going on inside. Too bad
    it's so close.

A very oddly laid out supermarket. the Deli isle is not very
    wide, the the walls are closing in on you, and they put the
    DIY olive cart in front to make it more cluttered. Just a
    poorly laid out store which is showing it's age.

[('store', 0.02825717462668952),
 ('the produce', 0.01719937359158404),
 ('pick save', 0.0171157817586613058),
 ('produce', 0.017000435507400078),
 ('this store', 0.016450186193483884),
 ('laid out', 0.01360566214521891),
 ('opticals', 0.012361992937075754),
 ('copps', 0.011805417634250547),
 ('hot cocoa', 0.011805417634250547),
 ('produce quality', 0.011805417634250547)]
```

Listing 3.11 Smallest topic: the ambiance and arrangement of stores

```
>>> dump_topic_and_docs("Median topic", n//2)
Median topic size: 28

**** Representative reviews ****
Cosmos Cafe is yet another venue that is really a restaurant,
    but doubles as a nightlife hot spot on the weekends. North
    Carolina's laws on serving alcohol make it nearly
    impossible to just open a \"club\", so you see a lot of
    these in Charlotte, especially downtown. \n\nThe staff is
    super friendly and doesn't hassle you for walking in and
    realizing \"Saturday night\" hasn't started yet because the
    dining patrons still haven't cleared out. So don't be
```

afraid to check it at 11pm and then come back again at midnight or 1 if it's still slow. I've never been here to eat but it's a great place to stop in for a late night weekend drink to see what's going on. People dress nice and behave well. So you can actually get an expensive drink and not worry about someone elbowing it across the room. \n\nThere's plenty of seating on both the first and second floors and they have a respectable, if predictable, Scotch selection that helps me keep them in mind when I'm downtown, so I'm sure the rest of the liquor options are pretty good. Coming from Illinois where you can buy booze at grocery stores, it's depressing to walk into a bar in Charlotte and only have one or two choices. Cosmos expands the horizons and I appreciate that.

Need a place in Charlotte to get black out drunk without fear of waking up missing vital organs? Than the Westin Charlotte is the place for you. Was witness to an amateur drunk who passed out. Rather than doing the typical bounce and toss the staff gave genuine care and concern to the help him through the this moment of self reflection. One employee went so far as to ice his neck in hope to help him sober up, if nothing else at least remeber his name. Even when the EMTs arrived and drunk punches were thrown the staff stood stoically ready to show their support for their customer. So, it became a dinner and a show. Five stars. NERD RAGE!

Festivals. Fun. Beer. Lots of beer. Charlotte Center City Partners (or Find Your Center) puts on a lot of these types of festivals Uptown and in South End. When you check out their website or their weekly newsletter you'll be able to see lots of events coming up like Beer, Blues and BBQ, Taste of Charlotte, Speedstreet and the like. \n\nMany of these events and festivals usually have beer available, hence why I'm a fan. And, yeah, I also really like supporting the local organization that's responsible for Uptown's development. If only there was a PBR festival...!

[('charlotte', 0.017158486331587473),
 ('in charlotte', 0.013092184112676906),
 ('beer', 0.01118926729742822),
 ('city', 0.007059710231581003),
 ('dance', 0.005752330716241153),
 ('selection', 0.005730672906147966),

```
('liquor', 0.005587858949299897),
('center city', 0.005496678910160935),
('beers', 0.005368697666709216),
('events', 0.005089779403417317)]
```

Listing 3.12 Median topic: Nightlife in Charlotte, NC

3.6 CASE STUDY: FINE-TUNING BERT

3.6.1 Goal

The goals of this case study is to provide a step-by-step demo of fine-tuning a standard BERT model for any sentence classification, we chose sentiment classification as a sample popular task.

3.6.2 Data, Tools, and Libraries

We chose the Google Play application review dataset. The dataset includes 15,746 samples in three categories; namely negative, neutral, and positive. We use the Huggingface transformer library to perform the fine-tuning task as well as standard Python data science stack for all other data handling and visualization [249] (Figs. 3.9–3.11).

We use BERT$_{\text{BASE}}$ as the starting pre-trained BERT mode. Listing 3.6.3 shows how to load the pre-trained BERT model from the Trans-

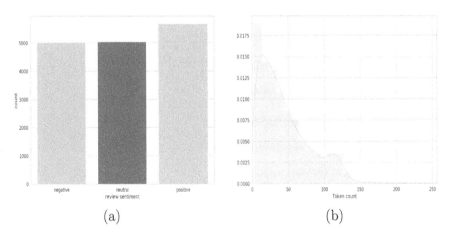

(a) (b)

Figure 3.9 Exploratory data analysis of the sentiment classification dataset.

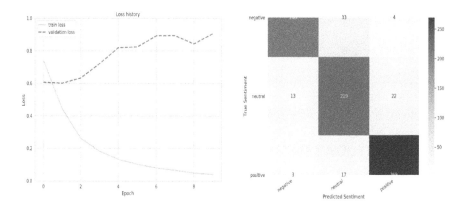

Figure 3.10 Training and validation loss throughout training.

Figure 3.11 Confusion matrix of
test set.

formers library and illustrates the output of tokenization that will be
used to fine-tune the BERT model [249].

3.6.3 Experiments, Results, and Analysis

```
PRE_TRAINED_MODEL_NAME = 'bert-base-cased'
tokenizer =
    BertTokenizer.from_pretrained(PRE_TRAINED_MODEL_NAME)

sample_txt = 'When was I last outside? I am stuck at home
    for 2 weeks.'
tokens = tokenizer.tokenize(sample_txt)
token_ids = tokenizer.convert_tokens_to_ids(tokens)
print(f' Sentence: {sample_txt}')
print(f'  Tokens: {tokens}')
print(f'Token IDs: {token_ids}')
encoding = tokenizer.encode_plus(
    sample_txt,
    max_length=32,
    truncation=True,
    add_special_tokens=True, # Add '[CLS]' and '[SEP]'
    return_token_type_ids=False,
    pad_to_max_length=True,
    return_attention_mask=True,
    return_tensors='pt', # Return PyTorch tensors
    )
print(f'Encoding keys: {encoding.keys()}')
```

```
print(len(encoding['input_ids'][0]))
print(encoding['input_ids'][0])
print(len(encoding['attention_mask'][0]))
print(encoding['attention_mask'])
print(tokenizer.convert_ids_to_tokens
      (encoding['input_ids'][0]))
```

Listing 3.6.3 provides the tooling to ingest our dataset as well as split the data into train, validation, and testing. It also creates data loader for each data split which to use throughout the fine-tuning iterations [249].

```
MAX_LEN = 160
class GPReviewDataset(Dataset):
  def __init__(self, reviews, targets, tokenizer, max_len):
    self.reviews = reviews
    self.targets = targets
    self.tokenizer = tokenizer
    self.max_len = max_len

  def __len__(self):
    return len(self.reviews)
  def __getitem__(self, item):
    review = str(self.reviews[item])
    target = self.targets[item]
    encoding = self.tokenizer.encode_plus(
        review, add_special_tokens = True, max_length =
            self.max_len, return_token_type_ids = False,
            return_attention_mask = True, truncation = True,
        pad_to_max_length = True, return_tensors = 'pt',
    )

    return {
        'review_text':review,
        'input_ids': encoding['input_ids'].flatten(),
        'attention_mask':encoding['attention_mask'].flatten(),
        'targets':torch.tensor(target, dtype=torch.long)
    }

def create_data_loader(df, tokenizer, max_len, batch_size):
  ds = GPReviewDataset(
      reviews = df.content.to_numpy(), targets =
          df.sentiment.to_numpy(), tokenizer = tokenizer,
          max_len = max_len
  )
  return DataLoader(ds, batch_size=batch_size, num_workers=4)
```

```
df_train, df_test = train_test_split(df, test_size = 0.1,
    random_state = RANDOM_SEED)
df_val, df_test = train_test_split(df_test, test_size = 0.5,
    random_state = RANDOM_SEED)
print(df_train.shape, df_val.shape, df_test.shape)
BATCH_SIZE = 16
train_data_loader = create_data_loader(df_train, tokenizer,
    MAX_LEN, BATCH_SIZE)
val_data_loader = create_data_loader(df_val, tokenizer,
    MAX_LEN, BATCH_SIZE)
test_data_loader = create_data_loader(df_test, tokenizer,
    MAX_LEN, BATCH_SIZE)

#Testing to see if the data loader works appropriately
data = next(iter(train_data_loader))
print(data.keys())
print(data['input_ids'].shape)
print(data['attention_mask'].shape)
print(data['targets'].shape)
```

Listing 3.6.3 creates the fine-tuned model and sets the parameters of the associated loss, optimizer, and learning rate scheduling [249].

```
EPOCHS = 10
optimizer = AdamW(model.parameters(), lr= 2e-5,
    correct_bias=False)
total_steps = len(train_data_loader) * EPOCHS
scheduler = get_linear_schedule_with_warmup(
    optimizer, num_warmup_steps = 0,
        num_training_steps=total_steps
)
loss_fn = nn.CrossEntropyLoss().to(device)

def train_epoch(model, data_loader, loss_fn, optimizer, device,
    scheduler, n_examples):
  model=model.train()
  losses = []
  correct_predictions = 0
  for d in data_loader:
    input_ids = d["input_ids"].to(device)
    attention_mask = d["attention_mask"].to(device)
    targets = d["targets"].to(device)
    outputs = model(input_ids=input_ids,
        attention_mask=attention_mask)
```

```
    _, preds = torch.max(outputs, dim = 1)
    loss = loss_fn(outputs, targets)
    correct_predictions += torch.sum(preds == targets)
    losses.append(loss.item())
    loss.backward()
    nn.utils.clip_grad_norm_(model.parameters(), max_norm=1.0)
    optimizer.step()
    scheduler.step()
    optimizer.zero_grad()

  return correct_predictions.double()/n_examples,
      np.mean(losses)

def eval_model(model, data_loader, loss_fn, device, n_examples):
  model = model.eval()
  losses = []
  correct_predictions = 0
  with torch.no_grad():
    for d in data_loader:
      input_ids = d["input_ids"].to(device)
      attention_mask = d["attention_mask"].to(device)
      targets = d["targets"].to(device)
      outputs = model(input_ids = input_ids, attention_mask =
          attention_mask)
      _,preds = torch.max(outputs, dim = 1)
      loss = loss_fn(outputs, targets)
      correct_predictions += torch.sum(preds == targets)
      losses.append(loss.item())
  return correct_predictions.double()/n_examples,
      np.mean(losses)
```

```
history = defaultdict(list)
best_accuracy = 0
for epoch in range(EPOCHS):
  print(f'Epoch {epoch + 1}/ {EPOCHS}')
  print('-'*15)
  train_acc, train_loss = train_epoch(model, train_data_loader,
      loss_fn, optimizer, device, scheduler, len(df_train))
  print(f'Train loss {train_loss} accuracy {train_acc}')
  val_acc, val_loss = eval_model(model, val_data_loader,
      loss_fn, device, len(df_val))
  print(f'Val loss {val_loss} accuracy {val_acc}')
  history['train_acc'].append(train_acc)
  history['train_loss'].append(train_loss)
```

```
history['val_acc'].append(val_acc)
history['val_loss'].append(val_loss)
if val_acc>best_accuracy:
  torch.save(model.state_dict(), 'best_model_state.bin')
  best_accuracy = val_acc

plt.plot(history['train_acc'], label='train accuracy')
plt.plot(history['val_acc'], label='validation accuracy')
plt.title('Training history')
plt.ylabel('Accuracy')
plt.xlabel('Epoch')
plt.legend()
plt.ylim([0,1])
```

```
plt.plot(history['train_loss'], label='train loss',linewidth=3)
plt.plot(history['val_loss'], '--',label='validation
    loss',linewidth=3)

plt.title('Loss history')
plt.ylabel('Loss')
plt.xlabel('Epoch')
plt.legend()
plt.ylim([0, 1]);
```

```
def get_predictions(model, data_loader):
  model = model.eval()
  review_texts = []
  predictions = []
  prediction_probs = []
  real_values = []
  with torch.no_grad():
    for d in data_loader:
      texts = d["review_text"]
      input_ids = d["input_ids"].to(device)
      attention_mask = d["attention_mask"].to(device)
      targets = d["targets"].to(device)
      outputs = model(input_ids = input_ids, attention_mask =
          attention_mask)
      _, preds = torch.max(outputs, dim=1)
      probs = F.softmax(outputs, dim =1)
      review_texts.extend(texts)
      predictions.extend(preds)
      prediction_probs.extend(probs)
```

```
    real_values.extend(targets)
  predictions = torch.stack(predictions).cpu()
  prediction_probs = torch.stack(prediction_probs).cpu()
  real_values = torch.stack(real_values).cpu()
  return review_texts, predictions, prediction_probs,
     real_values

def show_confusion_matrix(confusion_matrix):
  hmap = sns.heatmap(confusion_matrix, annot=True, fmt="d",
     cmap="Blues")
  hmap.yaxis.set_ticklabels(hmap.yaxis.get_ticklabels(),
     rotation = 0, ha='right')
  hmap.xaxis.set_ticklabels(hmap.xaxis.get_ticklabels(),
     rotation = 30, ha='right')
  plt.ylabel('True Sentiment')
  plt.xlabel('Predicted Sentiment')

y_review_texts, y_pred, y_pred_probs, y_test =
    get_predictions(model, test_data_loader)
print(classification_report(y_test, y_pred,
    target_names=class_names))

cm = confusion_matrix(y_test, y_pred)
df_cm = pd.DataFrame(cm, index=class_names, columns =
    class_names)
show_confusion_matrix(df_cm)
```

## CHAPTER 4

Multilingual Transformer Architectures

THE introduction of BERT [72] has transformed the area of Natural Language Processing (NLP) and resulted in state-of-the-art performance on a broad range of tasks. In the recent past, training NLP algorithms worked only with labeled data, which hindered their progress for years due to the limited availability and cost of collecting data for every new task and every new project. One major contribution of BERT is introducing a new pipeline for training NLP systems where algorithms can learn about core and generic natural language concepts from huge amount of cheap unlabeled data, a process also known as self-supervised learning or model pre-training. A pre-trained model is then fine-tuned for any specific downstream task using much smaller task-specific labeled datasets. This new pipeline of pre-training followed by fine-tuning constitutes the core of most advances in the machine learning field. The major success of BERT for English NLP tasks has motivated its use for other languages. However, using BERT's pipeline is only possible for languages with sufficiently large unlabeled data for pre-training. This motivated the development of multilingual models where models are pre-trained on multiple languages with the hope that the models will transfer core NLP knowledge from high-resource languages to low-resource ones and we end up with a polyglot model that aligns multilingual representations across languages.

This chapter covers the state-of-the-art developments in multilingual transformer architectures. A multilingual transformer architecture is fully defined using:

- Model Architecture (layers and components)

- Pre-training Tasks

- Pre-training Data

- Fine-tuning Tasks and Benchmarks

The chapter starts with different multilingual transformer architecture for Natural Language Understanding (NLU) and Natural Language Generation (NLG). Section 4.2 proceeds by describing the state-of-the-art in multilingual data, this includes unlabeled pre-training data and fine-tuning benchmarks for downstream NLP tasks. Section 4.3 provides some insights into the inner workings of multilingual transformer models. Finally, Section 4.4 provides a practical case study on zero-shot multilingual sentiment classification.

4.1 MULTILINGUAL TRANSFORMER ARCHITECTURES

This section discusses the different architectural designs for multilingual Transformers. We divide multilingual transformers into (i) Natural Language Understanding (NLU) architectures and (ii) Natural Language Generation (NLG) architectures. Table 4.1 [74] provides a summary of the impactful multilingual transformer models available at the time of publishing this book.

4.1.1 Basic Multilingual Transformer

Multilingual transformer models are typically based on the mBERT architecture [72]. In this section, we describe the basic components of a multilingual transformer architecture.

Input Layer A series of tokens is provided as input to the multilingual transformer. The token input is derived from a one-shot representation of a limited vocabulary, often a subword vocabulary. Typically, this vocabulary is learned by concatenating monolingual data from several languages using algorithms such as BPE [223], WordPiece [273], or SentencePiece [144]. To guarantee that diverse languages and scripts are well represented in the vocabulary, data may be sampled using exponential weighted smoothing or distinct vocabularies for clusters of languages can be learned [55] by dividing the vocabulary size.

TABLE 4.1 Summary of multilingual language models [74]

Model	Architecture	pre-training			#Langs.	Ref.
	#Params.	Objective Function	Mono.	Parallel		
IndicBERT	33M	MLM	IndicCorp	✗	12	[137]
mBERT	172M	MLM	Wikipedia	✗	104	[72]
Amber	172M	MLM, TLM, CLWA, CLSA	Wikipedia	✓	104	[121]
MuRIL	236M	MLM, TLM	CommonCrawl + Wikipedia	✓	17	[141]
VECO-small	247M	MLM, CS-MLM	CommonCrawl	✓	50	[175]
Unicoder	250M	MLM, TLM, CLWR, CLPC, CLMLM	Wikipedia	✓	15	[125]
XLM-15	250M	MLM, TLM	Wikipedia	✓	15	[63]
InfoXLM-base	270M	MLM, TLM, XLCO	CommonCrawl	✓	94	[48]
XLM-R-base	270M	MLM	CommonCrawl	✗	100	[61]
HiCTL-base	270M	MLM, TLM, HICTL	CommonCrawl	✓	100	[266]
Ernie-M-base	270M	MLM, TLM, CAMLM, BTMLM	CommonCrawl	✓	100	[194]
HiCTL-Large	559M	MLM, TLM, HICTL	CommonCrawl	✓	100	[266]
Ernie-M-Large	559M	MLM, TLM, CAMLM, BTMLM	CommonCrawl	✓	100	[194]
InfoXLM-Large	559M	MLM, TLM, XLCO	CommonCrawl	✓	94	[48]
XLM-R-Large	559M	MLM	CommonCrawl	✗	100	[61]
RemBERT	559M	MLM	CommonCrawl + Wikipedia	✗	110	[54]
X-STILTS	559M	MLM	CommonCrawl	✗	100	[198]
XLM-17	570M	MLM, TLM	Wikipedia	✓	17	[63]
XLM-100	570M	MLM, TLM	Wikipedia	✗	100	[63]
VECO-Large	662M	MLM, CS-MLM	CommonCrawl	✓	50	[175]

Transformer Layers Typically a multilingual Language Model (mLM) makes up the encoder of a multilingual transformer. It consists of a stack of N layers, each of which has k attention heads followed by a feed-forward neural network. An attention head computes an embedding for each token in the input sequence by combining the representations of all other tokens in the sentence using an attention weighted linear combination. Concatenating the embeddings from all the attention heads and passing them through a feed-forward network generates a d-dimensional embedding for each input word.

Output Layer Typically, the outputs of the final transformer layer are utilized as contextual representations for each token, while the embedding associated with the [CLS] token is considered to be the embedding of the entire input text. Alternatively, the text embedding may be generated by pooling the token embeddings together. The output layer has a basic linear transformation followed by a Softmax that accepts a token embedding from the previous transformer layer as an input and produces a probability distribution over the vocabulary's tokens.

4.1.2 Single-Encoder Multilingual NLU

4.1.2.1 Multilingual BERT (mBERT)

The multilingual BERT (mBERT) architecture is identical to that of the original BERT. Rather than being trained only on monolingual English data with an English-derived vocabulary, it is trained on the Wikipedia pages of 104 languages with a common WordPiece vocabulary. It makes no reference to the input language and lacks an explicit technique for ensuring that translation equivalent sentences have close representations. A 110k WordPiece vocabulary is shared amongst all 104 languages. To address Wikipedia's content imbalance, where for instance English Wikipedia has 120x the number of articles as Kurdish Wikipedia, minor languages were over-sampled while major languages were under-sampled. The same vocabulary enables some kind of cross-linguistic representation among other factors. Next, we briefly describe mBERT's pre-training tasks, namely multilingual Masked Language Model (mMLM) and Next Sentence Prediction (NSP).

Masked Language Model (MLM) This is the standard token-level unsupervised pre-training task introduced by BERT. However, in the context of multilingual transformers it is used with multiple languages pooled together with no alignment. It follows the same MLM procedure where 15% of the tokens are randomly picked then (i) with a probability of 80%, they are replaced by the [MASK] token, or (ii) with a probability of 10%, they are replaced with a random token, or (iii) they are kept the same with a probability of 10%. The objective of the MLM task is to predict the masked tokens using the unmasked ones on both sides of the input token sequence. Formally, let x be an input token sequence, and M_x be the set of masked tokens. The MLM loss is defined as follows:

$$\mathcal{L}_{MLM}^{(x)} = -\frac{1}{|M_x|} \sum_{i \in M_x} log P(x_i | x_{\backslash M_x}) \tag{4.1}$$

Fig. 4.1 illustrates the MLM task where x and y represent monolingual input sentences in different languages. Despite the fact that this task does not take into consideration any information about the multiple languages of the pooled masked input, it has shown great value in producing cross-lingual representations that are well aligned across languages. The insights section will provide more details on the factors behind this behavior.

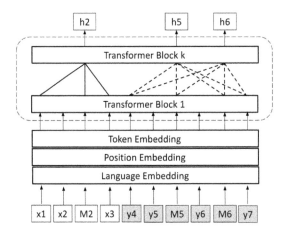

Figure 4.1 Illustration of multilingual MLM task [71, 194]. x and y are monolingual sentences in different languages that are not parallel.

Next Sentence Prediction (NSP) In the context of sentence-level pre-training tasks, NSP assists the model in learning associations between phrases [71]. It is a binary sentence pair classification problem that learns to identify consecutive sentences. For two sentences x and y, the [CLS] token vector representing the aggregate representation of the two sentences (x, y) is passed to the Sigmoid layer to obtain the probability of being consecutive sentences. To prepare for training, the phrase pairs are created such that fifty percent of the occurrences are consecutive and the remaining fifty percent are not consecutive. Pre-training the model at the sentence level is beneficial in downstream tasks like question answering (QA) , natural language inference (NLI), and semantic text similarity (STS), which need sentence pairs as input. Let $l \in \{1, 0\}$ represents two sentences (x, y) being consecutive or not, NSP loss is defined as follows:

$$\mathcal{L}_{NSP}^{(x,y)} = -logP(l|x, y) \tag{4.2}$$

4.1.2.2 *Cross-Lingual Language Model (XLM)*

Cross-Lingual Language Model (XLM) [146] is an improvement over the mBERT architecture by learning from monolingual and parallel corpora. For learning from monolingual data XLM uses the standard MLM pre-training task used by mBERT. XLM also proposes to use Causal Language Modeling (CLM) for monolingual pre-training.

Causal Language Modeling (CLM) CLM is the core pre-training task of classical language modeling where a model predicts the next word based on the previous words context Formally. Let $x = \{x_1, x_2, x_3, \ldots, x_{|x|}\}$ represents a sequence of tokens where $|x|$ represents the number of tokens in the sequence. CLM loss is defined as:

$$L_{CLM}^{(x)} = -\frac{1}{|x|}\sum_{i=1}^{|x|} \log P(x_i|x_{<i}) \tag{4.3}$$

where $x_{<i} = x_1, x_2, x_3, \ldots x_{i-1}$.

The main contribution of XLM is the introduction of a pre-training task that uses parallel corpora to explicitly encourage alignment of cross-lingual representations; namely Translation Language Model (TLM).

Translation Language Model (TLM) TLM is a variant of MLM that allows for the use of parallel corpora in cross-lingual pre-training [63]. The input to the encoder is a pair of parallel sentences (x, y). Similar to MLM, a total of k tokens are masked so that they might belong to either the x or y sentences. To predict a masked word in x, the model may depend on surrounding context in x or the translation y, and vice versa for masked tokens in y. This implicitly forces the encoder to acquire cross-lingual aligned representations. Essentially, if the context of masked token in x is insufficient, the model would pay more attention to the context in y to make better prediction of the masked token. Fig. 4.2 provides an illustration of how TLM performs cross-lingual attention. To define TLM for a parallel sentence pair (x, y), let M_x and M_y represent the set of masked positions in both sentences, then $x_{\backslash M_x}$ and $y_{\backslash M_y}$ will represent the masked versions of x and y. TLM loss function [138] is defined as follows:

$$\mathcal{L}_{TLM}^{(x,y)} = -\frac{1}{|M_x|}\sum_{i \in M_x} logP(x_i|x_{\backslash M_x}, y_{\backslash M_y}) - \frac{1}{|M_y|}\sum_{i \in M_y} logP(y_i|x_{\backslash M_x}, y_{\backslash M_y})$$

$$\tag{4.4}$$

XLM provided extensive evidence for how the MLM and CLM pre-training tasks provide strong cross-lingual features that could be used for unsupervised machine translations and other downstream supervised cross-lingual classification tasks. Cross-lingual Language Model (XLM) also shows the strong impact of using TLM with MLM on the quality of cross-lingual representations alignment as proven by their performance on the XNLI benchmark.

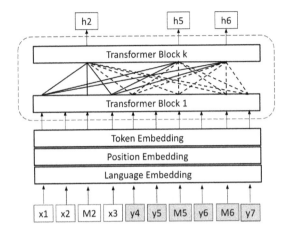

Figure 4.2 Illustration of TLM [146, 194] showing the attention mechanism across parallel sentences (x, y) which promotes cross-lingual alignment of the produced representations.

4.1.2.3 XLM-RoBERTa

XLM-RoBERTa (XLM-R) [61] is a multilingual transformer model based on MLM pre-training task only. XLM-R is trained on 2.5 TB of CommonCrawl data in 100 languages. XLM-R is a very important technique in the progress lineage of multilingual transformer models as it provided strong performance gains over mBERT and XLM on important downstream tasks such as sequence labeling and question answering. This is despite the fact that it does not use parallel corpora for pre-training. XLM-R follows the architectural design of XLM without using the language embeddings which allows for better handling of code-switching. The main contributions of XLM-R are achieving state-of-the-art performance with monolingual data and proving deep insights into the value of cleaner and larger training data, the size of the vocabulary, as well as the right level of hyperparameters tuning.

4.1.2.4 Alternating Language Model (ALM)

Alternating Language Model (ALM) ALM [282] is a pre-training task for cross-lingual representations that works in the same way as the TLM pre-training task except for the nature of the input data. TLM uses parallel sentences for input, however ALM uses code-switched sentences generated from parallel sentences. In code-switched sentences, some phrases of each sentence pair are randomly swapped with the corresponding translated phrase. For a parallel sentence pair (x, y) where the source sentence $x = \{x_1, x_2, \ldots, \}$ and the target sentence $y = \{y_1, y_2, \ldots, \}$, the input to the ALM model is a code-switched sequence $u = \{u_1, u_2, \ldots, \}$ composed of the pair (x, y). $u_{[i,j]}$ is assigned to either $x_{[a,b]}$ or $y_{[c,d]}$ where the constraint is that these two sequences are the translation counterpart in a parallel pair (x, y) such that $1 \leq a \leq b \leq |x|$ and $1 \leq c \leq d \leq |y|$. The proportion of the source tokens x in the code-switched sequence u is α. In other words, if $\alpha = 1$ then the entire input sequence is monolingual and composed of the source sentence x, if $\alpha = 0$ then input sequence is just the target sentence y, and we get code-switched sequences by using $0 < \alpha < 1$.

To construct the code-switched data, a tool is used to perform word alignment between source and target sentences in the parallel corpora and a bilingual phrase table is extracted using machine translation techniques. Next, code-switched data is constructed by replacing source and target phrases according to the ratio α. Given that α decides randomly which phrases are picked from source versus target sentence, each sentence pair can produce many code-switch sequences which is very useful in overcoming the usually limited size of available parallel corpora. ALM then proceeds by using a standard MLM pre-training task on the code-switched data. Formally, for a parallel sentence pair (x, y), let z be the code-switched sentence generated from x and y, then ALM loss is defined as:

$$\mathcal{L}_{ALM}^{(z(x,y))} = -\frac{1}{|M|} \sum_{i \in M} log P(z_i | z_{\backslash M}) \qquad (4.5)$$

where $z_{\backslash M}$ is the masked version of z and M is the set of masked token positions in $z_{\backslash M}$.

Fig. 4.3 illustrates how ALM creates a set of code-switched training data using a parallel sentence pair, which is in turn used to train a MLM transformer.

4.1.2.5 Unicoder

Unicoder [125] is another architecture for learning cross-lingual representations using parallel corpora. It uses the same architecture as XLM and introduces three new cross-lingual pre-training tasks; namely Cross-lingual Word Recovery (CLWR), Cross-lingual Paraphrase Classification (CLPC), and Cross-lingual Masked LM (CLMLM).

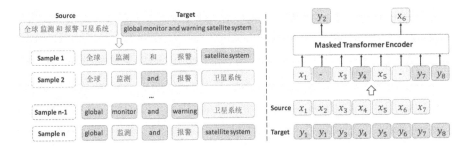

Figure 4.3 Illustration of Alternating Language Model (ALM) [282] where a parallel sentence pair (x, y) is used to generate multiple code-switch examples that are used to train an MLM transformer.

Cross-lingual Word Recovery (CLWR) CLWR [125] uses parallel corpora to learn word alignments between two languages. The pre-training task starts with a trainable attention matrix [17] that learns to represent the source language token embeddings in terms of the target language token embeddings. The transformation learned in the attention matrix is then provided to the cross-lingual model to learn to reconstruct the source token embedding. Formally, given a parallel sentence pair (x, y), where $x = (x_1, x_2, \ldots, x_m)$ is a sentence with m words from a source language s, and $y = (y_1, y_2, \ldots, y_n)$ is a sentence with n words from a target language t. CLWR starts by representing each x_i as $x_i^t \in R^h$ by all word embeddings of y [125]:

$$x_i^t = \sum_{j=1}^{n} \text{softmax}\,(A_{ij})\, y_j^t \tag{4.6}$$

where $x_i^s \in R^h$ and $y_j^t \in R^h$ are the representations of x_i and y_j, respectively, and h denotes the representation dimension, $A \in R^{m \times n}$ is the attention matrix defined as:

$$A_{ij} = W\left[x_i^s, y_j^t, x_i^s \odot y_j^t\right] \tag{4.7}$$

Note that $W \in R^{3*h}$ is a trainable weight matrix and $\odot$ is element-wise multiplication. Unicoder then takes $X^t = (x_1^t, x_2^t, \ldots, x_n^t)$ as input, and predicts the original word sequence x.

Cross-lingual Paraphrase Classification (CLPC) CLPC [125] introduces a different way of using parallel data by proposing a paraphrase classification pre-training task for parallel sentence pairs (x, y), where parallel sentence pairs (x, y) are the positive class and non-parallel pairs (x, z) are the negative class. The training data samples are picked using a smaller paraphrase detection model such that the for each (x, y) and (x, z) sentence pairs, z is chosen to be close to x but not equal to y.

Cross-lingual Masked LM (CLMLM) CLMLM [125] is an extension of TLM with the same cross-lingual attention scheme. However, while TLM takes in pairs of parallel sentences, CLMLM's input is created on the document level where multiple sentences from a parallel document (i.e., a full document with multiple parallel translations) are replaced with other language translations. This was inspired by some reported success on pre-training using longer monolingual text. Unicoder model is initialized with the XLM model and then pre-trained using the combined MLM, TLM, CLWR, CLPC, and CLMLM tasks and fine-tuned on XNLI and XQA benchmarks.

4.1.2.6 Information-Theoretic Cross-Lingual Model (INFOXLM)

Information-Theoretic Cross-Lingual Model (INFOXLM) [47] approaches the cross-lingual representation alignment problem from an information theoretic perspective, where it shows how multilingual pre-training tasks can in fact be viewed as maximizing the mutual information between multilingual contexts on different granularity. For instance, InfoXLM shows that the multilingual masked language model (mMLM) pre-training task essentially maximizes the mutual information between masked tokens and their context within the same language. On the other hand, anchor tokens across languages motivate cross-lingual contexts to be closely correlated. TLM also has an information theoretic explanation where it is shown to maximize the mutual information between masked tokens and parallel language contexts, which serves as an implicit cross-lingual representation alignment mechanism. Using the provided information theoretic framework, InfoXLM proposes a new cross-lingual pre-training task based on contrastive learning, namely Cross-lingual Contrastive Learning.

Cross-lingual Contrastive Learning (XLCO) XLCO [47] proposes an information theoretic approach to produce cross-lingual representations using parallel corpora. XLCO encourages a transformer encoder to maximize the mutual information between representations of parallel sentences in comparison to non-parallel sentences, thus performing contrastive learning. TLM is shown, within the information theoretic framework, to maximize token-sequence mutual information. On the other hand, XLCO maximizes sequence-level mutual information between parallel sentences. Let (x_i, y_i) be a parallel sentence pair, where y_i is a translation of x_i, and $\{y_j\}_{j=1, j \neq i}^N$ is the set of sentences of the same language as y_i but not a translation of x_i. XLCO maximizes the information content between x_i and y_i using the InfoNCE [251] based loss function defined as:

$$\mathcal{L}_{XLCO}^{(x,i,y_i)} = -\log \frac{\exp(f(x_i)^\top f(y_i))}{\sum_{j=1}^N \exp(f(x_i)^\top f(y_j))} \tag{4.8}$$

where $f(x_i)$ and $f(y_i)$ are the transformer encoder representations of sentences x_i and y_i, respectively. For negative sampling XLCO does not sample explicitly from $\{y_j\}_{j=1, j \neq i}^N$ but rather uses mixup contrast [47] and momentum [104] to construct harder negative samples.

INFOXLM is initialized with the XLM-R model parameters and then pre-trained using the combined mMLM, TLM, and XLCO tasks formulated as mutual information maximization tasks; monolingual token-sequence mutual information (MMLM), cross-lingual token-sequence mutual information (TLM), and cross-lingual sequence-level mutual information (XLCO).

4.1.2.7 Aligned Multilingual Bidirectional EncodeR (AMBER)

Aligned Multilingual Bidirectional EncodeR (AMBER) [121] is a technique that creates cross-lingual representations using parallel data with word-level and sentence-level alignment pre-training tasks, namely Cross-lingual Word Alignment (CLWA) and Cross-lingual Sentence Alignment (CLSA) tasks.

Cross-lingual Word Alignment (CLWA) Similar to CLWR, CLWA [121] also aims to learn word alignments between different languages using parallel corpora. CLWA uses two different attention masks as inputs to a transformer model. After training, two attention matrices are obtained in the top transformer layer, namely source-to-target attention $A_{x \to y}$ and target-to-source attention $A_{y \to x}$. Given that $A_{x \to y}$ measures the alignment of the source-to-target transformation, and vice versa for $A_{y \to x}$, it is desirable to have similar alignments for words using either $A_{x \to y}$ or $A_{y \to x}$ attention matrices. To that end the model is encouraged to minimize the distance between $A_{x \to y}$ and $A_{y \to x}$ during training.

Cross-lingual Sentence Alignment (CLSA) CLSA [121] is designed to enforce the alignment of sentence representations across languages using parallel data. Let $\mathcal{M}$ and $\mathcal{P}$ be the monolingual and parallel data, respectively. For each parallel sentence pair (x, y), distinct sentence embeddings for both x and y are generated separately, namely c_x and c_y, respectively. c_x and c_y are obtained by averaging the last layer's embeddings of the encoder. The embedding alignment takes place by encouraging the model to predict the correct translation y for an input sentence x by using the following loss function:

$$\mathcal{L}_{CLSA}^{(x,y)} = -\log \frac{e^{c_x^T c_y}}{\sum_{y' \in \mathcal{M} \cup \mathcal{P}} e^{c_x^T c_{y'}}} \tag{4.9}$$

where y' in $\mathcal{L}_{CLSA}^{(x,y)}$ can be any sentence and with no language restriction.

AMBER is trained using a combination of MLM, TLM, CLWA, CLSA tasks and is evaluated on the XTREME benchmark where it outperformed XLM-R and Unicoder.

4.1.2.8 ERNIE-M

Many techniques have shown the value of using parallel and monolingual corpora to get better aligned cross-lingual representations. However, parallel corpora are always limited in size relative to monolingual data, limiting the possible progress unless we collect sizable parallel corpora. ERNIE-M [194] uses large monolingual corpora and limited parallel corpora to produce cross-lingual representations. To enhance produced representations, ERNIE-M generates pseudo-parallel sentences using the large available monolingual corpora and then uses them along with the parallel data to improve the alignment of cross-lingual representations. ERNIE-M proposes two pre-training tasks, Cross-Attention masked Language Modeling (CAMLM) and Back-Translation Masked Language Modeling (BTMLM).

Cross-attention Masked LM (CAMLM) Cross-attention Masked LM (CAMLM) [194] is another parallel corpora pre-training task that is closely related to TLM. As described earlier, for a given parallel sentence pair (x, y), a masked token within x has access and can potentially

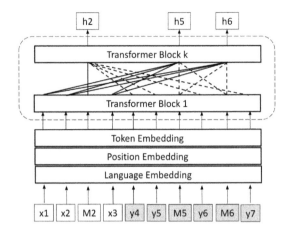

Figure 4.4 Cross-attention Masked LM (CAMLM) where a masked token can only attend to the opposite sentences for prediction [194].

attend to the context of x and the context of y, and the same applies to a masked token in y. On the other hand, CAMLM restricts TLM by only keeping access to the corresponding parallel sentence. Therefore, a masked token in x can only use y context for prediction, and vice versa for y. Prohibiting attending to the context of the same sentence as the masked token forces the algorithm to learn the representation in the parallel language. Otherwise, the algorithm might take the easier path and leans more towards using the same sentence of the masked token to make a prediction. Using the same setup in TLM, where for a sentence pair (x, y), let M_x and M_y represent the set of masked positions in both sentences, then $x_{\backslash M_x}$ and $y_{\backslash M_y}$ will represent the masked versions of x and y. The loss function for CAMLM is defined as follows:

$$\mathcal{L}_{CAMLM}^{(x,y)} = -\frac{1}{|M_x|} \sum_{i \in M_x} log P(x_i | y_{\backslash M_y}) - \frac{1}{|M_y|} \sum_{i \in M_y} log P(y_i | x_{\backslash M_x})$$

(4.10)

Fig. 4.4 illustrates the CAMLM cross-lingual attention. As depicted, token $h2$ attends to tokens in sentence y and not x, and tokens $h5$ and $h6$ attend only to tokens in sentence x and not y.

Back Translation Masked Language Modeling (BTMLM)
BTMLM [194] leverages back translation [222] to circumvent the issue of lack of parallel corpora for learning cross-lingual representations. It

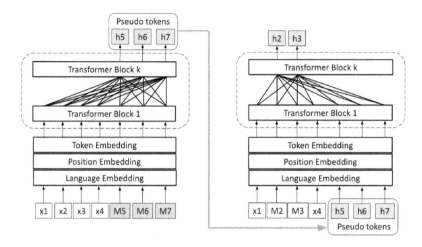

Figure 4.5 Illustration of BTMLM [194] pre-training task. The first step on the left is where a pre-trained CAMLM is used to generate pseudo-parallel sentences. The second step on the right is where the generated pseudo-parallel sentences are then used to further train the CAMLM.

consists of two steps; the first step generates pseudo-parallel data from a given monolingual corpus. ERNIE-M [194] constructs pseudo-parallel sentences by first pre-training the model using CAMLM and then adding placeholder masks to the end of the original monolingual sentence to show the location and language that the model should generate. The second step masks the tokens in the original monolingual sentence, then concatenates it with the created pseudo-parallel sentence. Finally, the model should predict the masked tokens. Fig. 4.5 shows the two steps of BTMLM.

Due to their superior performance in XLM architecture, the mMLM and TLM pre-training tasks are employed as part of training ERNIE-M as well. ERNIE-M is trained with monolingual and parallel corpora with 96 languages and is initialized with XLM-R weights. ERNIE-M has shown state-of-the-art performance on a diverse set of downstream tasks including NER, Cross-lingual Question Answering, Cross-lingual Paraphrase Identification, and Cross-lingual Sentence Retrieval.

4.1.2.9 Hierarchical Contrastive Learning (HICTL)

Hierarchical Contrastive Learning (HICTL) [266] is another cross-lingual pre-training task that uses InfoNCE [251] based loss functions. While

XLCO is sentence-based, HICTL provides both sentence and word-level cross-lingual representations.

Sentence level representations are constructed in the same manner as XCLO except for the negative sampling where instead of collecting samples from $\{y_j\}_{j=1, j\neq i}^N$ smoothed linear interpolation [31, 300] between sentence representations is used to construct hard negative samples.

For world-level representations, the contrastive loss similarity score is computed between a parallel sentence (x_i, y_i) [CLS] token representation and other words representations. For each parallel sentence pair input (x_i, y_i), a bag of words $\mathcal{W}$ is maintained, where all words in $\mathcal{W}$ are considered positive samples and all other words in the vocabulary are negative samples. For efficient negative words sampling, HICTL does not sample from the entire vocabulary but rather constructs a set of negative words that very close to parallel sentence (x_i, y_i) [CLS] token representation.

4.1.3 Dual-Encoder Multilingual NLU

4.1.3.1 *Language-agnostic BERT Sentence Embedding (LaBSE)*

Language-agnostic BERT Sentence Embedding (LaBSE) [88] is an architecture for training cross-lingual sentence representations which combines Masked Language Model (MLM) and Translation Language Model (TLM) pre-training tasks from XLM [146] with a translation ranking task using bi-directional dual-encoders with additive margin softmax loss[283]. The dual-encoders, as shown in Fig. 4.6, consist of two paired mBERT encoders. The [CLS] token sentence representation from both encoders are fed to a scoring function. Fig. 4.6 provide an illustration of the LaBSE architecture.

Bidirectional Dual Encoder with Additive Margin Softmax
The dual-encoder architecture [283] has proven to be very effective for ranking tasks such as the translation retrieval task employed by LaBSE for cross-lingual embedding. Formally, for a parallel sentence pair (x_i, y_i), translation retrieval is a ranking problem that aims to place y_i, the true translation of x_i, higher than all sentences in the space of translations $\mathcal{Y}$. $P(y_i \mid x_i)$ is formulated as:

$$P(y_i \mid x_i) = \frac{e^{\phi(x_i, y_i)}}{\sum_{\bar{y} \in \mathcal{Y}} e^{\phi(x_i, \bar{y})}} \tag{4.11}$$

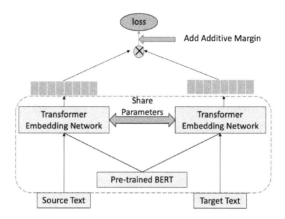

Figure 4.6 Illustration of Language-agnostic BERT Sentence Embedding (LaBSE) architecture [88].

where ϕ is the scoring function of the similarity between the representations of x_i and y_i

During training $P(y_i \mid x_i)$ is approximated by sampling negatives, y_n, from translation pairs in the same batch:

$$P_{\text{approx}}(y_i \mid x_i) = \frac{e^{\phi(x_i, y_i)}}{e^{\phi(x_i, y_i)} + \sum_{n=1, n \neq i}^{N} e^{\phi(x_i, y_n)}} \tag{4.12}$$

Therefore, for parallel source and target pairs (x_i, y_i), the model can be optimized using the log-likelihood objective [283]:

$$\mathcal{L}_s = -\frac{1}{N} \sum_{i=1}^{N} \log \frac{e^{\phi(x_i, y_i)}}{e^{\phi(x_i, y_i)} + \sum_{n=1, n \neq i}^{N} e^{\phi(x_i, y_n)}} \tag{4.13}$$

For each x_i, the loss $\mathcal{L}_s$ aims to identify the correct y_i. This means that using $\mathcal{L}_s$ will result in an asymmetric relationship between x_i and y_i representations. To overcome this issue, Yand et al. [283] introduced the bidirectional learning objective, $\overline{\mathcal{L}}_s$ that explicitly optimizes both forward and backward ranking of the parallel pair (x_i, y_i):

$$\mathcal{L}'_s = -\frac{1}{N} \sum_{i=1}^{N} \frac{e^{\phi(y_i, x_i)}}{e^{\phi(y_i, x_i)} + \sum_{n=1, n \neq i}^{N} e^{\phi(y_i, x_n)}} \tag{4.14}$$

$$\overline{\mathcal{L}}_s = \mathcal{L}_s + \mathcal{L}'_s$$

For added separation between the correct translations the closest non-translations that are very close, the scoring function ϕ is extended with additive margin softmax, which introduces a margin m around the positive parallel pairs (x_i, y_i).

$$\phi'(x_i, y_j) = \begin{cases} \phi(x_i, y_j) - m & \text{if } i = j \\ \phi(x_i, y_j) & \text{if } i \neq j \end{cases} \qquad (4.15)$$

Applying $\phi'(x_i, y_j)$ to the bidirectional loss $\overline{\mathcal{L}}_s$, the additive margin bidirectional loss becomes as follows [283]:

$$\mathcal{L}_{ams} = -\frac{1}{N} \sum_{i=1}^{N} \frac{e^{\phi(x_i, y_i) - m}}{e^{\phi(x_i, y_i) - m} + \sum_{n=1, n \neq i}^{N} e^{\phi(x_i, y_n)}} \qquad (4.16)$$

$$\overline{\mathcal{L}}_{ams} = \mathcal{L}_{ams} + \mathcal{L}'_{ams}$$

As mentioned earlier, LaBSE pre-trains its BERT based encoders with Masked Language Model (MLM) and Translation Language Model (TLM) pre-training tasks using monolingual and parallel corpora, respectively. LaBSE trains transformer encoders using a three-stage progressive stacking approach. For a L layer encoder, it first learning a model of $frac L4$ layers, then $frac L2$ layers, and lastly all L layers. During successive training steps, the parameters of the earlier steps models are copied to the subsequent ones.

4.1.3.2 Multilingual Universal Sentence Encoders (mUSE)

Multilingual Universal Sentence Encoders (mUSE) [284, 49] proposes an approach for cross-lingual sentence embedding learning by combining multitask learning of monolingual sentence representations, and dual-encoders for multilingual sentence embeddings learning for parallel text retrieval. By combining the two approaches, mUSE transfers the strong performance learned on monolingual tasks to zero-shot learning in other languages. Basically, for a certain language pair, source and target language, the model uses a multitask architecture to learn across (i) source language monolingual tasks, (ii) monolingual target language tasks, and (iii) a source-to-target language translation task that serves as a bridging task to encourage cross-lingual representation alignment across all the trained tasks. Fig. 4.7 provides an illustration of the architecture for QA, NLI and the bridging translation tasks.

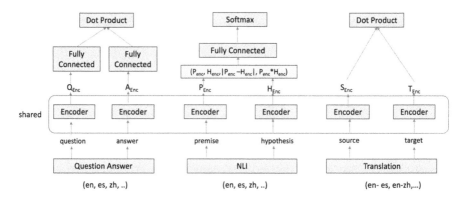

Figure 4.7 Illustration of mUSE architecture for QA, NLI and the bridging translation tasks [284].

mUSE uses dual-encoders to perform multitask learning on tasks that can be represented as ranking input-response sentence pairs. Some tasks fall naturally within this framework such as QA and translation tasks. Other tasks might need a special reformulation such as NLI. Input-response ranking can be formally described as follows: For an input-response pair (s_i^I, s_i^R), the goal is to get s_i^R to higher than all possible responses $s_j^R \in \mathcal{S}^R$. In other words, the conditional probability $P\left(s_i^R \mid s_i^I\right)$ should be defined as:

$$P\left(s_i^R \mid s_i^I\right) = \frac{e^{\phi\left(s_i^I, s_i^R\right)}}{\sum_{s_j^R \in \mathcal{S}^R} e^{\phi\left(s_i^R, s_j^R\right)}}$$

$$\phi\left(s_i^I, s_j^R\right) = g^I\left(s_i^I\right)^\top g^R\left(s_j^R\right)$$

(4.17)

where g^I is the input sentence encoding function and g^R is response sentence encoding function, g^I and g^R make up the dual-encoder. Both g^I and g^R are implemented using transformers and are trained with the log-likelihood loss function, $\widetilde{P}\left(s_i^R \mid s_i^I\right)$, for each task.

As illustrated in Fig. 4.7, mUSE uses a single shared encoder supporting multiple downstream tasks. The training tasks include: QA prediction task, NLI task, and translation ranking. Task-specific layers for the QA and NLI tasks are added after the shared encoder to help accommodating representational needs for each task.

4.1.4 Multilingual Natural Language Generation (Multilingual NLG)

All cross-lingual pre-training tasks discussed in the previous section are used for Natural Language Understanding (NLU) tasks only. This section discusses a few of the pre-training tasks used by generative multilingual models such as MASS [231], BART [155], mBART [169], and XNLG [46].

Sequence-to-Sequence LM (Seq2SeqLM) As discussed earlier, Masked Language Model (MLM) is handled as a token-level classification problem over the masked tokens, in which the original words are predicted by feeding the masked token vectors to a Softmax layer over the vocabulary. MLM also is used to pre-train encoder-only transformer architectures which are then used for NLU tasks. Seq2SeqLM extends conventional MLM to pre-train encoder-decoder transformer models such as T5[205], mT5 [281], and MASS [231]. While the context of MLM includes all tokens in the input sequence, the context of Seq2SeqLM includes all tokens in the input masked sequence and the left side tokens in the predicted target sequence. With the encoder's masked sequence as input, the decoder predicts the masked words sequentially from left to right. This allows transformer architectures pre-trained with Seq2SeqLM to be used for NLG tasks. For a given input sequence of tokens x, let $\hat{x}$ be the masked version of x, that is x with masked n-gram span. With l_s defined as the length of masked n-gram span, then Seq2SeqLM loss is defined as

$$\mathcal{L}^{(x)}_{Seq2SeqLM} = -\frac{1}{l_s} \sum_{s=i}^{j} logP(x_s|\hat{x}, x_{i:s-1}) \tag{4.18}$$

Denoising Auto-Encoder (DAE) Similar to Seq2SeqLM, DAE [155, 169] is a pre-training task for encoder-decoder transformer architectures. While Seq2SeqLM is based on predicting masked tokens, DAE does not mask textual elements but rather corrupts them and then reconstructs the original values. DAE corrupts text at the token level by token deletion and token masking, at the sentence level by sentence permutation, at a text span level by text infilling, or at the document level by document rotation. DAE is more sample efficient than Seq2SeqLM since it provides more signals for model training. DAE generates more training signal since it reconstructs the complete original text, while Seq2SeqLM reconstructs just the masked tokens. BART [155] encodes corrupted input sequences using a bidirectional encoder and reconstructs the original text using a left-to-right decoder. Similar to Seq2SeqLM definition, for a given input text x , let $\hat{x}$ be the corrupted version of x, then DAE loss is defined as

$$\mathcal{L}_{DAE}^{(x)} = -\frac{1}{|x|} \sum_{i=1}^{|x|} log P(x_i|\hat{x}, x_{<i}) \qquad (4.19)$$

Cross-lingual Auto-Encoding (XAE) While DAE is trained on a variety of languages, the encoding input and decoding output are always identical. As a result, models detect improper correlations between linguistic symbols and produced phrases. In other words, models may disregard the provided language symbols and create sentences directly in the input language. XNLG [46] offers the cross-lingual auto-encoding (XAE) job to overcome this problem. Unlike DAE, XAE's encoding input and decoding output are in distinct languages, comparable to machine translation. Additionally, XNLG does a two-stage optimization of parameters. It initially trains the encoder using MLM and TLM jobs. Then, in the second step, it repairs the encoder and trains the decoder using the DAE and XAE tasks. This method effectively pre-trains all parameters, and also bridges the gap between MLM pre-training and autoregressive decoding fine-tuning.

4.2   MULTILINGUAL DATA

4.2.1   Pre-Training Data

Multilingual Language Models (mLMs) use different sources of data during the pre-training stage. More specifically, large monolingual corpora are commonly used in individual languages and parallel corpora are used between some languages. The source of the monolingual corpora varies for the different existent mLMs. For example, mBERT [72] uses Wikipedia for pre-training. Whereas, in [61], Conneau et al. used a much larger common-crawl corpus to train XML-R. Other models use custom crawled data. For example, IndicBERT [137] is trained on custom crawled data in Indian languages. Table 4.1 provides a summary for the datasets used for pre-training the different mLMs.

Some models such as IndicBERT [137] and MuRIL [141] are designed to support only small set of languages. Other mLMs such as XLM-R are massively multilingual and can support ∼ 100 languages. Managing large number of languages poses a challenge of the possible imbalance between the amount of data used for pre-training for the different languages. For example, when using Wikipedia and CommonCrawl for pre-training, it is obvious that the number of available articles in English is much higher than other languages such as Persian or Urdu. Similarly, the amount of parallel data available for pairs of languages differ highly depending of the popularity of such languages. To overcome these challenges, most mLMs use exponentially smoothed weighting of the data while creating the pre-training data. This weighting prevents the low resource languages from being under represented. More specifically, if $m\%$ of the total pre-training data belongs to language i, then the probability of this language is $p_i = \frac{k}{100}$. Each probability is then modulated by an exponential factor α, then the resulting values are normalized to provide the final probability distribution over the languages. This probability distribution is used to the sample the pre-training data from the different languages. Therefore, low-resource languages will be over sampled while high-resource languages will be under sampled. Such process guarantees the use of a reasonable set of vocabulary (while training the Word-Piece [220] or SentencePiece model [144]) in the low resource languages. Table 4.1 summarizes the number of languages supported by different mLMs and the total vocabulary used by them. Typically, mLMs which support more languages have a larger vocabulary.

4.2.2 Multilingual Benchmarks

The most often used methods for evaluating mLMs is cross-lingual performance on downstream tasks, which requires fine-tuning the model using task-specific data from a high-resource language such as English and evaluating it on other languages. XGLUE [160], XTREME [122], XTREME-R [216] are some of the state-of-the-art cross-lingual learning benchmarks. As shown in Table 4.2, these benchmarks provide training/evaluation data for a broad range of tasks and languages. These tasks can be categorized into: classification, structure prediction, question answering, and semantic retrieval.

4.2.2.1 Classification

For classification, the downstream task is to categorize an input consisting of a single sentence or a pair of sentences into one of k classes. One example is the problem of Natural Language Inference (NLI), which requires the input to be a pair of phrases and the output to be one of three classes: implies, neutral, or contradicts. XNLI [64], PAWS-X [285], XCOPA [200], NC [160], QADSM [160], WPR [160], and QAM [160] are

TABLE 4.2   Multilingual language models benchmarks categorized by NLP task [74]

Task	Corpus	Train	Dev	Test	Test Sets	#Langs.	Task	Metric	Domain	Benchmark
	XNLI	392,702	2,490	5,010	Translations	15	NLI	Acc.	Misc.	XT, XTR, XG
	PAWS-X	49,401	2,000	2,000	Translations	7	Paraphrase	Acc.	Wiki / Quora	XT, XTR, XG
	XCOPA	33,410+400	100	500	Translations	11	Reasoning	Acc.	Misc	XTR
Classification	NC	100k	10k	10k	-	5	Sent. Labeling	Acc.	News	XG
	QADSM	100k	10k	10k	-	3	Sent. Relevance	Acc.	Bing	XG
	WPR	100k	10k	10k	-	7	Sent. Relevance	nDCG	Bing	XG
	QAM	100k	10k	10k	-	7	Sent. Relevance	Acc.	Bing	XG
	UD-POS	21,253	3,974	47-20,436	Ind. annot.	37(104)	POS	F1	Misc.	XT, XTR, XG
Struct. Pred	WikiANN-NER	20,000	10,000	1,000-10,000	Ind. annot.	47(176)	NER	F1	Wikipedia	XT, XTR
	NER	15k	2.8k	3.4k	-	4	NER	F1	News	XG
	XQuAD	87,599	34,736	1,190	Translations	11	Span Extraction	F1/EM	Wikipedia	XT, XTR
QA	MLQA			4,517-11,590	Translations	7	Span Extraction	F1/EM	Wikipedia	XT, XTR
	TyDiQA-GoldP	3,696	634	323-2,719	Ind. annot.	9	Span Extraction	F1/EM	Wikipedia	XT, XTR
	BUCC	-	-	1,896-14,330	-	5	Sent. Retrieval	F1	Wiki / News	XT
Retrieval	Tatoeba	-	-	1,000	-	33(122)	Sent. Retrieval	Acc.	Misc.	XT
	Mewsli-X	116,903	10,252	428-1,482	ind. annot.	11(50)	Lang. agn. retrieval	mAP@20	News	XTR
	LAReQA XQuAD-R	87,599	10,570	1,190	translations	11	Lang. agn. retrieval	mAP@20	Wikipedia	XTR

some of the prominent cross-lingual text classification datasets used to evaluate mLMs.

4.2.2.2 Structure prediction

The task is to predict a label for each word in an input sentence. Two often performed tasks are Part-of-Speech (POS) tagging and Named Entity Recognition (NER). The WikiANN-NER [193], CoNLL 2002 [246] and CoNLL 2003 [247] shared task datasets are popular for NER, and the Universal Dependencies dataset [192] is used for POS tagging.

4.2.2.3 Question answering

QA task involves extracting a response span from a context and a question. Typically, training data is only accessible in English, but assessment sets are available in a variety of languages. XQuAD [9], MLQA [156], and TyDiQA-GoldP [56] datasets are often used for QA evaluation.

4.2.2.4 Semantic retrieval

Semantic retrieval is concerned with finding a matched sentence in the target language from a collection of sentences given a sentence in the source language. This task is evaluated using the following datasets: BUCC [305], Tatoeba [11], Mewsli-X [216], and LAReQA XQuAD-R [215]. Mewsli-X and LAReQA XQuAD-R are believed to be more challenging since they involves matching sentence recovery in the target language from a pool of multilingual sentences.

4.3 MULTILINGUAL TRANSFER LEARNING INSIGHTS

4.3.1 Zero-Shot Cross-Lingual Learning

One of the ultimate goals of multilingual transfer learning is to create mLMs with zero-shot cross-lingual performance commensurate with supervised monolingual models. The standard workflow to create a zero-shot cross-lingual model entails using many languages to pre-train a mLM, where the mLM learns cross-lingual representations. The model is then fine-tuned with a task-specific supervised dataset from a source language. Finally, the fine-tuned model is then used to perform inference on the same task from multiple different target languages. Transformers has shown remarkable progress in cross-lingual transfer learning, especially when it comes to zero-shot learning. The details of how transformers perform cross-lingual transfer learning is still an active research area. This section discusses the active areas of research to understand the main factors affecting cross-lingual transfer learning [74]. The discussed factors include: (i) data related factors, (ii) model architecture factors, and (iii) training tasks factors.

4.3.1.1 Data factors

Shared Vocabulary Prior to training a mLM, text from all languages is tokenized using a WordPiece [220] or SentencePiece [144] models. The main concept is to tokenize each word into its most often occurring subwords. The model's vocabulary is then composed of all of these subwords recognized across all languages. This combined tokenization assures that subwords are shared across a large number of closely related or even distant languages. Thus, if a subword that exists in the target language's test set also appears in the source language's training set, some model performance may be transmitted through this common vocabulary. The relationship between cross-lingual zero-shot transferability and the size of vocabulary overlap between languages has been examined in [199] and [271], where strong positive correlation was found and the positive effect on downstream tasks has been shown to be consistent across several diverse areas including NER [246, 247], POS [192], XNLI [64], MLDoc [221], and Dependency parsing [192]. These observations are intuitive and provide some explanation for cross-lingual representation alignment when performing multilingual training using monolingual corpora. However, this area of research is still new and additional evidence is still being examined to validate these observations. For instance, Karthikeyan et al.

[135] synthetically reduced the vocabulary overlap to zero, however the observed performance drop in cross-lingual zero-shot learning was minimal, which undermines the observed effect of vocabulary overlapping has on cross-lingual zero-shot transfer learning. Another work [10] shows that even if there's no vocabulary overlap, cross-lingual transfer learning still takes place by properly fine-tuning all transformer layers except for the input embedding layer.

Pre-training Data Size   The effect of pre-training data size on cross-lingual has been evaluated in [165] which demonstrates that when mBERT is pre-trained on big corpora, cross-lingual transfer is improved. Also Lauscher et al. [148] show that the performance of zero-shot transfer is strongly correlated with the quantity of data in the target language utilized to pre-train the mLM for higher level tasks such as XNLI and XQuAD. There is also a positive connection for lower level tasks like as POS, dependency parsing, and NER, although it is not as strong as the association for XNLI and XQuAD.

Using Parallel Corpora   While mLMs perform well even when not specifically trained with cross-lingual signals, it is intuitive that purposeful training with such signals should boost performance. In fact, XLMs in [63] and InfoXLM in [47] demonstrate that using parallel corpora in conjunction with the TLM pre-training task improves performance. If no parallel corpus is available, [79] argue that training mLMs using similar corpora (such as Wikipedia or CommonCrawl) is preferable than utilizing corpora from disparate sources across languages.

4.3.1.2 Model architecture factors

A multi-language model's capacity is dependent on its layer count, number of attention heads, and the size of the hidden representations. Karthikeyan et al. [135] demonstrate that cross-lingual transfer learning performance is highly dependent on the network's depth while not as much on the number of attention heads. They demonstrate, in particular, that enough cross-lingual transfer is possible even with single-headed attention. Moreover, the total number of parameters in the model has less bearing on the efficacy of cross-lingual transfer than the number of layers. Interestingly, in [79] mBERT's cross-lingual transfer is argued to be a result of its small parameter set and thus limited capacity, which compels it to use shared structures to align representations across languages.

Another critical architectural decision is the self-attention context window, which refers to the number of tokens given into the mLM during training. Liu et al. [165] demonstrate that although using smaller context windows is more desirable when pre-training data is sparse, utilizing longer context windows is better when huge quantities of pre-training data are available.

In [260] and [45] it is contended that since mLMs have limited model capacity that gets used by multiple languages, they cannot capture all the subtleties of several languages as a pre-trained monolingual model can. They demonstrate how knowledge distillation from a monolingual model may enhance a mLM's cross-lingual performance.

4.3.1.3 Model tasks factors

Fine-tuning Strategies In [171] it is discussed that fine-tuning a mLM changes its parameters, impairing its cross-lingual capacity by erasing part of the alignments learned during pre-training. They demonstrate this by showing that when a mLM is fine-tuned for POS tagging, its cross-lingual retrieval performance decreases significantly. To overcome this issue, they recommend utilizing a continual learning framework for fine-tuning the model so that it does not forget the original task (MLM) on which it was trained. They claim improved results in cross-lingual POS tagging, NER, and sentence retrieval using this fine-tuning method.

Representations Alignment In [261, 168] the performance of zero-shot cross-lingual transfer is examined using implicitly aligned representations learned by mLMs and representations from monolingual models that are subsequently explicitly aligned using parallel corpora. They note that the explicit alignment provide improved performance. Taking this into account, Wang et al. [263] provide an explicit strategy for aligning the representations of matched word pairs across languages during mBERT training. This is accomplished by including a loss function that minimizes the Euclidean distance between aligned words' embeddings. Zhao et al. [298] also report comparable results when the representations of word pairs are explicitly aligned and the vector spaces are further normalized.

4.3.2 Language-Agnostic Cross-Lingual Representations

Despite the big success of transformer models, such as BERT, in advancing the NLP field and machine learning in general, the inner workings of how such models extract and store knowledge is still not completely understood and is the focus of active research. Multilingual transformers is certainly no exception but even more intriguing as they appear to use and share knowledge across multiple languages; i.e., cross-lingual transfer learning. This raises the question if multilingual transformers learn language-agnostic cross-lingual representations. Several approaches have been proposed to answer this question, each with a different angle of attack; (i) Ablation Studies, (ii) Task Probes, and (iii) Parallel Corpora Representations.

Ablation Studies Several ablation studies have been proposed to examine several hypotheses about the validity of language-agnostic representations in multilingual transformers. First hypothesis tested in [199] is that the joint script between high resource language is a confounding factor for good multilingual transformers performance. However this was shown to be true as multilingual transfer occur between languages that do not share script such as Urdu written in Arabic script and Hindi in Devanagari script [199]. Other work [229] examined the input tokenization as a confounding factor and found that using subword tokenization biases the models towards learning language-agnostic representations more than word-level or character-level tokenization. Pre-training tasks has also been examined as a possible confounding factor, it was shown that models trained with parallel corpora pre-training tasks such as XLM retain language-agnostic representations within the higher encoder layers in a stronger manner than models trained on monolingual corpora such as mBERT and XLMR [52].

Parallel Corpora Representations Another way to approach the language-agnostic representation hypothesis is to use parallel corpora in different languages and examine their parallel representations for alignment in the model embedding space. Canonical Correlation Analysis (CCA) is one techniques used to analyze the alignment of parallel representations. In [229] CCA analysis showed that mBERT does not project parallel representations on the same space. Machine translation has also been used to examine language-agnostic representations, where on one hand a sentence in a source language is provided and on the other hand multiple sentences in a target language are available and the task is to use the nearest neighbors algorithm to identify the correct translation among the target candidates. In [199] it is observed that the proper translation (i.e., representations alignment) is dependent on the layer in the model that produced the representations. It is shown that the mBERT middle layers, 5–8, produces a nearest neighbors accuracy of 75% for languages from the same family such as English-German and Hindi-Urdu. It has been argued that one proper conclusion is that the large capacity of multilingual transformer models allows to produce create and preserve language-agnostic and language-specific representations. The language-agnostic representations are rich enough to properly align multilingual words and retrieves semantically similar sentences. However, the representations are not powerful enough to approach hard problems such as machine translation [161].

Probing tasks   Another way to investigate language-agnostic representations is to use probing tasks on the representations acquired at various layers. Consistent dependency trees, for example, may be learned from the representations of intermediate layers in mBERT that indicate syntactic abstractions [44, 162]. However, the dependency trees for Subject-Verb-Object (SVO) languages (such as English, French, and Indonesian) were more accurate than those for SOV languages (such as Turkish, Korean, and Japanese). This discrepancy between SOV and SVO languages is also seen in the labeling of POS [199]. Each layer has distinct specialties, and it is therefore advantageous to mix data from many layers for optimal results, rather than picking a single layer based on its overall performance, as proved for Dutch on a variety of NLU tasks [68]. In the same experiment, it was discovered that a multilingual model had more informative representations for POS tagging in early layers when compared to a monolingual Dutch model.

4.4   CASE STUDY

4.4.1   Goal

In this section, we provide a practical example of training a multilingual sentiment classifier. Our goal is to illustrate the zero-shot classification abilities of multilingual models where the model is only trained English data and then used to predict on non-English data with no further training.

4.4.2   Data, Tools, and Libraries

For this case study we use the binary sentiment classification Yelp Polarity dataset [297]. The dataset consists of 560K highly polar Yelp reviews for training and 38K reviews for testing. Original Yelp reviews take numerical score from 1 to 5 stars. This dataset is constructed by grouping the 1 and 2 stars reviews into the negative sentiment class and the 3 and 4 stars reviews into the positive sentiment class.

Our model will use the Multilingual Universal Sentence Encoder (mUSE) [49, 284] for feature generation. mUSE is a Transformer encoder trained such that text which is in different languages, but has similar meaning, will result in a similar encoding. This is analogous to the way two words with similar meaning (and usage) will have similar word embeddings. mUSE supports 16 languages: Arabic, Chinese-simplified, Chinese-traditional, English, French, German, Italian, Japanese, Korean, Dutch, Polish, Portuguese, Spanish, Thai, Turkish, Russian.

In this case study, we'll use TensorFlow Hub to load the mUSE model, Huggingface Datasets to load the Yelp Polarity dataset, and PyTorch Lightning for make training a bit simpler. mUSE internally uses TensorFlow Text for tokenization, so we install that as well. They can be installed by running the shell command shown in Listing 4.1.

```
pip install tensorflow_hub tensorflow_text>=2.0.0rc0
    pytorch_lightning==1.4.7 datasets==1.12.1
```

Listing 4.1   Python environment setup

4.4.3   Experiments, Results, and Analysis

Once the environment is setup, the encoder can be loaded, as shown in Listing 4.2. We also define a simple function that accepts a list of strings as inputs and returns a list of Numpy arrays. Note that we include Python 3's type annotations for clarity. They do not have to be used.

```
import tensorflow_hub as hub
import tensorflow_text
import numpy as np
from typing import List, Dict

model_URL =
    "https://tfhub.dev/google/universal-sentence-encoder-
    multilingual-large/3"
```

```
encoder = hub.load(model_URL)

def embed_text(text: List[str]) -> List[np.ndarray]:
    "Encode text and convert TensorFlow tensors to Numpy arrays"
    vectors = encoder(text)
    return [vector.numpy() for vector in vectors]
```

Listing 4.2 Load universal sentence encoder

4.4.3.1 Data preprocessing

To make training the model easy, this case study uses PyTorch Lightning. PyTorch Lightning has you implement the LightningDataModule class, which encapsulates all the data loading, preprocessing, and batching. We show how one might do this for the Yelp Polarity dataset in Listing 4.3. We use a small subset of the full train and test sets to keep model training time to a minimum. We leave it as an exercise to the reader to expand to larger subsets or to the entire dataset.

```
import pytorch_lightning as pl
import torch
from torch.utils.data import DataLoader
from datasets import Dataset, load_dataset


# set seed (this is optional)
pl.seed_everything(445326, workers=True)


class YelpDataModule(pl.LightningDataModule):
    def __init__(self,
                 batch_size: int = 32,
                 num_workers: int = 2):
        super().__init__()
        self.batch_size = batch_size
        self.num_workers = num_workers
        self.pin_memory = torch.cuda.is_available()

    def prepare_data(self):
        """
        This method loads a subset of the train and test sets.
        It uses the first 2% of the train and test sets to
            train and test, respectively.
        It uses the last 1% of the training set for validation.
```

```python
        """
        self.test_ds = load_dataset('yelp_polarity',
            split="test[:2%]")
        self.train_ds = load_dataset('yelp_polarity',
            split="train[:2%]")
        self.val_ds = load_dataset('yelp_polarity',
            split="train[99%:]")

        # Map class labels to an integer
        self.label_names = self.train_ds.unique("label")
        label2int = {str(label): n for n, label in
            enumerate(self.label_names)}
        self.encoder = encoder_factory(label2int)

    def setup(self):
        # Compute embeddings in batches, to speed things up
        self.train = self.train_ds.map(self.encoder,
            batched=True, batch_size=self.batch_size)
        self.train.set_format(type="torch",
            columns=["embedding", "label"],
                            output_all_columns=True)

        self.val = self.val_ds.map(self.encoder, batched=True,
            batch_size=self.batch_size)
        self.val.set_format(type="torch", columns=["embedding",
            "label"],
                            output_all_columns=True)

        self.test = self.test_ds.map(self.encoder,
            batched=True, batch_size=self.batch_size)
        self.test.set_format(type="torch",
            columns=["embedding", "label"],
                            output_all_columns=True)

    def train_dataloader(self):
        return DataLoader(self.train,
                        batch_size=self.batch_size,
                        num_workers=self.num_workers,
                        pin_memory=self.pin_memory,
                        shuffle=True)

    def val_dataloader(self):
        return DataLoader(self.val,
                        batch_size=self.batch_size,
                        num_workers=self.num_workers,
```

```
                         pin_memory=self.pin_memory)

    def test_dataloader(self):
        return DataLoader(self.test,
                          batch_size=self.batch_size,
                          num_workers=self.num_workers)


def encoder_factory(label2int: Dict[str, int]):
    "Returns a function that encodes each text example and each
        label"
    def encode(batch):
        batch["embedding"] = embed_text(batch["text"])
        batch["label"] = [label2int[str(x)] for x in
            batch["label"]]
        return batch

    return encode
```

Listing 4.3 Load model and tokenizer

4.4.3.2 Experiments

Next, we define the model architecture in Listing 4.4.

```
import torch
import torch.nn as nn
import torch.nn.functional as F
from datasets import load_metric


class Model(pl.LightningModule):
    def __init__(self,
                 hidden_dims: List[int] = [768, 128],
                 dropout_prob: float = 0.5,
                 learning_rate: float = 1e-3):
        super().__init__()
        self.train_acc = load_metric("accuracy")
        self.val_acc = load_metric("accuracy")
        self.test_acc = load_metric("accuracy")
        self.hidden_dims = hidden_dims
        self.dropout_prob = dropout_prob
        self.learning_rate = learning_rate

        self.embedding_dim = 512
```

```python
        layers = []
        prev_dim = self.embedding_dim

        if dropout_prob > 0:
            layers.append(nn.Dropout(dropout_prob))

        for h in hidden_dims:
            layers.append(nn.Linear(prev_dim, h))
            prev_dim = h
            if dropout_prob > 0:
                layers.append(nn.Dropout(dropout_prob))
            layers.append(nn.ReLU())
            if dropout_prob > 0:
                layers.append(nn.Dropout(dropout_prob))
        # output layer
        layers.append(nn.Linear(prev_dim, 2))

        self.layers = nn.Sequential(*layers)

    def forward(self, x):
        # x will be a batch of USEm vectors
        logits = self.layers(x)
        return logits

    def configure_optimizers(self):
        optimizer = torch.optim.Adam(self.parameters(),
            lr=self.learning_rate)
        return optimizer

    def __compute_loss(self, batch):
        "Runs the forward pass and computes the loss"
        x, y = batch["embedding"], batch["label"]
        logits = self(x)
        preds = torch.argmax(logits,
            dim=1).detach().cpu().numpy()
        loss = F.cross_entropy(logits, y)
        return loss, preds, y

    def training_step(self, batch, batch_idx):
        "Computes forward pass, loss, and logs metrics for a
            training batch"
        loss, preds, y = self.__compute_loss(batch)
        self.train_acc.add_batch(predictions=preds,
            references=y)
```

```
    acc = self.train_acc.compute()["accuracy"]
    values = {"train_loss": loss, "train_accuracy": acc}
    self.log_dict(values, on_step=True, on_epoch=True,
                prog_bar=True, logger=True)
    return loss

def validation_step(self, batch, batch_idx):
    "Computes forward pass, loss, and logs metrics for a
        validation batch"
    loss, preds, y = self.__compute_loss(batch)
    self.val_acc.add_batch(predictions=preds, references=y)
    acc = self.val_acc.compute()["accuracy"]
    values = {"val_loss": loss, "val_accuracy": acc}
    self.log_dict(values, on_step=True, on_epoch=True,
                prog_bar=True, logger=True)
    return loss

def test_step(self, batch, batch_idx):
    "Computes forward pass, loss, and logs metrics for a
        test batch"
    loss, preds, y = self.__compute_loss(batch)
    self.test_acc.add_batch(predictions=preds, references=y)
    acc = self.test_acc.compute()["accuracy"]
    values = {"test_loss": loss, "test_accuracy": acc}
    self.log_dict(values, on_step=False, on_epoch=True,
                prog_bar=True, logger=True)
    return loss
```

Listing 4.4 Multilingual binary classifier architecture

Now that the model is defined, we can load the data and then train and evaluate the model. We'll train for at most five epochs, will monitor the validation loss during training, will save the three model checkpoints (one per epoch) that contain the lowest validation loss. The checkpoints will be stored in a directory called 'model'. These options are passed to PyTorch Lightning's Trainer object via a ModelCheckpoint callback.

```
data = YelpDataModule()
data.prepare_data()
data.setup()
print(len(data.train)) # >> 11200
print(len(data.val)) # >> 5600
print(len(data.test)) # >> 760

model = Model()
```

```
MAX_EPOCHS = 5

checkpoint_callback = pl.callbacks.ModelCheckpoint(
    monitor="val_loss",
    dirpath="model",
    filename="yelp-sentiment-multilingual-{epoch:02d}-
            {val_loss:.3f}",
    save_top_k=3,
    mode="min")

# Create the Trained, and use a GPU (if available)
# It is best to train this model with a GPU.
if torch.cuda.is_available():
    trainer = pl.Trainer(gpus=1, max_epochs=MAX_EPOCHS,
                    callbacks=[checkpoint_callback])
else:
    trainer = pl.Trainer(max_epochs=MAX_EPOCHS,
                    callbacks=[checkpoint_callback])

# Train the model, passing it the train and validation data
    loaders
trainer.fit(model, data.train_dataloader(),
    data.val_dataloader())

# Test the model
trainer.test(test_dataloaders=data.test_dataloader())
#>> [{'test_accuracy': 0.8644737005233765, 'test_loss':
    0.32756760716438293}]
```

Listing 4.5 Load data, train, and evaluate the model

We've trained a model, now let's try it out. In Listing 4.6, we define a function that predicts sentiment for input text using the model checkpoint with lowest validation loss.

```
best_model = Model.load_from_checkpoint(checkpoint_callback.
            best_model_path)

def predict(text: List[str]):
    embeddings = torch.Tensor(embed_text(text))
    logits = best_model(embeddings)
    preds = torch.argmax(logits, dim=1).detach().cpu().numpy()
    scores = torch.softmax(logits, dim=1).detach().cpu().numpy()

    results = []
```

```
for t, best_index, score_pair in zip(text, preds, scores):
    results.append({
        "text": t,
        "label": "positive" if best_index == 1 else
            "negative",
        "score": score_pair[best_index]
    })
return results
```

```
predict(["I love that restaurant!", "I hate italian food."])
#>> [{"label": 'positive', "score": 0.99751616, "text": 'I love
    that restaurant!'},
#   {"label": 'negative', "score": 0.9791407, "text": 'I hate
    italian food.'}]
```

Listing 4.6   Load best model and run inference

Since we used USEm embeddings, we should be able to predict sentiment for non-English languages. Let's try it out. As mentioned earlier, USEm supports 16 languages: Arabic, Chinese-simplified, Chinese-traditional, English, French, German, Italian, Japanese, Korean, Dutch, Polish, Portuguese, Spanish, Thai, Turkish, Russian. In Listing 4.7, we compare sentiment predictions between pairs of languages, finding that even though our model was trained on a small subset of the Yelp Polarity training set, it can still perform well. We also find that the model can make accurate predictions for at least one language that is *not* one of the 16 supported languages. We use input text in four languages in Listing 4.7: English, German, Italian, and Finnish.

```
from pprint import PrettyPrinter
pp = PrettyPrinter()

# English vs. German
english_text = "Our server was horrid. He messed up the order
    and didn't even apologize when he spilled wine on my
    sister's hair!"
german_translation = "Unser Server war schrecklich. Er hat die
    Bestellung durcheinander gebracht und sich nicht einmal
    entschuldigt, als er Wein in die Haare meiner Schwester
    verschuttet hat!"

pp.pprint(predict(best_model, [english_text,
    german_translation]))
```

```
#>> [{"label": "negative",
#     "score": 0.9564845,
#     "text": "Our server was horrid. He messed up the order
    and "
#             "didn't even apologize when he spilled wine on my "
#             "sister's hair!"},
#    {"label": "negative",
#     "score": 0.9694613,
#     "text": "Unser Server war schrecklich. Er hat die
    Bestellung "
#             "durcheinander gebracht und sich nicht einmal "
#             "entschuldigt, als er Wein in die Haare meiner "
#             "Schwester verschuttet hat!"}]


# English vs. Italian & Finnish
english_text = "My least favorite film is Showgirls. I hate it
    so much. In fact, it's so bad that it makes me angry."
italian_translation = "Il mio film meno preferito e Showgirls.
    Lo odio cosi tanto. In effetti, e cosi brutto che mi fa
    arrabbiare."
finnish_translation = "Minun lempi elokuva on Showgirls. Vihaan
    sita niin paljon. Itse asiassa se on niin paha, etta se saa
    minut vihaiseksi."


pp.pprint(predict(best_model, [english_text,
    italian_translation, finnish_translation]))
#>> [{"label": "negative",
#     "score": 0.98994666,
#     "text": "My least favorite film is Showgirls. I hate it
    so much. "
#             "In fact, it's so bad that it makes me angry."},
#    {"label": "negative",
#     "score": 0.974451,
#     "text": "Il mio film meno preferito e Showgirls. Lo odio
    cosi "
#             "tanto. In effetti, e cosi brutto che mi fa
    arrabbiare."},
#    {"label": "negative",
#     "score": 0.7616636,
#     "text": "Minun lempi elokuva on Showgirls. Vihaan sita
    niin paljon. "
#             "Itse asiassa se on niin paha, etta se saa minut
    vihaiseksi."}]
```

Listing 4.7 Load best model and run inference

USEm even works on Finnish. But why? Without digging into things, it would be difficult to know for sure. Our guess is that in the training process, the subword units used in USEm's tokenization let the Transformer learn which subword units are used across languages, similar to what has been seen with the speech subunits in wav2vec2 [16]. The layers we added onto USEm, which are trained for classification, then let the model learn which subword units are related to positive or negative sentiment. Perhaps the subword units used in Finnish are close enough to those in one of the 16 languages that USEm supports.

## CHAPTER 5

Transformer Modifications

T HERE have been many modifications made to the Transformer architecture introduced in *Attention Is All You Need* [254]. As discussed in section 1.2.1, there are two broad types of modifications: changes to the organization of the Transformer block itself and changes to the submodules inside the Transformer block. This chapter discusses specific examples the Transformer block changes in section 1.2.1.1 and the Transformer submodule changes in section 1.2.1.2.

5.1 TRANSFORMER BLOCK MODIFICATIONS

In this section we'll take a detailed look at several models with altered Transformer blocks.

5.1.1 Lightweight Transformers

5.1.1.1 Funnel-transformer

Funnel-Transformer [66] compresses the output of a transformer encoder layer via pooling before it is passed to the next layer, thus reducing computation cost. It then uses the saved computation to support a deeper or wider model, thereby increasing the model capacity.

Encoder The standard transformer uses the same sequence length for all layers. Funnel-Transformer changes this by placing a pooling layer between the transformer layers to reduce the sequence length. It typically has multiple transformer layers in a block of the same sequence length

DOI: 10.1201/9781003170082-5

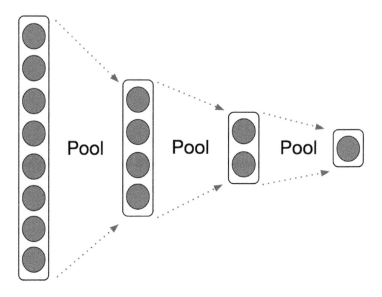

Figure 5.1 Schematic architecture diagram for Funnel-Transformer's encoder. Each layer represents a block composed of several transformer layers with the same sequence length. Shows three pooling operations between blocks, with each decreasing the sequence length of the output by half.

before the pooling operation. This is shown in Fig. 5.1. If the output of a given layer is $\mathbf{h}$, then the output of the pooling layer is $\mathbf{h}' = Pooling(\mathbf{h})$, where $\mathbf{h} \in \mathbb{R}^{T \times d}$ and $\mathbf{h}' \in \mathbb{R}^{T' \times d}$, for some $T' < T$.

$\mathbf{h}'$ is used to construct the query and the residual connection for the self-attention block, $\mathbf{h}$ is used for the key and value vectors:

$$\mathbf{Q} = \mathbf{h}' \mathbf{W}_Q, \in \mathbb{R}^{T' \times d_k} \tag{5.1}$$

$$\mathbf{K} = \mathbf{h} \mathbf{W}_K, \in \mathbb{R}^{T \times d_k} \tag{5.2}$$

$$\mathbf{V} = \mathbf{h} \mathbf{W}_V, \in \mathbb{R}^{T \times d_v} \tag{5.3}$$

This relationship between the unpooled and pooled outputs and the query, key, and value matrices of the next layer is shown in Fig. 5.2. The output of the $(n+1)^{st}$ layer is then

$$\mathbf{h}^{(n+1)} = LayerNorm(\mathbf{h}'^{(n)} + multihead(\mathbf{Q}(\mathbf{h}'^{(n)}), \mathbf{K}(\mathbf{h}^{(n)}), \mathbf{V}(\mathbf{h}^{(n)}))) \tag{5.4}$$

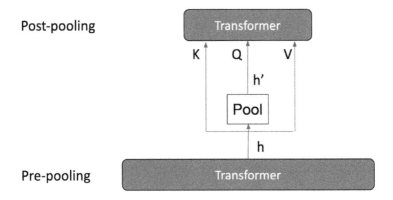

Figure 5.2 Shows how the pooling operation between Funnel-Transformer's encoder layers affect the input of the next layer. **h** is the output of the layer before the pooling and **h'** is the output of the pooling operation. The query matrix for the next layer is constructed from the pooled output, **h'**. The key and value matrices for the next layer are made from the unpooled output, **h**.

The attention weight matrix of each attention head is $(T' \times T)$, which has decreasing complexity for each successive layer. The output of multi-head attention has the same dimensions as **h'**.

By constructing the query from the pooled sequence and the key and value from the unpooled sequence, the attention mechanism tries to learn how the pooled and unpooled sequences should best attend to each other to result in high quality compression. Funnel-Transformer uses mean pooling with stride and window size both set to two.

Decoder To support token-level prediction tasks where the model needs to produce a full output sequence, like machine translation, Funnel-Transformer has an optional decoder that upsamples the compressed encoder output to a full sequence length. M encoder layers will have the output sequence $\mathbf{h}^{(M)}$ that has length $T_M = T/2^{M-1}$. It will be upsampled in a single step to $\mathbf{h}^{(up)} = [h_1^{(up)}, \ldots, h_T^{(up)}]$ by repeating each hidden vector 2^{M-1} times:

$$h_i^{up} = h_{i//2^{N-1}}^{(M)}, \forall i = 1, \ldots, T \qquad (5.5)$$
$$x//y = floor(x/y) \qquad (5.6)$$

To address the duplicate information in Funnel-Transformer's up-sampling process, the hidden state output of the first encoder layer is added to the upsampled representation: $\mathbf{g} = \mathbf{h}^{(up)} + \mathbf{h}^{(1)}$. This acts as a residual connection. They then add a few transformer layers on top of $\mathbf{g}$ for it to learn how to best combine the features.

Scaling   The time complexity of Funnel-Transformer is $O(d \cdot T^2 + T \cdot d^2)$. Since T decreases by half at successive encoder layers, the complexity decreases by a factor of four for each layer. Since $O(T \cdot d^2)$ has the large constant d^2, it tends to dominate, providing a linear speedup, instead of a quadratic one.

Due to the complexity reduction afforded by the pooling between layers, it is possible to add additional encoder layers or make existing layers wider without increasing the computational load in any significant manner.

Performance   Three sizes of the standard transformer were compared to several configurations of Funnel-Transformer, each with fewer or similar numbers of expected floating-point operations to the transformer to which it was being compared:

- large: 24 layers, $d = 1024$

- base: 12 layers, $d = 768$

- small: 6 layers, $d = 768$

Quality comparisons are made for GLUE and when Funnel-Transformer decreases the sequence length and adds more layers, it performs better than the standard transformer on text classification and all GLUE datasets except for STS-B. When the sequence length is decreases but the depth is not increased, performance decreases on GLUE text classification datasets.

5.1.1.2 DeLighT

DeLighT [180] is a modified Transformer architecture that performs as well as the standard transformer on machine translation and language modeling; all while using far fewer parameters and FLOPs. It introduces a transformation on the input to a Transformer block that comes before the projections into query, key, value spaces.

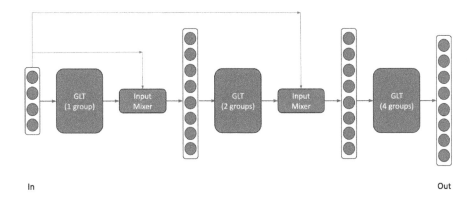

Figure 5.3 The expansion phase of the DeLight transformation, showing the three grouped linear transformations (GLT).

DeLighT block The DeLighT block uses N layers of the grouped linear transformation (GLT) [181] to first transform a d-dimensional vector into a higher-dimensional space of $d_{max} = w_m d_{in}$ in the first $\lceil N/2 \rceil$ layers, and then transform the d_{max} vector into a lower-dimensional space, d_o, using the other $N - \lceil N/2 \rceil$ layers. The d_o vector is what is then projected in the query, key, and value spaces. DeLighT blocks closer to the output of the model are made wider and deeper than those closer to the model input. DeLighT used $d_o = d/2$ and also shuffles the features between the groups in the GLT, using a mixer connection [182] to combine the shuffled features with the input, similar to a residual connection. The expansion phase of the DeLighT block is shown in Fig. 5.3.

Mehta et al. proposed that by increasing the depth of the DeLighT block and the width of its intermediate GLT layers, the transformer will have an increased representational capacity and that one can then replace multi-head attention with single-head attention. Similarly, they propose that the DeLighT block's wide linear layers let one decrease the size of the feedforward layer by up to 16x.

Performance DeLighT performed as well as or better than the standard transformer on machine translation, despite having considerably fewer parameters. But, when DeLighT is given more parameters, it outperforms the standard transformer. It also obtains similar or better quality to SOTA models on machine translation. Also, performance increases with the number of network parameters in the DeLighT block.

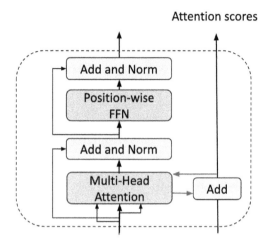

Figure 5.4 RealFormer's residual attention connection.

5.1.2   Connections between Transformer Blocks

5.1.2.1   RealFormer

RealFormer, the Residual Attention Layer Transformer [107], adds residual scores to the raw attention logits (query-key dot product) of all attention heads from the previous layer of a transformer. The attention weights are then the softmax of the summed attention logits. This is shown schematically in Fig. 5.4 and mathematically in (5.7)–(5.9).

$$ResidualMultiHead(\mathbf{Q}, \mathbf{K}, \mathbf{V}, \mathbf{Prev}) = \text{concat}(head_1, \ldots, head_h)\mathbf{W}_o$$
(5.7)

$$head_i = ResidualAttn(\mathbf{Q}_i, \mathbf{K}_i, \mathbf{V}_i, \mathbf{Prev}_i)$$
(5.8)

$$ResidualAttn(\mathbf{Q}', \mathbf{K}', \mathbf{V}', \mathbf{Prev}') = \text{softmax}\left(\frac{\mathbf{Q}'\mathbf{K}'^T}{\sqrt{d_k}} + \mathbf{Prev}'\right)\mathbf{V}'$$
(5.9)

where $\mathbf{Prev} \in \mathbb{R}^{h \times d_{in} \times d_{out}}$ are the attention logits from the previous transformer layer. d_{in} is the layer's input sequence dimension and d_{out} is the layer's output sequence dimension. The argument of the softmax, the attention logits or attention scores, is passed to the next RealFormer layer.

This method can be applied to other transformer architectures, including to decoder layers. When there are multiple types of attention modules in a transformer, one can skip edges to support one residual connection for each type of attention.

Performance RealFormer generally performs better than the standard transformer architecture, including its use in BERT, all without increasing the number of model parameters.

5.1.3 Adaptive Computation Time

5.1.3.1 Universal transformers (UT)

As seen in the previous chapters, transformers overcome the issues associated with RNNs, namely the bottlenecks of sequential computation and the vanishing gradient problems amongst the many. Furthermore, self-attention, the critical innovation in the transformers, helps in parallelizing the computation of per-symbol context-based vectors and creates a global receptive field where the symbol gets information from all the symbols. On the other hand, the absence of recurrent inductive bias of RNNs becomes an issue when solving tasks with inherent hierarchical structures or when the lengths vary significantly between the training and the unseen data the model predicts. Also, the number of sequential computations in transformers is independent of the input size but only dependent on the number of layers, making it computationally non-universal or Turing incomplete. Transformers apply the same amount of computation to all the inputs leading to inefficiencies in many cases where computations can be conditioned on the complexity.

Universal transformers (UT) by Dehghani et al. [69] is an extension of transformers where the parallelizability and global receptive field benefits get supplemented by the recurrent inductive bias of RNNs while being computationally universal. Instead of a fixed number of layers in the transformers, Universal transformers have a Universal transformer block, i.e., a self-attention mechanism followed by a recurrent transformation that provides a recurrent inductive bias for each input symbol in parallel. As shown in Fig. 5.5, the Universal Transformer is a recurrent function not in time but in depth that evolves the hidden states corresponding to every input in parallel, based at each step on the sequence of previous hidden states.

UT has many commonalities with the existing neural architectures, such as the Neural GPU [136] and the Neural Turing Machine [98]. It can also be shown to be equivalent to a multi-layer transformer with tied parameters across its layers. Graves proposed Adaptive Computation Time (ACT), which allows RNNs to learn dynamically how many computational steps to take between accepting input and emitting an output (ponder time) to overcome the issues of a fixed number of

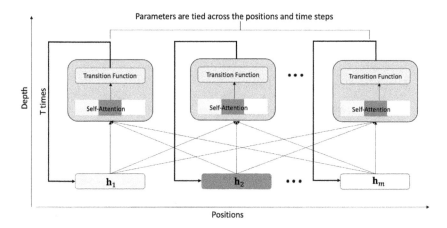

Figure 5.5 Universal Transformer with information from different positions using self-attention and applying a recurrent transition function.

computational steps per symbol. UT incorporates a dynamic ACT halting mechanism to each position inspired by Graves's ACT to condition the computation per symbol based on the complexity. The research shows that UTs outperform standard transformers on a wide range of NLP and NLU and achieve a new state-of-the-art in complex tasks such as the LAMBADA language modeling.

5.1.4 Recurrence Relations between Transformer Blocks

5.1.4.1 Transformer-XL

The Transformer-XL [67] models dependencies beyond a fixed length, while respecting sentence boundaries. It was introduced because the standard transformer architecture's fixed-width context window prevents it from learning to model dependencies at ranges outside of its fixed window. Transformer-XL can handle dependencies 450% longer than the standard transformer and inference is ~ 1800 times faster than the Transformer.

Segment-level recurrence Transformer-XL extends its context beyond a fixed window by using a method called Segment-level recurrence. Segment-level recurrence works by using the previous segment of text as additional context when processing the current segment of text. For this to work, the previous segment has to be cached, along with the transformer output of each layer for that segment.

In the standard transformer, the nth transformer layer takes the output of the previous layer $(n-1)$ as input:

$$\mathbf{h}_t^{(n)} = Transformer(\mathbf{h}_t^{(n-1)}) \tag{5.10}$$

and internally generates the query, key, and value from $\mathbf{h}_t^{(n-1)}$:

$$\begin{aligned}
\mathbf{Q}_t^{(n)} &= \mathbf{h}_t^{(n-1)}\mathbf{W}_q \\
\mathbf{K}_t^{(n)} &= \mathbf{h}_t^{(n-1)}\mathbf{W}_k \\
\mathbf{V}_t^{(n)} &= \mathbf{h}_t^{(n-1)}\mathbf{W}_v
\end{aligned} \tag{5.11}$$

Note that $n = 1$ is being considered as the first transformer layer and $n = 0$ is the input to the first transformer layer, so $\mathbf{h}_t^{(0)} = \mathbf{X}$.

Eqns. (5.11) change when the previous segment is included. Consider two consecutive segments of text, which have embedded representations $\mathbf{X}_t$ and $\mathbf{X}_{t+1}$, where t is just used to signify the segment ordering. When computing the output of the nth transformer layer for the current segment, $\mathbf{X}_{t+1}$, we have a contribution from $\mathbf{h}_t^{(n-1)}$, which is the previous transformer layer's output for the previous segment,

$$\mathbf{h}_{t+1}^{(n)} = \text{TransformerXL}(\mathbf{h}_{t+1}^{(n-1)}, \mathbf{h}_t^{(n-1)}). \tag{5.12}$$

The dependency on the previous segment comes in when computing the key and value for the current segment:

$$\begin{aligned}
\mathbf{Q}_{t+1}^{(n)} &= \mathbf{h}_{t+1}^{(n-1)}\mathbf{W}_q \\
\mathbf{K}_{t+1}^{(n)} &= \tilde{\mathbf{h}}_{t+1}^{(n-1)}\mathbf{W}_k \\
\mathbf{V}_{t+1}^{(n)} &= \tilde{\mathbf{h}}_t^{(n-1)}\mathbf{W}_v
\end{aligned} \tag{5.13}$$

$$\tilde{\mathbf{h}}_{t+1}^{(n-1)} = [\text{StopGradient}(\mathbf{h}_t^{(n-1)}); \mathbf{h}_{t+1}^{(n-1)}] \tag{5.14}$$

where StopGradient means the gradient is not computed during the operation.

Eqns. (5.13) and (5.14) show that the attention mechanism is being used to compute a modified attention that incorporates information from the previous input sequence to compute a representation of the current input sequence. And yet there is more to it than that. The transformer output for the current sequence depends on the transformer output for

TABLE 5.1 At a layer depth of three, the output of the transformer on the fourth segment has contributions from the first segment. For brevity, the T shown above is the Transformer-XL operation as described in (5.12)

Layer (n) S_1	S_2	S_3	S_4
0 (input) $h_1^{(0)} = S_1$	$h_2^{(0)} = S_2$	$h_3^{(0)} = S_3$	$h_4^{(0)} = S_4$
1 $\quad h_1^{(1)} = T(h_1^{(0)})$	$h_2^{(1)} = T(h_2^{(0)}, h_1^{(0)})$	$h_3^{(1)} = T(h_3^{(0)}, h_2^{(0)})$	$h_4^{(1)} = T(h_4^{(0)}, h_3^{(0)})$
2 $\quad h_1^{(2)} = T(h_1^{(1)})$	$h_2^{(2)} = T(h_2^{(1)}, h_1^{(1)})$	$h_3^{(2)} = T(h_3^{(1)}, h_2^{(2)})$	$h_4^{(2)} = T(h_4^{(1)}, h_3^{(1)})$
3 $\quad h_1^{(3)} = T(h_1^{(2)})$	$h_2^{(3)} = T(h_2^{(2)}, h_1^{(2)})$	$h_3^{(3)} = T(h_3^{(2)}, h_2^{(3)})$	$h_4^{(3)} = T(h_4^{(2)}, h_3^{(2)})$

the previous sequence. The transformer output for the previous sequence depends on the sequence before that one and on the previous transformer layer. This means that as the number of transformer layers increases, the effective context size the model can process also increases. Formally, we can say that the output of the nth transformer layer on the tth segment has contributions from segments as far back as $t - n$. An example of this is shown in Table 5.1, for four text segments and three Transformer-XL layers.

Positional encodings in Transformer-XL

Positional encodings   As discussed in Ch. 1, since a Transformer doesn't contain recurrent or convolutional layers, word order is explicitly built in via positional encodings. Each input sequence is given a positional encoding, $\mathbf{P} \in \mathbb{R}^{L \times d}$, where L is the maximum sequence length and d is the embedding dimension, and word embeddings $\mathbf{E} \in \mathbb{R}^{L \times d}$. Note that the full input sequence is represented by $\mathbf{X} = \mathbf{E} + \mathbf{P}$; this is the same $\mathbf{X}$ used throughout this chapter, e.g., as seen in (5.22).

Row i of $\mathbf{P}$, $\mathbf{p}_i$, contains the positional encoding for the token in position i. Similarly, $\mathbf{e}_i$ is the word embedding for the token in position i. Since the positional encodings are deterministic and are independent of the tokens in the sequence, any word in position i will have the same positional encoding. This introduces a problem for segment-level recurrence.

Consider two consecutive text sequences $\mathbf{X}_{t+1}$ and $\mathbf{X}_t$, and the output of the first TransformerXL layer for each sequence. (5.12) tells us that

$$\mathbf{h}_{t+1}^{(1)} = \text{TransformerXL}(\mathbf{X}_{t+1}, \mathbf{X}_t) \tag{5.15}$$

and (5.14) says that

$$\tilde{\mathbf{h}}_{t+1}^{(0)} = [\text{StopGradient}(\mathbf{X}_t); \mathbf{X}_{t+1}] \qquad (5.16)$$

Since $\mathbf{X}_t = \mathbf{E}_t + \mathbf{P}$ and positional encodings are independent of the tokens in the sequence, $\tilde{\mathbf{h}}_{t+1}^{(0)}$ is concatenating identical copies of the positional encodings. This is problematic because $\tilde{\mathbf{h}}_{t+1}^{(0)}$ represents the expanded effective context size and thus each position in the sequence should have distinct positional encodings. Without distinct positional encodings, the model loses information about word order. The solution to this problem is to use relative positional encodings.

Relative positional encodings Earlier work [224, 124] introduced relative positional encodings as a way to let an attention mechanism learn from the distance between two positions in a sequence, rather than using the absolute positional encodings from the standard transformer, which biases the attention mechanism to consider the absolute position as important. Instead, information about the relative distance between $\mathbf{q}_i$ and $\mathbf{k}_j$ would be incorporated into the attention weight calculation, biasing the attention mechanism to consider the distance $i - j$ as the important quantity, rather the positions i and j.

Transformer XL modified the attention matrix calculation to use sinusoidal relative positional encodings [67]. We can see how by first expanding the (i, j) term of $\mathbf{Q}\mathbf{K}^T$ in (5.23), $\mathbf{q}_i\mathbf{k}_j^T$. Recalling (5.22), (5.24), and (5.25), we can see that the ith row of $\mathbf{X}$ is $\mathbf{x}_i = \mathbf{e}_i + \mathbf{p}_i$, and that

$$\begin{aligned} \mathbf{q}_i &= \mathbf{x}_i\mathbf{W}_q \\ \mathbf{k}_j &= \mathbf{x}_j\mathbf{W}_k \end{aligned} \qquad (5.17)$$

Using (5.17), we expand $\mathbf{q}_i\mathbf{k}_j^T$ to get

$$\begin{aligned} A_{ij} &= (\mathbf{e}_i\mathbf{W}_q + \mathbf{p}_i\mathbf{W}_q)(\mathbf{W}_k^T\mathbf{e}_j^T + \mathbf{W}_k^T\mathbf{p}_j^T) \\ &= \mathbf{e}_i\mathbf{W}_q\mathbf{W}_k^T\mathbf{e}_j^T + \mathbf{e}_i\mathbf{W}_q\mathbf{W}_k^T\mathbf{p}_j^T \\ &\quad + \mathbf{p}_i\mathbf{W}_q\mathbf{W}_k^T\mathbf{e}_j^T + \mathbf{p}_i\mathbf{W}_q\mathbf{W}_k^T\mathbf{p}_j^T \end{aligned} \qquad (5.18)$$

Transformer XL reparameterizes A_{ij} in terms of five new quantities: $\mathbf{R}_{i-j}$, $\mathbf{u}$, $\mathbf{v}$, $\mathbf{W}_{k,E}$, and $\mathbf{W}_{k,R}$ [67]:

1. $\mathbf{R}_{i-j}$ are the relative positional encodings for a token pair with distance $i - j$ and replaces $\mathbf{p}_j$ in (5.18). $\mathbf{R}_{i-j}$ is the $(i - j)^{th}$ row of the relative positional encoding matrix $\mathbf{R} \in \mathbb{R}^{L \times d}$.

2. $\mathbf{u}$ replaces $\mathbf{p}_i \mathbf{W}_q$ in the third term of (5.18).

3. $\mathbf{v}$ replaces $\mathbf{p}_i \mathbf{W}_q$ in the fourth term of (5.18).

4. TransformerXL replaces the keys K with two sets of keys: content-based and location-based. This change results in a replacement of the key weight matrix, $\mathbf{W}_k$, with two weight matrices, $\mathbf{W}_{k,E}$ and $\mathbf{W}_{k,R}$, where $\mathbf{W}_{k,E}$ generates content-based keys and $\mathbf{W}_{k,R}$ generates location-based keys [67].

As a result, (5.18) becomes

$$A_{ij} = \mathbf{e}_i \mathbf{W}_q \mathbf{W}_{k,E}^T \mathbf{e}_j^T + \mathbf{e}_i \mathbf{W}_q \mathbf{W}_{k,R}^T \mathbf{R}_{i-j}^T + \mathbf{u} \mathbf{W}_{k,E}^T \mathbf{e}_j^T + \mathbf{v} \mathbf{W}_{k,R}^T \mathbf{R}_{i-j}^T \quad (5.19)$$

Note that by removing the explicit position dependence, that $\mathbf{x}_i = \mathbf{e}_i$ implies $\mathbf{X} = \mathbf{E}$, and thus $\mathbf{q}_i = \mathbf{e}_i \mathbf{W}_q$ and $\mathbf{k}_j = \mathbf{e}_j \mathbf{W}_{k,E}$.

Using (5.19), we arrive at the final form of Transformer-XL's attention mechanism for the nth model layer

$$\mathbf{Attn}_t^{(n)} = \text{softmax}\left(\frac{\mathbf{A}_t^{(n)}}{\sqrt{d_k}}\right) \mathbf{V}_t^{(n)}, \quad (5.20)$$

where $A_t^{(n)}$ is (5.19) modified as prescribed in (5.13)

$$A_{t,ij}^{(n)} = \mathbf{q}_{t,i}^{(n)} \mathbf{k}_{t,j}^{(n)T} + \mathbf{q}_{t,i}^{(n)} \mathbf{W}_{k,R}^{(n)T} \mathbf{R}_{i-j}^T + \mathbf{u} \mathbf{k}_{t,j}^{(n)T} + \mathbf{v} \mathbf{W}_{k,R}^{(n)T} \mathbf{R}_{i-j}^T \quad (5.21)$$

Note that the sum in the softmax denominator is a masked sum over the set of key positions that the query attends to, S_i, as shown in (5.27). Also, since $\mathbf{x} = \mathbf{e}_i$, $\mathbf{h}_t^{(0)} = \mathbf{X}_t$.

5.1.5 Hierarchical Transformers

Two examples of hierarchical transformers are the Vision Transformer [78], for image recognition, and TimeSformer [29], for video classification/action recognition. Both models will be covered in Chapter 6.

5.2 TRANSFORMERS WITH MODIFIED MULTI-HEAD SELF-ATTENTION

5.2.1 Structure of Multi-Head Self-Attention

Multi-head attention is a way of combining multiple attention mechanisms that lets a model learn different types of dependencies between the input and output. The multi-head attention mechanism is the core of every transformer block. The encoder and decoder blocks both use multi-head self-attention, and the decoder block has a second multi-head attention that attends to the output of the encoder block, with the appropriate causal constraint.

In this section, we'll describe the structure of the multi-head self-attention calculation for a single input sequence of L tokens, with embedding dimension d. The input sequence can be represented by a matrix $\mathbf{X} \in \mathbb{R}^{L \times d}$:

$$
\mathbf{X} = \begin{bmatrix} \mathbf{x}_1 \\ \vdots \\ \mathbf{x}_L \end{bmatrix} \tag{5.22}
$$

where $\mathbf{x}_i = (x_0^{(i)}, \dots, x_{d-1}^{(i)})$ is the embedding vector of the ith token.

As we saw in section 2.4.2.1, the output of the attention mechanism (before the heads are concatenated) can be represented by

$$
\mathbf{Attn}(\mathbf{Q}, \mathbf{K}, \mathbf{V}) = \mathrm{softmax}\left(\frac{\mathbf{Q}\mathbf{K}^T}{\sqrt{d_k}}\right)\mathbf{V}, \tag{5.23}
$$

where $\mathbf{Q}, \mathbf{K}, \mathbf{V}$ are the query, key, and value matrices, respectively. Each is the result of transforming the input sequence into a different vector space:

$$
\begin{aligned}
\mathbf{Q} &= \mathbf{X}\mathbf{W}_q, \in \mathbb{R}^{L \times d_k} \\
\mathbf{K} &= \mathbf{X}\mathbf{W}_k, \in \mathbb{R}^{L \times d_k} \\
\mathbf{V} &= \mathbf{X}\mathbf{W}_v, \in \mathbb{R}^{L \times d_v}
\end{aligned} \tag{5.24}
$$

where d_k is the dimension of the query and key spaces and is typically set to d, and d_v is the value dimension. The matrices $\mathbf{W}_q, \mathbf{W}_k \in \mathbb{R}^{d \times d_k}$, and $\mathbf{W}_v \in \mathbb{R}^{d \times d_v}$ are basically rotation matrices. Each row of a query/key/value matrix corresponds to the query/key/value vector of the ith token:

$$
\mathbf{Q} = \begin{bmatrix} \mathbf{q}_1 \\ \vdots \\ \mathbf{q}_L \end{bmatrix}, \mathbf{K} = \begin{bmatrix} \mathbf{k}_1 \\ \vdots \\ \mathbf{k}_L \end{bmatrix}, \mathbf{V} = \begin{bmatrix} \mathbf{v}_1 \\ \vdots \\ \mathbf{v}_L \end{bmatrix} \tag{5.25}
$$

Note that (5.24) can be adapted for the case of multi-head attention between two sequences, $\mathbf{X}_1$ and $\mathbf{X}_2$, of lengths L_1 and L_2, respectively.

For two sequences, the query matrix is formed from $\mathbf{X}_1$ and the key and value matrices are formed from $\mathbf{X}_2$:

$$
\begin{aligned}
\mathbf{Q} &= \mathbf{X}_1 \mathbf{W}_k, \in \mathbb{R}^{L_1 \times d_k \times h} \\
\mathbf{K} &= \mathbf{X}_2 \mathbf{W}_k, \in \mathbb{R}^{L_2 \times d_k \times h} \\
\mathbf{V} &= \mathbf{X}_2 \mathbf{W}_v, \in \mathbb{R}^{L_2 \times d_v \times h}
\end{aligned}
\tag{5.26}
$$

where $\mathbf{X}_1 \in \mathbb{R}^{L_1 \times d}$ and $\mathbf{X}_2 \in \mathbb{R}^{L_2 \times d}$. This is generally what happens in a transformer decoder block. $\mathbf{X}_1 \in \mathbb{R}^{L \times d}$

The softmax portion of (5.23) is the attention weight matrix A_{ij}:

$$
A_{ij} = \frac{\exp\left(\frac{\mathbf{q}_i \mathbf{k}_j^T}{\sqrt{d_k}}\right)}{\sum_{r \in S_i} \exp\left(\frac{\mathbf{q}_i \mathbf{k}_r^T}{\sqrt{d_k}}\right)},
\tag{5.27}
$$

where S_i is the set of key positions that query $\mathbf{q}_i$ can attend to.

5.2.1.1 Multi-head self-attention

So far, we have only discussed single-head self-attention. Multi-head attention is mainly partitioning the matrices shown above into h pieces, where h is the number of attention heads.

Each attention head has its own query/key/value that is obtained by breaking the single-head versions into h equally sized pieces, that are indexed by $n = 1, \ldots, h$:

$$
\begin{aligned}
\mathbf{Q}_n &= \mathbf{X}\mathbf{W}_n^{(q)}, \in \mathbb{R}^{L \times d_k/h} \\
\mathbf{K}_n &= \mathbf{X}\mathbf{W}_n^{(k)}, \in \mathbb{R}^{L \times d_k/h} \\
\mathbf{V}_n &= \mathbf{X}\mathbf{W}_n^{(v)}, \in \mathbb{R}^{L \times d_v/h}
\end{aligned}
\tag{5.28}
$$

This does not mean that we now have h query, key, and value matrices, but that the matrices shown in (5.28) are a part of the matrices shown in (5.24). This is explicitly shown for the query in Fig. 5.6.

The key and value matrices are partitioned into attention heads in a similar way to $\mathbf{Q}$ and the attention calculation for the nth head proceeds as expected:

$$
\mathbf{Attn}^{(n)}(\mathbf{Q}_n, \mathbf{K}_n, \mathbf{V}_n) = \text{softmax}\left(\frac{\mathbf{Q}_n \mathbf{K}_n^T}{\sqrt{d_k/h}}\right) \mathbf{V}_n,
\tag{5.29}
$$

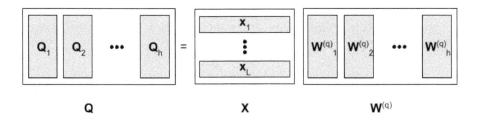

Figure 5.6 The query matrix, $\mathbf{Q}$, can be partitioned into h heads, as described in (5.28).

Note that for the multihead case, $\mathbf{Q}_n\mathbf{K}_n^T$ is divided by $\sqrt{d_k/h}$ instead of $\sqrt{d_k}$. This change account s for the change in effective dimension of the query and key spaces to d_k/h. The attention heads are then combined as described in (2.19).

5.2.1.2 Space and time complexity

Computing the attention weight matrix described in section 5.27 takes $O(L^2 \cdot d_k)$ matrix multiplications and computing the context vector in section 5.23 needs $O(L^2 \cdot d_v)$ matrix multiplications, so the time complexity of self-attention is $O(L^2 \cdot d_k + L^2 \cdot d_v)$.

Consider a single input sequence of L tokens and that the query, key, and value share the same dimensionality, so $d_k = d_v = d_{model}$. This means that $\mathbf{Q}, \mathbf{K}, \mathbf{V}$ are $L \times d_{model}$ matrices and the attention weight matrix from (5.23) is $L \times L$. Assuming 32-bit floating points numbers, the memory usage grows quickly, as shown in Table 5.2. More memory is required when including the batch size. For example, if the batch size were 32 and the sequence length were 20,000, then 51.2 GB would be needed to store the self-attention weights. The time complexity is also quadratic in L. This kind of scaling becomes prohibitive as the sequence

TABLE 5.2 Memory usage for self-attention weights, for 32-bit floats [142]

L	Memory
600	4 MB
1K	1.4 MB
20K	1.6 GB
64K	16.384 GB

length increases. For example, if the sequence length doubles, the amount of time needed to compute and store the attention weights will increase fourfold.

5.2.2 Reducing Complexity of Self-Attention

This section discusses several transformer models that reduce the computational complexity of multi-head self-attention.

5.2.2.1 Longformer

When calculating self-attention (omitting the causal requirement for the self-attention between the encoder and decoder blocks) there are usually no restrictions on which positions in the sequence can attend to each other. This means that, in principle, the matrix of attention weights for every head could be dense. When viewed as a graph, it corresponds to a fully-connected, weighted bipartite graph. If the sequence has L tokens, then there would be $L(L-1)/2$ edges. Longformer [25] changes this by restricting which positions can attend to each other according to specific patterns. This results in sparse attention weights across all heads and corresponds to deleting edges from the attention graph.

Longformer combines a global attention with two types of short-range attention, sliding window and dilated sliding window. Each attention pattern corresponds to a type of attention mask.

Sliding window attention   Rather than being able to attend to any token in the sequence, each token in a sequence is given a fixed-sized context window, w, so it can only attend to its neighbors. For example, if we had a sequence of nine tokens, $(w_1, \ldots, w_9)$, and window size $w = 4$, then the context of the middle token, w_5, would extend right (w_3, w_4) and left (w_6, w_7) by two tokens each. This is shown in Fig. 5.7.

In the graph view, this means that each vertex would be linked to at most $w - 1$ vertices. So, this change reduces the number of edges from $L(L-1)/2$ to $L(w-1)$. This simple change reduces the complexity from one that is quadratic in the sequence length to one that is linear in the sequence length, $O(Lw)$, since the sliding window attention weight matrix would have Lw nonzero values in each row (or column).

Dilated sliding window attention   This attention pattern extends the breadth of the sliding window attention by add gaps of size d in the

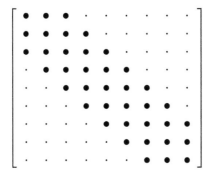

Figure 5.7 Sliding window attention pattern, for $L = 9$ and $w = 4$. Row i corresponds to query i. Columns with a • are keys that query i attends to and · represents a lack of attention (a missing edge).

context window. This actually extends the effective size of the context window. For example, in the sequence of nine tokens used above, suppose we added a dilation $d = 2$. In generating the context of w_5, we would now skip one word in between. Thus, the left context of w_5 would be (w_1, w_3) and the right context would be (w_7, w_9). Note that even though the overall context width has grown, this attention pattern also prevents a token from attending to its immediate neighbor, or to any token that is a distance $d - 1$ away from the center of the window or to any position it attends to that are inside the window. Different attention heads can use different values of d, which mitigates the issue mentioned above. Fig. 5.8 shows dilated sliding window attention for $L = 2$, $w = 4$, and $d = 2$.

Global attention The global attention pattern chooses lets some tokens attend to any other token in the sequence. In such cases, all tokens in the sequence attend to that token. This corresponds to choosing specific rows of an attention weight matrix and their transposed columns.

Longformer decides which tokens are allowed to have global attention based on the training task. For instance, in question and answer tasks, all tokens in the question have global attention. The number of tokens with global attention is generally independent of sequence length, so global attention is also linear in sequence length. The Longformer combines this global attention with the sliding window attention.

Weights for the global and short-ranged attention patterns are computed separately by giving the global and sliding window patterns their

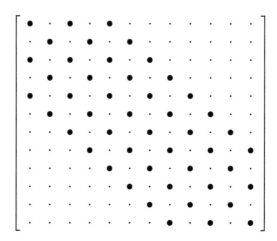

Figure 5.8 Dilated sliding window attention pattern, for $L = 12$, $w = 4$, and $d = 2$. Row i corresponds to query i. Columns with a ● are keys that query i attends to and · represents a lack of attention (a missing edge).

own query, key, and value matrices: $\mathbf{Q}_g$, $\mathbf{K}_g$, $\mathbf{V}_g$ and $\mathbf{Q}_s$, $\mathbf{K}_s$, $\mathbf{V}_s$, respectively.

Longformer uses small window sizes for lower layers and larger window sizes for higher layers. This gives the higher layers a hierarchical nature. In fact, dilated sliding windows are only used for higher layers, so that lower layers can focus on local context.

5.2.2.2 Reformer

Reformer, introduced in [142], addresses attention mechanism complexity by modifying the attention mechanism and reduces memory usage by using reversible residual networks. These tricks let the Reformer include context windows that are several orders of magnitude larger than a Transformer (up to $1,000,000$ words).

Attention and locality-sensitive hashing As discussed in section 5.2.1.1, the scaled dot-product attention which is at the core of the transformer has time complexity $O(L^2)$, which becomes prohibitive as the number of tokens in the sequence, L, increases. The Reformer model addresses this by modifying attention mechanism with locality-sensitive hashing. This changes the time complexity to $O(L \log L)$.

Recall that in the scaled dot-product attention, the query, key, and value matrices are the result of transforming the matrix of d_{model}-dimensional input vectors into queries and keys of dimension d_k and values of dimension d_v.

In the equation for A, the computationally expensive term is the product $\mathbf{QK}^T$, moreover, once the softmax function is applied, only the largest terms along each d_{model} dimension are important. This means that for each query vector in $\mathbf{Q}$, we only need the keys in $\mathbf{K}$ that are closest to it. To make this easier, they set $\mathbf{Q} = \mathbf{K}$, meaning that for each query vector, we only need to find the closest queries. This is an approximate nearest neighbors problem, so we can use locality-sensitive hashing (LSH).

Locality-sensitive hashing Locality-sensitive hashing, or LSH, was introduced in 1998, in [129] as a method of approximate similarity search based on hashing. In formal terms, LSH is based on a family of hash functions $\mathcal{F}$ that operate on a collection of items where, if any two such items x and y, $Prob_{h \in \mathcal{F}}[h(x) = h(y)] = sim(x, y)$, where $sim(x, y) \in [0, 1]$ in a similarity function defined on the collection of items [39]. Or, in other words, you have an LSH method whenever you can hash the items in a dataset such that the collision probability of any two items is much higher when those items are close together than when they're far apart.

There are many ways to implement an LSH scheme. The Reformer uses the angular LSH scheme defined in [6]. Recall that the query matrix $\mathbf{Q}$ (and key matrix $\mathbf{K}$) has shape $l \times d_k$. To compute a hash for $\mathbf{Q}$, begin by generating a random $d_k \times b/2$ matrix $\mathbf{R}$, where each column has a single nonzero value sampled uniformly from ± 1 and b is the number of hashes. Next, compute $\mathbf{QR}$, which rotates the query (and key) matrix. Finally, the hash is $h(\mathbf{Q}) = \arg\max([\mathbf{QR}; -\mathbf{QR}])$ [142]. Once the query and key have been hashed, you can permute the indices so that sequence positions that hashed into the same bucket are side by side. Then, within each hash bucket, compute the full attention.

We can use this information to see how LSH affects the attention calculation by first rewriting the equation for self-attention, (5.23), using (5.27):

$$a_i = \sum_{j \in S_i} \exp\left(\frac{\mathbf{q_i k}_j^T}{\sqrt{d_k}} - \log Z(i, S_i)\right) \mathbf{v}_j, \qquad (5.30)$$

where S_i is the set of key positions that query i attends to and $Z(i, S_i) = \sum_{r \in S_i} \exp\left(\frac{\mathbf{q_i k}_r^T}{\sqrt{d_k}}\right)$ is the softmax normalization term.

Without a loss in generality, we can rewrite (5.30) as a sum over an expanded set of key positions, $\tilde{S}_i \supseteq S_i$, that can include positions that $\mathbf{q}_i$ does not attend to:

$$a_i = \sum_{j \in \tilde{S}_i} \exp\left(\frac{\mathbf{q_i k}_j^T}{\sqrt{d_k}} - m(i, S_i) - \log Z(i, S_i)\right) \mathbf{v}_j \quad (5.31)$$

$$m(i, S_i) = \begin{cases} \infty, & j \notin S_i \\ 0, & \text{otherwise} \end{cases} \quad (5.32)$$

The term $m(i, S_i)$ in (5.31) is a masking term that ensures that key positions that $\mathbf{q_i}$ does *not* attend to does not contribute to the sum.

As mentioned above, the set S_i is the set of key positions that query i attends to. Under the LSH scheme defined above, S_i should only contain key positions that hash into the same bucket as the query, or in other words

$$S_i = \{j : h(\mathbf{q_i}) = h(\mathbf{k}_j)\} \quad (5.33)$$

A priori, there are no guarantees that a query will have any keys to attend to. To address this, and ensure that $h(\mathbf{q_i}) = h(\mathbf{k}_j)$, [142] fixes key $\mathbf{k}_j$ so that $\mathbf{k}_j = \frac{\mathbf{q}_j}{\|\mathbf{q}_j\|}$. To make the computation more efficient, Reformer does two simple things

1. Queries are sorted so those in the same hash bucket are adjacent. Within the hash bucket, original sequence order is preserved

2. The sorted queries are grouped into blocks of m consecutive queries

$$m = \frac{2L}{\text{Number of buckets}} \quad (5.34)$$

Within each block, each position is allowed to attend to the others in the block and to those in the preceding block. These two changes define a new set of key positions that query i can attend to:

$$\tilde{S}_i = \left\{j : \left\lfloor \frac{s_i}{m} \right\rfloor - 1 \le \left\lfloor \frac{s_j}{m} \right\rfloor \le \left\lfloor \frac{s_i}{m} \right\rfloor\right\}, \quad (5.35)$$

where s_i is the position in the sorted matrix that position i was moved to. (5.35) can be used in (5.31) to compute the attention under the LSH scheme described above.

Multi-round LSH Due to the randomness inherent to LSH, its easy for similar things to hash into different buckets. To address this, it's common practice to do multiple rounds of LSH. For instance, when approximating a feature vector with LSH, one might hash the vector multiple times to generate an LSH signature. Then, instead of comparing two feature vectors with, say, cosine similarity, you would compare their LSH signatures using the Hamming distance. Similarly, in Reformer, you can compute multiple hashes for queries and keys and then combine them.

As discussed above, a query at position i can attend to the key positions in S_i. However, if we perform n rounds of LSH, then we end up with n sets of key positions that query position i can attend to

$$S_i = \bigcup_{r=1}^{n} S_i^{(r)}, \tag{5.36}$$

where $S_i^{(r)} = \{j : h^{(r)}(\mathbf{q_i}) = h^{(r)}(\mathbf{q}_j)\}$. Then, regarding sorting queries by hash bucket, (5.35) becomes

$$\tilde{S}_i^{(r)} = \left\{ j : \left\lfloor \frac{s_i^{(r)}}{m} \right\rfloor - 1 \leq \left\lfloor \frac{s_j^{(r)}}{m} \right\rfloor \leq \left\lfloor \frac{s_i^{(r)}}{m} \right\rfloor \right\}. \tag{5.37}$$

We can similarly update (5.31) for multi-round LSH:

$$a_i = \sum_{r}^{n} \exp\left(\log Z(i, S_i^{(r)}) - \log Z(i, S_i) \right) a_i^{(r)} \tag{5.38}$$

$$a_i^{(r)} = \sum_{j \in \tilde{S}_i^{(r)}} \exp\left(\frac{\mathbf{q_i k}_j^T}{\sqrt{d_k}} - m_{i,j}^{(r)} - \log Z(i, S_i^{(r)}) \right) \mathbf{v}_j \tag{5.39}$$

$$m_{i,j}^{(r)} = \begin{cases} \infty & j \notin S_i^{(r)} \\ 10^5 & \text{if } i = j \\ \log N_{i,j} & \text{otherwise} \end{cases} \tag{5.40}$$

$$N_{i,j} = \left| \{ r' : j \in S_i^{(r')} \} \right| \tag{5.41}$$

Note that in the multi-round LSH case, Reformer modifies the masking term to include (and downweight) the case where query at position i attends to a key at position i. This case is added because, while the standard transformer allows a position to attend to itself, this is unhelpful when $\mathbf{Q} = \mathbf{K}$, as is the case in LSH attention. It is unhelpful because the LSH hash $h(\mathbf{q}_i)$ of any position i is trivially equal to itself.

Reversibility and memory The Reformer also addressed the memory usage of the standard transformer using reversible residual layers.

Residual layers were designed to address the problem of training error increasing with network depth while avoiding the problem of vanishing gradients. By rewriting a neural network in terms of a residual function, training accuracy could be made to increase with network depth:

$$y = x + F(x), \tag{5.42}$$

where x is layer input and y is layer output [105]. ResNets are stacks of these residual layers.

In the standard transformer, each transformer layer has more than one residual layer. For example, a single transformer encoder block has two residual blocks. The first residual block is multi-head attention [254], followed by layer normalization [13]. The second residual block is the position-wise feedforward network (FFN) [254], followed by layer normalization. Note that the layer normalization operation has the form $x + Sublayer(x)$, where *Sublayer* represents the incoming layer. For the first residual block, the sublayer is the Multi-head attention and for the second residual block it is the FFN layer.

Reversible residual layers are a reversible variant of the residual layers used in image recognition and were introduced as a less memory-intensive replacement [94]. Each reversible layer takes a pair (x_1, x_2) as input and returns a pair (y_1, y_2) as output:

$$\begin{aligned} y_1 &= x_1 + F(x_2) \\ y_2 &= x_2 + G(y_1) \end{aligned} \tag{5.43}$$

To reverse the layer, simply subtract the residual from both sides:

$$\begin{aligned} x_2 &= y_2 - G(y_1) \\ x_1 &= y_1 - F(x_2) \end{aligned} \tag{5.44}$$

Now, suppose we have a stack of n such reversible layers, so that the input to the nth layer is the output of layer $n-1$. Eqns. (5.43) and (5.44) become recurrence relations:

$$\begin{aligned} y_1^{(n)} &= y_1^{(n-1)} + F(y_2^{(n-1)}) & (5.45) \\ y_2^{(n)} &= y_2^{(n-1)} + G(y_1^{(n)}) & (5.46) \\ y_2^{(n-1)} &= y_2^{(n)} - G(y_1^{(n)}) & (5.47) \\ y_1^{(n-1)} &= y_1^{(n)} - F(y_2^{(n-1)}) & (5.48) \end{aligned}$$

Thus, the output activations of layer $n-1$ can be computed from the output activations of layer n and the value of the residuals F and G for layer n. This is why the activations for a reversible residual layer do not need to be stored to perform backpropagation. Because the activations for intermediate layers do not need to be stored, the model will use less memory (without sacrificing performance).

Reversible layers in a transformer Now that we understand what reversible residual layers are and how they save memory, we can look at how they're used in the Reformer [142]. The attention mechanism serves as the residual function F and the position-wise feed-forward network is G. The layer normalization becomes part of the residual block since it has the form $x + Sublayer(x)$, where $Sublayer$ represents the appropriate residual function. Ref. [142] shows that a transformer using reversible residual layers has the same performance as the standard transformer.

5.2.2.3 Performer

The Performer [53] model reduces attention mechanism complexity using a method called *Fast Attention Via positive Orthogonal Random features* (FAVOR+). Performer does not bias the attention mechanism ahead of time by using attention patterns, instead FAVOR+ approximates the softmax calculation using kernels.

Attention as a kernel By rewriting the formula for self-attention ((5.23)) the kernel formalism becomes apparent:

$$Attn(\mathbf{Q}, \mathbf{K}, \mathbf{V}) = \text{softmax}\left(\frac{\mathbf{Q}\mathbf{K}^T}{\sqrt{d_k}}\right)\mathbf{V} \qquad (5.49)$$

$$\Rightarrow \left[\frac{\exp\left(\frac{\mathbf{q}_i \mathbf{k}_j^T}{\sqrt{d_k}}\right)}{\sum_{r \in S_i} \exp\left(\frac{\mathbf{q}_i \mathbf{k}_r^T}{\sqrt{d_k}}\right)}\right]\mathbf{V} \qquad (5.50)$$

$$= \mathbf{D}^{-1}\left[\exp\left(\frac{\mathbf{q}_i \mathbf{k}_j^T}{\sqrt{d_k}}\right)\right]\mathbf{V}, \qquad (5.51)$$

where $\mathbf{D}$ is the diagonal matrix of terms $D_{ij} = \delta_{ij} \sum_{r \in S_i} \exp\left(\frac{\mathbf{q}_i \mathbf{k}_r^T}{\sqrt{d_k}}\right)$. Note that each diagonal element is part of the sum in the softmax denominator and the inverse of $\mathbf{D}$ is simply the matrix of reciprocals. Within the Reformer, we can then redefine the attention weights as

$A_{ij} = \exp\left(\frac{\mathbf{q}_i \mathbf{k}_j^T}{\sqrt{d_k}}\right)$, so that $D_{ij} = \delta_{ij} \sum_{r \in S_i} A_{ir}$. Thus $Attn(\mathbf{Q}, \mathbf{K}, \mathbf{V}) = \mathbf{D}^{-1}\mathbf{A}\mathbf{V}$. The queries and keys can be scaled so that the key dimension is absorbed into them, A_{ij} is simply $\exp(\mathbf{q}_i \mathbf{k}_j^T)$.

Since A_{ij} depends on the inner product of the query and key vectors, it is a measure of similarity between $\mathbf{q}_i$ and $\mathbf{k}_j$. These attention weights can be approximated using the FAVOR+ algorithm:

$$A_{ij} = \langle \phi(\mathbf{q}_i^T)^T \phi(\mathbf{k}_j^T) \rangle, \tag{5.52}$$

where mapping ϕ maps $\mathbf{Q}, \mathbf{K} \in \mathbb{R}^{L \times d_k}$ to $\mathbf{Q}', \mathbf{K}' \in \mathbb{R}^{L \times r}$, respectively, with $r > 0$. The rows of $\mathbf{Q}'$ are $\phi(\mathbf{q}_i^T)^T$ and the rows of $\mathbf{K}'$ are $\phi(\mathbf{k}_j^T)^T$; then (5.49) becomes

$$\widehat{Attn}(\mathbf{Q}, \mathbf{K}, \mathbf{V}) = \hat{\mathbf{D}}^{-1}(\mathbf{Q}'((\mathbf{K}')^T \mathbf{V}), \quad \hat{D}_{ij} = \delta_{ij} \sum_{m \in S_i} \phi(\mathbf{q}_i^T) \phi(\mathbf{k}_m^T)^T. \tag{5.53}$$

When the kernel functions $\phi(\mathbf{x})$ are as defined in [53], the attention weights $A_{ij} = \exp\left(\mathbf{q}_i \mathbf{k}_j^T\right)$ can be approximated by

$$\exp(\mathbf{q}_i \mathbf{k}_j^T) = \Lambda \langle \cosh(\omega^T(\mathbf{q}_i + \mathbf{k}_j)) \rangle_\omega, \tag{5.54}$$

where $\Lambda = \exp(-(\|\mathbf{q}_i\|^2 + \|\mathbf{k}_j\|^2)/2)$ and ω is sampled from the d_k-dimensional standard normal distribution. If ω in (5.54) is replaced with $\sqrt{d}\frac{\omega}{\|\omega\|}$, then ω is any point on the surface of the d_k-dimensional sphere of radius $\sqrt{d_k}$.

This kernel approximation of the softmax calculation reduces the quadratic complexity to one that is nearly linear in sequence length, and the approximation error can be decreased by periodically resampling ω.

5.2.2.4 Big Bird

Big Bird is another effort to give the Transformer a sparse attention mechanism that allows for linear scaling. It is also proven to be Turing complete and a universal sequence function approximator [292].

An Attention mechanism is a directed graph Big Bird describes the attention mechanism as a directed graph. The vertices represent the L positions in the input sequence. The directed edges represent the pre-softmax attention weights. In other words, the directed edges are the inner products between the query and key vectors, where the ith vertex will only have directed edges with the vertices that correspond to the key positions that it can attend to, as described by the set S_i in (5.27).

Adjacency matrix The graph representation casts the problem of reducing the complexity of the attention mechanism as a graph sparsification problem, which can be tackled with graph theory. Big Bird describes the attention graph with its $L \times L$ adjacency matrix, $\mathbf{A}$:

$$A(i,j) = \begin{cases} 1, & j \in S_i \\ 0, & \text{otherwise} \end{cases} \tag{5.55}$$

When the adjacency matrix is all ones, $A(i,j) = 1$, $\forall\,(i,j)$, then we have a fully connected graph where each vertex is connected to every other vertex and an attention mechanism with quadratic complexity. Whenever $A(i,j) = 0$, it means that edge (i,j) does not exist and thus query position i ($\mathbf{q}_i$) cannot attend to key position j ($\mathbf{k}_j$).

Attention graph patterns Using the graph theoretical framework, Big Bird combines three attention patterns: random attention, sliding window attention, and a global attention. Each attention pattern corresponds to a particular way of initializing the adjacency matrix.

Random attention Big Bird's random attention pattern is inspired by the type of Erdős-Renyi random graph [84] that connects vertices at random with a uniform probability. In Big Bird's random attention, each query $\mathbf{q}_i$ attends to a random number of keys. In terms of the adjacency matrix, $A(i,:) = 1$ for r key positions that are chosen at random, with equal probability. An example adjacency matrix for the random attention pattern is shown in Fig. 5.9.

Sliding window attention Big Bird's local attention is derived from a Watts-Strogatz [265] small world graph on a ring lattice, where each vertex is connected to w neighbors, so there are $w/2$ neighbors to either side. This allows the query at position i to attend to keys at positions in the window $[i - w/2, i + w/2]$. In terms of the adjacency matrix, $A(i, i - w/2 : i + w/2) = 1$. This is similar to the sliding window attention in the Longformer that was discussed in Sec. 5.2.2.1. An example adjacency matrix for the sliding window attention is shown in Fig. 5.10.

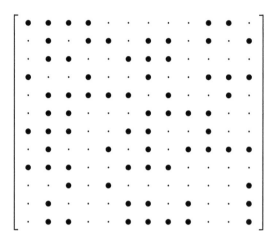

Figure 5.9 Random adjacency matrix, for $L = 12$ and $r = 7$. Row i corresponds to query i. Columns with a • are keys that query i attends to and · represents a lack of attention (a missing edge).

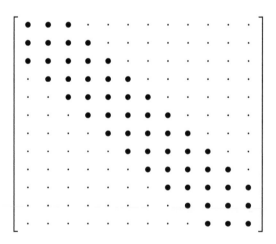

Figure 5.10 Sliding window attention adjacency matrix, for $L = 12$ and $w = 4$. Row i corresponds to query i. Columns with a • are keys that query i attends to and · represents a lack of attention (a missing edge).

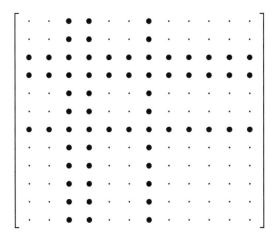

Figure 5.11 Global attention adjacency matrix for the internal transformer construction, for $L = 12$ and $G = 3, 4, 7$. Row i corresponds to query i. Columns with a • are keys that query i attends to and · represents a lack of attention (a missing edge).

Global attention   Big Bird also allows some tokens to attend to all tokens in the sequence. These global tokens are also attended to by all tokens. Big Bird uses two types of global tokens: internal transformer construction and external transformer construction.

In the internal transformer construction, a subset of the L vertex, G, are promoted to global tokens. Thus the queries or keys in those positions attend to all other positions. Here, $A(i, :) = A(:, i) = 1, \forall i \in G$. The expanded adjacency matrix B is shown in Fig. 5.11.

The external transformer construction adds g additional tokens to the existing L tokens. The additional tokens are global. Examples include special tokens used in transformers, like [CLS]. This essentially creates a new adjacency matrix, B, that includes the special tokens by prepending g rows and columns onto A. Here, $B(i, :) = B(:, i) = 1$, where $i = 1, \ldots, g$, and $B(g + i, g + j) = A(i, j)$, where i and $j = 1, \ldots, L$. The expanded adjacency matrix B is shown in Fig. 5.12.

Finally, an example adjacency matrix for the combination of random, sliding window, and global attention (external construction) is shown in Fig. 5.13.

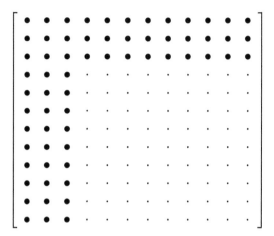

Figure 5.12 Global attention adjacency matrix for the external transformer construction, for $L = 9$ and $g = 3$. Row i corresponds to query i. Columns with a • are keys that query i attends to and · represents a lack of attention (a missing edge).

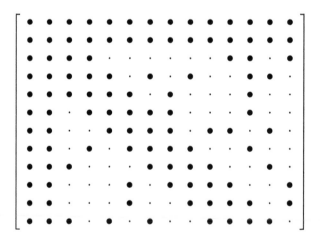

Figure 5.13 Big Bird attention adjacency matrix for the external transformer construction, for $L = 12, g = 2, w = 4$, and $r = 4$. Row i corresponds to query i. Columns with a • are keys that query i attends to and · represents a lack of attention (a missing edge).

Efficient sparse matrix multiplication By making the adjacency matrix (and the corresponding attention matrix) sparse, the speedups provided by GPUs are removed. This is because multiplication of matrices with arbitrary sparsity is not efficient on GPUs. However, matrices whose sparsity is grouped into blocks can be efficiently multiplied on GPUs [100].

To address this, Big Bird groups blocks of queries and keys together and then adds sparsity by block rather than by individual sequence position [292]. Select a block size, b, and then divide the sequence length L into L/b blocks. So, instead of L queries and keys, there will be L/b queries and keys. This modifies each attention pattern discussed above in relatively simple ways:

1. **Random attention** The random number of keys for a query to attend to, r, becomes the random number of key blocks that a query block attends to.

2. **Sliding window attention** The query block i attends to key blocks $i - (w - 1)/2$ through $i + (w - 1)/2$.

3. **Global attention** The definition of global attention is unchanged, except it is defined in terms of blocks rather than sequence position.

5.2.3 Improving Multi-Head-Attention

Now we focus on some of the ways the attention mechanism has been changed to improve performance of the transformer.

5.2.3.1 Talking-heads attention

Vaswani et al. [254] showed that multi-head attention allows the transformer to perform h (number of attention heads) separate attention calculations. Talking-Heads Attention [227] instead allows the attention heads to share information. It works by adding two linear layers that project the product of the query and key matrices, $\mathbf{QK}^T$ (attention logits), into a new space and projects the attention weights, $Softmax(\mathbf{QK}^T)$, into a new space.

Talking-Heads Attention (THA) also partitions the attention heads into three types: heads for the queries and keys, heads for the value, and heads for the attention logits and attention weights. Let's look at this in detail.

Recall from section 5.2.1.1 that the multi-head attention between two sequences $\mathbf{X}_1, \mathbf{X}_2$, with lengths L_1 and L_2 is:

$$
\begin{aligned}
\mathbf{Q} &= \mathbf{X}_1\mathbf{W}_q, \in \mathbb{R}^{L_1 \times d_k \times h} \\
\mathbf{K} &= \mathbf{X}_2\mathbf{W}_k, \in \mathbb{R}^{L_2 \times d_k \times h} \\
\mathbf{V} &= \mathbf{X}_2\mathbf{W}_v, \in \mathbb{R}^{L_2 \times d_v \times h}
\end{aligned}
\tag{5.56}
$$

where $\mathbf{X}_1 \in \mathbb{R}^{L_1 \times d}$, $\mathbf{X}_2 \in \mathbb{R}^{L_2 \times d}$, $\mathbf{W}_q, \mathbf{W}_k \in \mathbb{R}^{d \times d_k \times h}$, and $\mathbf{W}_v \in \mathbb{R}^{d \times d_v \times h}$, with

$$
\begin{aligned}
\alpha &= \mathbf{Q}\mathbf{K}^T, \in \mathbb{R}^{L_1 \times L_2 \times h} \tag{5.57} \\
\mathbf{A}(\mathbf{Q}, \mathbf{K}) &= \operatorname{softmax}\left(\frac{\alpha}{\sqrt{d_k}}\right), \in \mathbb{R}^{L_1 \times L_2 \times h} \tag{5.58} \\
\mathbf{C}(\mathbf{Q}, \mathbf{K}, \mathbf{V}) &= \sum_{L_2} \mathbf{A}(\mathbf{Q}, \mathbf{K})\mathbf{V}, \in \mathbb{R}^{L_1 \times d_v \times h} \tag{5.59}
\end{aligned}
$$

where α is the attention logits, $\mathbf{A}(\mathbf{Q}, \mathbf{K})$ are the attention weights, and $\mathbf{C}(\mathbf{Q}, \mathbf{K}, \mathbf{V})$ is the "context" vector representing the output of the h attention heads prior to concatenation of the attention heads and the final projection layer.

Partitioning the attention heads THA modifies the attention mechanism in a few ways from that shown in (5.56)–(5.59). First, it changes the attention head dimension of $\mathbf{Q}$ and $\mathbf{K}$ to be the number of query-key attention head h_k, and changes the attention head dimension of $\mathbf{V}$ to be the number of value attention heads h_v. This happens by changing the dimension of the projection matrices that generate the query, key, and value matrices from the input sequences. In other words, (5.56) becomes

$$
\begin{aligned}
\mathbf{Q} &= \mathbf{X}_1\mathbf{W}_q, \in \mathbb{R}^{L_1 \times d_k \times h_k} \\
\mathbf{K} &= \mathbf{X}_2\mathbf{W}_k, \in \mathbb{R}^{L_2 \times d_k \times h_k} \\
\mathbf{V} &= \mathbf{X}_2\mathbf{W}_v, \in \mathbb{R}^{L_2 \times d_v \times h_v}
\end{aligned}
\tag{5.60}
$$

where $\mathbf{W}_q, \mathbf{W}_k \in \mathbb{R}^{d \times d_k \times h_k}$, and $\mathbf{W}_v \in \mathbb{R}^{d \times d_v \times h_v}$.

Projecting the attention logits Next, the attention logits α are projected with a linear layer that mixes the query-key attention heads with the attention logit/weight heads, $\mathbf{W}_\alpha \in \mathbb{R}^{h_k \times h}$, and the attention weights are projected with a linear layer that mixes the value attention heads with the attention logit/weight heads, $\mathbf{W}_A \in \mathbb{R}^{h \times h_v}$. In other words, (5.57)–(5.59) becomes

$$\alpha = \mathbf{Q}\mathbf{K}^T, \in \mathbb{R}^{L_1 \times L_2 \times h_k} \tag{5.61}$$

$$\mathbf{P}_\alpha = \alpha \mathbf{W}_\alpha, \in \mathbb{R}^{L_1 \times L_2 \times h} \tag{5.62}$$

$$\mathbf{A}(\mathbf{Q}, \mathbf{K}) = \mathrm{softmax}\left(\frac{\mathbf{P}_\alpha}{\sqrt{d_k}}\right), \in \mathbb{R}^{L_1 \times L_2 \times h} \tag{5.63}$$

$$\mathbf{P}_A(\mathbf{Q}, \mathbf{K}) = \mathbf{A}\mathbf{W}_A, \in \mathbb{R}^{L_1 \times L_2 \times h_v} \tag{5.64}$$

$$\mathbf{C}(\mathbf{Q}, \mathbf{K}, \mathbf{V}) = \sum_{L_2} \mathbf{P}_A \mathbf{V}, \in \mathbb{R}^{L_1 \times d_v \times h_v} \tag{5.65}$$

where $\mathbf{P}_\alpha$ are the projected attention logits and $\mathbf{P}_A(\mathbf{Q}, \mathbf{K})$ are the projected attention weights.

Performance Talking-Heads Attention (THA) was evaluated by training a T5 model using THA and the same hyperparameters as the T5 paper (except for omitting dropout during pre-training) and similarly training an ALBERT model. The authors found that THA consistently performed better than multi-head attention [227]. Just projecting the attention logits or just the attention weights is only *slightly* better than using pure multi-head attention. Significant performance increases came from using both projections. Using talking-heads attention on the encoder block's self-attention layers has a larger effect on model performance than using talking-heads attention on the decoder block's attention layers.

Multi-head attention already comes at a cost and the projections that THA adds, $\mathbf{W}_\alpha$ and $\mathbf{W}_A$, increase that cost. Computing the projected attention logits, $\mathbf{P}_\alpha$, adds $L_1 \cdot L_2 \cdot h_k \cdot h$ matrix multiplications and computing the projected attention weights, $\mathbf{P}_A$, adds $L_1 \cdot L_2 \cdot h \cdot h_v$ matrix multiplications. Together, THA adds $L_1 \cdot L_2 \cdot h \cdot (h_k + h_v)$ matrix multiplications, which will make the calculation more costly. The authors note that if $h < d_k$ and $h < d_v$, then the cost of the THA projections are less than the cost of the existing multi-head attention calculations. So, in summary, Talking-Heads Attention improves model quality at the cost of increased computation time; allowing the user to decide what kind of tradeoffs they wish to make.

5.2.4 Biasing Attention with Priors

This section discusses a few models that bias the attention mechanism by fixing which positions can attend to which. The Longformer model, discussed in section 5.2.2.1, and Big Bird model, discussed in section 5.2.2.4 are both examples of attention with priors, since each uses specific attention patterns, like sliding window attention in sections 5.2.2.1 and 5.2.2.4. We also discussed another example of biasing attention with priors in section 5.1.2.1, the Realformer.

5.2.5 Prototype Queries

5.2.5.1 Clustered attention

Clustered attention [256] is a method to avoid self-attention's $O(L^2 \cdot d_k + L^2 \cdot d_v)$ time complexity that linearizes the self-attention weight computation by clustering LSH hashed queries with the k-means clustering algorithm. And using the query centroids as the queries to compute the attention matrix.

Clustering query vectors Clustered attention happens in two stages. First, each query vector is hashed with locality-sensitive hashing. The hashed queries are then grouped into C clusters with k-means. The distance metric used for k-means is the Hamming distance. The centroid of the jth cluster is given by

$$\mathbf{q}_j^c = \frac{\sum_{i=1}^{L} S_{ij}\mathbf{q}_i}{\sum_{i=1}^{L} S_{ij}} \tag{5.66}$$

where $\mathbf{q}_j^c$ is the centroid of the jth cluster and the matrix $S \in \{0,1\}^{L \times C}$ partitions the query vectors into C non-overlapping clusters, so if $S_{ij} = 1$, then $\mathbf{q}_i$ is in cluster j. The centroid queries are grouped into $\mathbf{Q}^c, \in \mathbb{R}^{C \times d_k}$, the matrix of centroid vectors. We can then substitute the real query matrix with the query centroid matrix, $\mathbf{Q}^c$ and compute the clustered attention matrix:

$$\mathbf{A}^c = \text{softmax}\left(\frac{\mathbf{Q}^c\mathbf{K}^T}{\sqrt{(d_k)}}\right), \in \mathbb{R}^{C \times L} \tag{5.67}$$

You can stop here and just use the clustered attention weights to compute the output of the attention mechanism. This calculation has time complexity of $O(CL \cdot d_k + LC \cdot d_v)$, which is explicitly linear in the sequence length. But, the clustered attention approximation can be improved finding k keys that have the highest attention score within each of the C clusters. And, for each of the top-k keys for a cluster, compute the attention with the queries in that cluster:

$$
A_{il}^t = \begin{cases} \dfrac{\hat{m}_j \exp\left(\mathbf{q}_i \mathbf{k}_l^T\right)}{\sum_{r=1}^{L} T_{jr} \exp\left(\mathbf{q}_i \mathbf{k}_r^T\right)}, & \text{if } T_{jl} = 1 \\[2ex] A_{jl}^c, & \text{otherwise} \end{cases} \tag{5.68}
$$

where $\hat{m}_j = \sum_{i=1}^{L} T_{ij} A_{ij}^c$ and $T \in \{0,1\}^{C \times L}$: if $T_{ij} = 1$, then $\mathbf{k}_i$ is one of the top-k keys for in cluster j.

Then compute the context vectors (weighted average of the values) of the clustered attention and use it as the value matrix: $\hat{\mathbf{V}} = \mathbf{A}^t \mathbf{V}, \in \mathbb{R}^{L \times d_v}$. This makes the complexity of the clustered attention calculation to $O(CL \cdot d_k + LC \cdot d_v + kL \max(d_k, d_v))$, which is linear in the sequence length.

Performance Clustered attention outperforms standard transformer and Reformer on automatic speech recognition with WSJ and Switchboard audio datasets. It also approximates pre-trained RoBERTa on GLUE and SQuAD, with minute performance loss. It performs better on GLUE that RoBERTa, but not SQuAD, where it is slightly worse.

As number of clusters increases, the approximation becomes more accurate. It converges up to twice as fast as the standard transformer, for long sequence lengths and, for short sequence lengths, clustered attention is *not* faster than the standard transformer.

5.2.6 Compressed Key-Value Memory

5.2.6.1 Luna: Linear Unified Nested Attention

Luna [177], which stands for Linear Unified Nested Attention, replaces the attention weight computation in each attention head with two nested linear attention computations using an extra, learnable, input sequence that learns to encode contextual information: $\mathbf{P} \in \mathbb{R}^{l \times d}$, where l is the length of the sequence.

As discussed earlier, the output of an attention head between a query sequence, $\mathbf{X} \in \mathbb{R}^{n \times d}$ and a context sequence, $\mathbf{C} \in \mathbb{R}^{m \times d}$, can be written as

$$
\mathbf{Y} = Attn(\mathbf{X}, \mathbf{C}) = \text{softmax}\left(\frac{\mathbf{X}\mathbf{W}_q(\mathbf{C}\mathbf{W}_k)^T}{\sqrt{d_k/h}}\right)\mathbf{C}\mathbf{V}, \in \mathbb{R}^{n \times d} \tag{5.69}
$$

where $\mathbf{W}_q, \mathbf{W}_k, \mathbf{W}_v$ are the linear projections that project an input sequence into the query, key, and value spaces, respectively, as in (5.24).

Luna attention

Pack attention The first of the nested attention layers computes the attention between the extra sequence $\mathbf{P}$ and the context sequence $\mathbf{C}$. Luna calls this "pack attention". Its output is the "packed context", $\mathbf{Y}_P = Attn(\mathbf{P}, \mathbf{C}), \in \mathbb{R}^{l \times d}$, and it has the same dimensionality as $\mathbf{P}$. It's complexity is $O(lm)$.

Unpack attention The second of the nested attention layers computes the attention between the input sequence and the packed context sequence, $\mathbf{Y}_P$. Luna calls this the "unpack attention": $\mathbf{Y}_X = Attn(\mathbf{X}, \mathbf{Y}_P), \in \mathbb{R}^{n \times d}$. Its output has the same dimensionality as the input sequence $\mathbf{X}$. It's complexity is $O(ln)$.

Luna attention Luna combines the pack and unpack attention layers in sequence, forming the Luna layer: $\mathbf{Y}_X, \mathbf{Y}_P = LunaAttn(\mathbf{X}, \mathbf{P}, \mathbf{C})$, which encompasses the two multi-head attention layers shown in Fig. 5.14. $\mathbf{P}$ is initialized to the transformer's positional encodings, and for subsequent transformer blocks, $\mathbf{Y}_P$ is used in place of $\mathbf{P}$.

Because the pack attention and unpack attention layers are composed in sequence, their combined complexity is $O(lm + ln)$. Since the extra input sequence $\mathbf{P}$ has fixed length, the combined complexity of Luna's multi-head attention mechanism is linear in the length of the input sequence $\mathbf{X}$. With slight modifications, Luna can also support causal cross-attention.

Performance Luna was compared to the performance of the standard transformer and 11 other efficient transformers on the Long Range Arena benchmark (LRA) [242]. It performed well on all tasks, outperforming most, but not all, models; obtaining the highest average accuracy. Luna was consistently faster than the standard transformer and many, but not all, of the efficient transformers to which it was compared. It was also more memory efficient than the standard transformer, with memory usage comparable to other efficient transformers and beating a few.

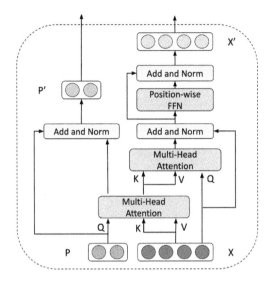

Figure 5.14 Architecture of a Luna encoder block. **P** is the extra sequence for the block and **X** is the input sequence of the block. **P'** will be the extra sequence for the next Luna block and **P'** will be the input sequence of the next Luna block.

5.2.7 Low-Rank Approximations

5.2.7.1 Linformer

In [259], Wang et al. prove that the standard transformer's [254] self-attention weight matrix can be approximated with a low-rank matrix [83], reducing the complexity from $O(L^2)$ to $O(L)$, where L is the sequence length.

Linformer introduces two linear projection matrices that transform the key and value matrices of the ith attention head: $\mathbf{E}_i = \delta \mathbf{R}$ and $\mathbf{F}_i = \exp^{-\delta} \mathbf{R}$, where $\mathbf{R} \in \mathbb{R}^{k \times L}$ and its components are drawn from $\mathcal{N}(0, 1/k)$, $\delta = \theta(1/L)$, $k = 5 \log(dL)/(\epsilon^2 - \epsilon^3)$, and ϵ is the approximation error. Also, $d_k = d_v = d$. This approximation means that the output of each attention head in the mechanism can be approximated by $\overline{head}_i = \overline{\mathbf{A}}_i \cdot \mathbf{F}_i \mathbf{V}_i$, where

$$\overline{\mathbf{A}}_i = \text{softmax}\left(\frac{\mathbf{Q}_i(\mathbf{E}_i\mathbf{K}_i)^T}{\sqrt{d_k/h}}\right), \in \mathbb{R}^{L \times k} \qquad (5.70)$$

$\overline{\mathbf{A}}_i$ is a low-rank approximation of the attention weight matrix for the ith attention head. It's complexity is $O(kL)$, which is why Linformer is also a way of reducing the space and time complexity of the attention mechanism and thus fits in with the methods discussed in section 5.2.2.

The authors consider three variants of parameter sharing to make Linformer even more efficient:

1. Share E and F across all attention heads (headwise sharing): $\mathbf{E}_i = \mathbf{E}$, $\mathbf{F}_i = \mathbf{F}$

2. Share projections across heads and key/value matrices: $\mathbf{E}_i = \mathbf{F}_i = \mathbf{E}$

3. Share projections across heads, key/value matrices, and model layers (layerwise sharing)

Inference speed was first tested against the standard transformer [254]. As sequence length L increased, the standard transformer became slower. The Linformer speed remained largely constant and was significantly faster for long sequences. Wang et al. kept the sequence length fixed and varied the batch size to process the text sequences. This behavior is expected since the sequence length was held fixed.

To test performance, Linformer was trained in the same way as RoBERTa [170] and compared using validation perplexities and performance on downstream tasks. Based on perplexities, Linformer performance increases as k increases and Linformer's quality nearly matches that of the standard transformer for $L = 512, k = 128$ and $L = 1024, k = 256$. Based on downstream task performance, Linformer performance is comparable to RoBERTa when $L = 512, k = 128$, and outperforms RoBERTa at $k = 256$. Performance for $L = 1024, k = 256$ and $L = 512, k = 256$ are similar, suggesting that performance for Linformer is controlled more by k than by L/k. There are two key results:

1. Layerwise parameter sharing performs the best.

2. Performance when using layerwise sharing is nearly identical to the performance of using no parameter sharing. This suggests that the number of parameters introduced by Linformer can be reduced without quality taking a hit.

The Performer model, which was discussed in section 5.2.2.3, is also based on a low-rank approximations of attention.

5.3 MODIFICATIONS FOR TRAINING TASK EFFICIENCY

5.3.1 ELECTRA

ELECTRA [58] introduces a new pre-training task, replaced token detection, that combines the best of masked language models and regular language models, allowing ELECTRA to learn more efficiently than its predecessors. ELECTRA is a bidirectional model, like a masked language model. However, unlike a masked language model, it learns from all positions in the input sequence.

5.3.1.1 Replaced token detection

Replaced token detection (RTD) helps the model learn which tokens are most likely to be in a given position in a sequence because the model learns to replace and identify each token in the training data. In this way, ELECTRA is like the discriminator in a Generative adversarial network (GAN). Here, unlike a GAN, the generator is not being trained to trick the discriminator and a noise vector is not added to the generator's input.

ELECTRA is trained using combination of a generator and a discriminator. The generator is a masked language model and the discriminator is ELECTRA itself. As a result, ELECTRA needs less training data than earlier masked language models, like BERT, because masked language models do not mask every token in the training data. Generator and discriminator are both transformer encoders.

Training begins with the generator chooses a random set of k positions, $\mathbf{m} = (m_1, \ldots, m_k)$, from the input sequence, such that each position m_i, with $i = 1, \ldots, k$, is drawn uniformly from $[1, L]$, where L is the sequence length. Each token in the input sequence $\mathbf{x} = (x_1, \ldots, x_L)$ that is at the positions in $\mathbf{m}$ will be replaced with the [MASK] token. The masked sequence is

$$\mathbf{x}^{\text{masked}} = \text{REPLACE}(\mathbf{x}, \mathbf{m}, [MASK]) \tag{5.71}$$

The generator then learns the unmasked versions of the masked tokens in $\mathbf{x}$. The probability that the generator outputs a particular token x_t is

$$Prob_G(x_t|\mathbf{x}) = \frac{\exp\left(\mathbf{e}_t^T \mathbf{h}_G(\mathbf{x})_t\right)}{\sum_{t'} \exp\left(\mathbf{e}(x')^T \mathbf{h}_G(\mathbf{x})_t\right)}, \tag{5.72}$$

where $\mathbf{e}_t$ is the embedding vector for the token x_t.

The discriminator learns to tell which tokens in a sequence were produced by the generator. This works by creating a sequence where the masked tokens have been replaced with samples ("corrupt" tokens) from the generator:

$$\mathbf{x}^C = \text{REPLACE}(\mathbf{x}, \mathbf{m}, \hat{\mathbf{x}}_i) \tag{5.73}$$

where $\hat{\mathbf{x}}_i$ are the tokens generated by the generator:

$$\hat{\mathbf{x}}_i \sim Prob_G(x_i|\mathbf{x}^{\text{masked}}) \tag{5.74}$$

where $i \in \mathbf{m}$. The discriminator then learns to identify which tokens in $\mathbf{x}^C$ were in the original input $\mathbf{x}$. Here, unlike a GAN, the generator is not being trained to trick the discriminator and a noise vector is not added to the generator's input.

5.3.2 T5

T5, the Text-to-Text Transfer Transformer [205], is the result of a survey aimed at understanding which transfer learning methods work best. It reframed standard NLP tasks as text-to-text transformations, where the input and output are strings. This is in contrast to masked language models like BERT, which output either class labels or a span of the input.

The reformulation of training tasks means you can use the same model and loss function on any NLP task. Using text-to-text transformations (sequence transduction) allows you to train one model on multiple tasks at once, reusing model architecture, loss functions, and hyperparameters. Appendix D of Raffel et al. has examples of how input was formatted for each of the datasets the T5 model was trained or fine-tuned on.

5.4 TRANSFORMER SUBMODULE CHANGES

This section discusses modifications to the Transformer that do not modify the attention mechanism or the model's memory profile.

5.4.1 Switch Transformer

The Mixture of Experts (MoE) model has contributed to many successes at the expense of complexity and training cost [225]. However, the mixture of expert models does not share the parameters, resulting

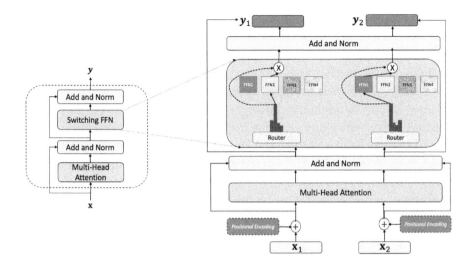

Figure 5.15 Switch Transformer encoder block illustrating two input tokens $\mathbf{x}_1$ and $\mathbf{x}_2$ being processed through the network. The dense FFN is replaced with switching FFN as one of the experts.

in a sparse model with a substantial computational cost and training instabilities. Switch transformers address most of these issues with a novel routing algorithm between the experts, enabling an increase in the number of the parameters without an increase in computational cost [87]. The core innovation of switch transformers is replacing the feed-forward layer in the transformer with a switching feed-forward layer, as shown in Fig. 5.15.

In the standard transformer, a single feed-forward network follows the outputs from the multi-head attention layer. It is responsible for translating the representation token-by-token to the next transformer input block. As shown in Fig. 5.15, in a switch transformer, instead of one feed-forward network, there are multiple feed-forward networks, also known as the experts. After the multi-head attention, each token representation, $\mathbf{x}$, gets routed to only *one* expert. The expert is chosen from a set of N experts, $\{E_i(\mathbf{x})\}_{i=1}^{N}$ by computing a probability distribution over the experts:

$$\mathbf{p}(\mathbf{x}) = \operatorname{softmax}\left(\mathbf{W}_r \cdot \mathbf{x}\right) \tag{5.75}$$

where $\mathbf{W}_r \in \mathbb{R}^{N \times d}$ is a learnable weight matrix that determines which expert is selected and d is the dimensionality of the token representation, $\mathbf{x}$. The expert with largest probability corresponds to the largest component of 5.75: $\mathbf{p}(\mathbf{x}) = (p_1, \ldots, p_N)$, call it p_j, and is used to compute the updated token representation. Thus, though the parameters have increased four times because of four feed-forward networks, hard routing guarantees that the computational cost remains the same. Thus the switching feed-forward network enables the scaling of experts to any number (bound by memory capacity) without increasing computational cost and not needing any transfer helps in the sharding process.

Model parallelism shards the model across the devices (cores/machines) while consuming the same data in the batch, resulting in a large model with slower processing due to sequential flow; the bottleneck introduced by communication. On the other hand, data parallelism keeps the model weights constant and shards the data across, allowing improved computational speed but a lower capacity model due to size. Switch Transformer employs data and expert parallelism—i.e., each data gets sharded to one expert on one device, which uses its expert weights for computations. The experts themselves are distributed and not communicating with each other, resulting in total parallelism and lower computation overheads. The authors use experts, data, and model parallelism to scale up to a gigantic model where even a single expert doesn't fit a device.

Compared to T5-Base and T5-large, the switch transformers show that given the same FLOPS, the models can be substantially large and excel across a diverse set of natural language tasks and in different training regimes, such as pre-training, fine-tuning and multi-task training. The multilingual results are more impressive as they show the gain compared to an equivalent MT5 model across 101 languages.

5.5 CASE STUDY: SENTIMENT ANALYSIS

5.5.1 Goal

This case study examines the attention weights of a T5 model that was fine-tuned for sentiment span extraction. The input to this span extraction model is a span of text containing positive or negative sentiment. The output is the subsequence of the input text that causes the span to have the specified sentiment.

5.5.2 Data, Tools, and Libraries

```
pip install torch transformers sentencepiece bertviz
```

Listing 5.1 Python environment setup

To use this model, we'll need three Python libraries: Huggingface's transformers, Google's sentencepiece, and the bertviz library. They can be installed by running the shell command shown in Listing 5.1. Once the environment is setup, the model and tokenizer can be loaded into memory, as shown in Listing 5.2.

```python
import torch
from transformers import T5ForConditionalGeneration,
    AutoTokenizer
import numpy as np

# Use GPU, if available
device = torch.device("cuda" if torch.cuda.is_available()
    else "cpu")
model_name =
    "mrm8488/t5-base-finetuned-span-sentiment-extraction"
tokenizer = AutoTokenizer.from_pretrained(model_name)
model =
    T5ForConditionalGeneration.from_pretrained(model_name)
model = model.to(device)
```

Listing 5.2 Load model and tokenizer

To make extract sentiment spans with this model, you can use the function defined in Listing 5.3.

```python
def get_sentiment_span(text, sentiment):
    query = f"question: {sentiment} context: {text}"
    input_ids = tokenizer.encode(query, return_tensors="pt",
                    add_special_tokens=True)
    input_ids = input_ids.to(device)
    generated_ids = model.generate(input_ids=input_ids,
        num_beams=1,
                        max_length=80).squeeze()
    predicted_span = tokenizer.decode(generated_ids,
                        skip_special_tokens=True,
                        clean_up_tokenization_spaces=True)
    return predicted_span


text = "You're a nice person, but your feet stink."
get_sentiment_span(text, "positive")
# > 'nice person,'

get_sentiment_span(text, "negative")
# > 'your feet stink.'
```

Listing 5.3 Extract sentiment span from input text

The model takes input in the following form:

question: [positive/negative] context: [text of specified sentiment].

This case study focuses on positive sentiment in a sequence of text with both positive and negative sentiment. The text is *"You're a nice person, but your feet stink."* Thus, for positive sentiment, the full input text to the span extraction model is *"question: positive context: You're a nice person, but your feet stink."*

5.5.3 Experiments, Results, and Analysis

There are a variety of methods that have been used to analyze the influence of attention mechanisms on model output.

We will look at just one: simply visualizing attention weights (with BertViz [255]).

5.5.3.1 Visualizing attention head weights

The T5 model has 12 layers, each of which has three attention mechanisms:

1. encoder self-attention

2. decoder self-attention

3. cross-attention

Each attention mechanism has 12 heads, and thus has 144 sets of attention weights, one for each choice of layer and attention head. We'll use the BertViz [255] library to view the weights of the attention heads, this is shown in Listing 5.4.

```python
from bertviz import head_view

def view_cross_attn_heads(text, sentiment, layer=None,
    heads=None):
    query = f"question: {sentiment} context: {text}"
    input_ids = tokenizer.encode(query, return_tensors="pt",
                            add_special_tokens=True)
    input_ids = input_ids.to(device)

    with torch.no_grad():
```

```
        output = model.forward(input_ids=input_ids,
                               decoder_input_ids=input_ids,
                               output_attentions=True,
                               return_dict=True)

    tokens = tokenizer.convert_ids_to_tokens(input_ids[0])
    head_view(output.cross_attentions, tokens, layer=layer,
        heads=heads)


def view_decoder_attn_heads(text, sentiment, layer=None,
    heads=None):
    query = f"question: {sentiment} context: {text}"
        input_ids = tokenizer.encode(query, return_tensors="pt",
                                     add_special_tokens=True)
    input_ids = input_ids.to(device)

    with torch.no_grad():
        output = model.forward(input_ids=input_ids,
                               decoder_input_ids=input_ids,
                               output_attentions=True,
                               return_dict=True)

    tokens = tokenizer.convert_ids_to_tokens(input_ids[0])
    head_view(output.decoder_attentions, tokens, layer=layer,
        heads=heads)


def view_encoder_attn_heads(text, sentiment, layer=None,
    heads=None):
    query = f"question: {sentiment} context: {text}"
    input_ids = tokenizer.encode(query, return_tensors="pt",
                                 add_special_tokens=True)
    input_ids = input_ids.to(device)

    with torch.no_grad():
        output = model.forward(input_ids=input_ids,
                               decoder_input_ids=input_ids,
                               output_attentions=True,
                               return_dict=True)

    tokens = tokenizer.convert_ids_to_tokens(input_ids[0])
    head_view(output.encoder_attentions, tokens, layer=layer,
        heads=heads)
```

```
view_cross_attn_heads(text, "positive")
view_decoder_attn_heads(text, "positive")
view_encoder_attn_heads(text, "positive")
```

Listing 5.4 Visualizing attention weights

For starters, we want to see if the weights of any of the attention heads show the word "positive" in the input text attending to any of the tokens in the extracted subsequence.

We can see that "positive" attends to "nice" in three heads of the encoder attention. These are shown in Fig. 5.16. In five heads of the cross-attention mechanism, "positive" and "nice" both attend to "person". These are shown in Fig. 5.17.

5.5.3.2 Analysis

While there are 11 attention heads (out of 432) that show strong attention between "positive" and attention, there are even more that do not. Many of the other attention heads in the span extraction model fall into the type of attention patterns shown in [57], particularly the broad attention where each token attends to nearly every other token and the type where each token attends to the following token.

The analysis above calls into question the ability to use attention weights themselves to explain predictions. And recently, [143] found the attention weight analysis shown above to be a poor method for analyzing

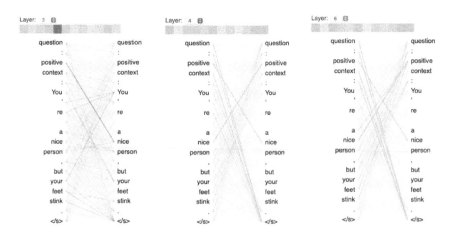

Figure 5.16 Encoder attention heads from layers 3 (head 5), 4 (head 11), and 6 (head 11), from left to right.

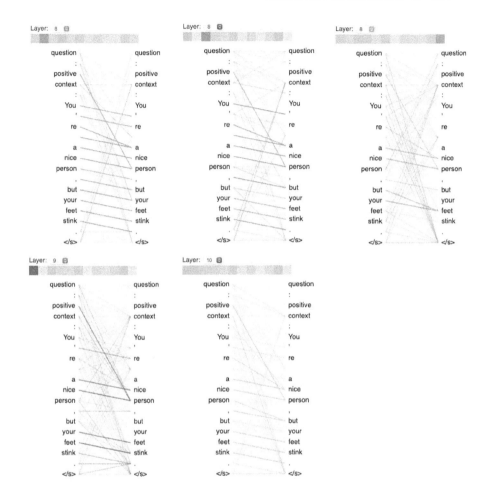

Figure 5.17 Cross-attention heads from layers 8, 9, and 10. The top row shows heads 1, 2, and 11 of layer 8 (left to right). The bottom row shows head 0 of layer 9 and head 1 of layer 10.

an attention mechanism. There are several papers that suggest other analysis methods. We'll describe one of them below.

Attention mechanism output norm Analyzing an attention mechanism using the norm of the components of its output was suggested by [143]. Recall (5.29), which shows how self-attention is defined in the standard transformer, for a single attention head. As shown in (2.19), after the attention heads are concatenated, we apply a linear layer to obtain the output of the attention mechanism. The linear layer has weights $\mathbf{W}_O$, giving the mechanism the following output:

$$\mathbf{y}_i \;=\; \left(\sum_{j=1}^{L} A_{ij}\mathbf{v}(\mathbf{x}_j) \right) \mathbf{W}_O \tag{5.76}$$

$$=\; \sum_{j=1}^{L} A_{ij}\mathbf{f}(\mathbf{x}_j) \tag{5.77}$$

where A_{ij} are the attention weights from (5.27), $\mathbf{v}(\mathbf{x}_j)$ is a value vector from 5.25, and $f(\mathbf{x}_j) = \mathbf{v}(\mathbf{x}_j)\mathbf{W}_O$. $f(\mathbf{x}_j)$ is the output of the attention mechanism corresponding to the jth input token $\mathbf{x}_j$.

In [143], Kobayashi et al. specifically suggest using $\|A_{ij}f(\mathbf{x}_j)\|$ as it's the degree to which token i attends to token j. They also show that $\|f(\mathbf{x}_j)\|$ and A_{ij} are meaningful quantities and sometimes play opposing roles in determining model behavior.

## CHAPTER 6

Pre-trained and Application-Specific Transformers

THE transformer architecture was introduced as a language model that transformed text in one language into text in another language [254]. Since that initial application to machine translation, the transformer architecture has been applied to computer vision, audio processing, and video processing, as well as other problems in NLP. The transformer architecture has been shown to be a somewhat reliable way of taking in an input sequence and converting it into something else.

6.1 TEXT PROCESSING

This section describes some of the ways that transformers have been applied to domain-specific text processing and a recent advancement made in text sequence to text sequence processing.

6.1.1 Domain-Specific Transformers

Transformers have been made for domain-specific applications by fine-tuning pre-trained models like BERT. We'll look at a few.

6.1.1.1 BioBERT

BioBERT [152] is domain-specific language model constructed by fine-tuning BERT on a large collection of biomedical text. BioBERT was created because ELMo and BERT did not perform well on biomedical text because their training data did not include it. BioBERT outperformed previous models on three NLP tasks useful for biomedical text mining: named entity recognition (NER), relationship extraction, and question answering (QA).

There are three steps to go from a pre-trained BERT model to a BioBERT model. The starting point is a pre-trained BERT model. The next step is to pre-train the model on PubMed abstracts and PubMed Central full-text articles. Finally, after the pre-training is over, BioBERT is further fine-tuned on the NER, relationship extraction, and question answering tasks, using task-specific datasets.

BioBERT used the cased BERT vocabulary, unchanged. Had they not done this, they would not have been able to start with a pre-trained BERT model. BioBERT was trained in 23 days, on eight NVIDIA Volta V100 GPUs.

6.1.1.2 *SciBERT*

SciBERT [24] is a language model built to process scientific text. It uses the BERT architecture, but was trained on the full text and abstracts of 1.4 million papers from the Semantic Scholar website (semanticscholar.org).

Like BERT, SciBERT uses WordPiece tokenization with 30,000 tokens, but it does not use BERT's vocabulary. Instead, SciBERT's vocabulary is built from Semantic Scholar corpus. SciBERT was evaluated on five NLP tasks: NER, PICO extraction, text classification, relationship extraction, and dependency parsing. PICO extraction is a sequence labeling task applied to papers about clinical trials where a model extracts spans that mention the participants, interventions, comparisons, or outcomes of a clinical trial. Training took one week on single 8-core TPU.

6.1.1.3 *FinBERT*

With the ULMFit model [119], Howard and Ruder showed that tuning an already pre-trained language model on a corpus from a target domain results in improved classification metrics. FinBERT [7] is the result of seeing if the same idea can be applied to BERT, with equal or greater success. FinBERT attempts this in two ways: (1) further pre-train on a large financial corpus and (2) pre-train only on the sentences from a financial sentiment analysis corpus. For pre-training, FinBERT uses a subset of the Reuters TRC2 dataset that has been filtered for financial keywords. The resulting corpus has more than 29M words, across 46,143 documents. For sentiment analysis, the Financial Phrasebank dataset is used. It has 4845 sentences from LexisNexis.

6.1.2 Text-to-Text Transformers

As discussed in section 5.3.2, the T5 model from Raffel et al. [205] reframed standard NLP tasks as text-to-text transformations, where the input and output are strings. Since the introduction of T5, there have been two important advancements: a multilingual version named mT5 [281], supporting 101 languages, and a token-free variant that operates directly on UTF-8 bytes, ByT5 [280]. In this section, we discuss ByT5.

6.1.2.1 ByT5

ByT5 [280] is a byte-level model, to take advantage of strings being encoded as a sequence of UTF-8 bytes. Part of the motivation for this ByT5 was that token-free models would be more robust to out-of-vocabulary words, misspellings, casing, and morphological changes. A token-free model would not use a fixed vocabulary to map test to tokens. A byte-level model would only need 256 embedding vectors, rather than the large number needed when using a fixed vocabulary. The massive decrease in vocabulary size that comes with using bytes means more parameters can be used elsewhere in the model.

Since byte sequences are longer than token sequences and transformer computational complexity is quadratic in sequence length (except for linearized attention), earlier work has tried to mitigate the increased complexity that comes with using byte-level and character-level sequences. ByT5 starts with the mT5 architecture, but differs from mT5 in a few ways. Firstly, there is no SentencePiece tokenization. Raw UTF-8 bytes are used as input and embeddings are learned for each of the 256 bytes. In addition, there are three special tokens added to the vocabulary: a padding token, an EOS token, and an unknown token. The pre-training task is changed so that the length of the masked portion of input spans is longer than in is in T5. in T5, the encoder and decoder modules have the same number of layers. That restriction is removed in ByT5 and it the encoder is three times as many layers as the decoder. Lastly, illegal UTF-8 bytes are removed from the output.

As discussed above, robustness is one of the hypothesized benefits of working with bytes instead of tokens. To test the hypothesized robustness, they authors add six kinds of noise to the data and see how it affects performance:

1. Make deletions by giving each character has a 10% chance of being deleted.

2. Give each character a 10% chance of added, deleted, or mutated (with equal likelihood).

3. Give each character a 20% chance of being duplicated 1-3 times.

4. Capitalize each character and pad it with spaces.

5. Make each character uppercase, when the language uses case.

6. Set the case of each character randomly when the language uses case.

The noise is injected in one of two ways: into the fine-tuning and evaluation data or just into the evaluation data. For the question answering task, noise is added to the context but not to the question or answer. For the sentence entailment training task, noise is added to the premise and hypothesis. For both types of noise, the paper shows that ByT5 is indeed more robust to noise than mT5.

6.1.3   Text Generation

One of the most well-known successes of transformer-based language models has been text generation with the GPT-2 and GPT-3 language models, which are built from stacks of transformer-decoder layers.

6.1.3.1   *GPT: Generative pre-training*

The family of generative pre-training models are part of the language modeling trend where a model is first trained on unsupervised data, in a task-agnostic fashion, and later fine-tuned for a specific task. The first model in this family, the eponymous GPT [202], first pre-trains a stack of transformer decoder layers on a large body of unlabeled text and is then fine-tuned on labeled, task-specific data. GPT is an autoregressive model, which means it uses inputs from previous steps of a sequence to predict values later in the sequence. GPT was evaluated on four kinds of natural language understanding tasks: natural language inference, question answering, semantic similarity, and text classification.

Unsupervised pre-training   In this phase, GPT starts with a corpus of tokens and, moving through it, learns how to predict the next token, given some preceding context. More formally, given an unlabeled corpus $U = (w_1, \ldots, w_n)$, the model learns the conditional probability of predicting token w_t given the preceding k tokens, $P(w_t|w_{t-1}, \ldots, w_{t-k})$, by minimizing the negative log-likelihood

$$L_1(U) = -\sum_t \log P(w_t|w_{t-1}, \ldots, w_{t-k}; \Theta) \qquad (6.1)$$

where Θ represents the model parameters. Optimization was with stochastic gradient descent.

Supervised fine-tuning   In this phase, the model is fine-tuned on labeled, task-specific corpus, C, where each data point is a token sequence $\mathbf{x} = (x_1, \ldots, x_m)$ and a class label y. The pre-trained decoder model is used as a feature generator for the labeled data and a fully-connected linear layer, with softmax activation and weight matrix $\mathbf{W}$, is appended to it and trained by minimizing a second negative log-likelihood

$$L_2(C) = -\sum_{(\mathbf{x},y)} \log P(y|\mathbf{x}; \mathbf{W}) \qquad (6.2)$$

Radford et al. found that the model converged faster and generalized better when the language modeling objective from the unsupervised phase, (6.1), was added to (6.2). So, the full objective was the weighted sum $L_2(C) + \lambda L_1(C)$.

Formatting data for fine-tuning   Data for each of the four training tasks is formatted differently:

- Text classification data has a simple format; each instance is bracketed with a start and an end token, so the input is formatted like $[\langle s \rangle, text, \langle /s \rangle]$.

- A natural language inference (NLI) instance has two parts, the premise, p, and the hypothesis, h. Labels can be entailment, contradiction, or neutral. The input is formatted like $[\langle s \rangle, p, \$, h, \langle /s \rangle]$, where $\$$ is a delimiter token.

- A text similarity instance has two text sequences, which can be in any order; so both orders are included. The input is formatted like an entailment instance.

- For question-answering and commonsense reasoning, AKA multiple-choice questions, each instance is context sequence, a question, and a set of k possible answers, $\{a_k\}$. From one such instance, k model inputs are constructed by concatenating the context, the question, the $ delimiter token, and one of the possible answers. Each is used as a separate input.

Model training The model was a stack of 12 transformer decoder layers, with 12 masked self-attention heads. Model dimension is 768, the feedforward layers use $d_{ff} = 3072$. Positional embeddings were learned, instead of the fixed embeddings used in the standard Transformer.

Pre-training data Language model pre-training was on the BooksCorpus [303] and 1B Word Benchmark [197] datasets.

Fine-tuning data Some of the data was from the GLUE multi-task benchmark [257]. Five NLI datasets were used: SNLI, MNLI, QNLI, SciTail, and RTE. Multiple-choice data was from the RACE dataset [145]. Evaluation was on the Story Cloze Test dataset [190]. Semantic Similarity was on the Microsoft Paraphrase corpus (MRPC) [75], the Quora Question Pairs (QQP) dataset [43], and Semantic Textual Similarity benchmark (STS-B) [38]. Text classification was evaluated on The Corpus of Linguistic Acceptability (CoLA) [264] and Stanford Sentiment Treebank (SST-2) [230].

6.1.3.2 GPT-2

If the first GPT model demonstrated the power of generative pre-training, then GPT-2 [203] showed that a language model can learn specific NLP tasks without being explicitly trained on those tasks. This is the same kind of zero-shot application of a model discussed in Chapters 3 and 4.

Model architecture Similar to GPT, GPT-2 uses a stack of transformer decoder blocks. The decoders are slightly modified. In the standard transformer, the layer norm module comes after the multi-head attention and after the position-wise feedforward network, as part of the residual connection. In GPT-2, the layer norm module instead comes before the multi-head attention and before the position-wise feedforward. The residual connection now only includes addition, rather than addition and layer norm. One additional layer norm module is placed in the final decoder block, after the multi-head attention. The weights of the residual layers are initialized differently than in the GPT model. The weights for a residual layer are divided by $1/\sqrt{N}$, where N is the number of residual layers in the entire model.

GPT-2 uses byte-pair encoding (BPE) tokenization [92] so that any UTF-8 string can be represented using a vocabulary that of only 256 bytes. Computing with the raw UTF-8 bytes was not done here, since byte-level language models were not performing at the level of word-level language models. [1]

Four variants with the described architecture were trained. The largest model of the four is the one called "GPT-2". It has 1.542 billion parameters and uses 48 transformer decoder layers. Each was evaluated on several language modeling datasets without any additional training. GPT-2 achieved state-of-the-art on seven out of eight datasets.

6.1.3.3   GPT-3

GPT-3 [32] is part of the trend in transformer language models where an increase in the number of parameters leads to an increase in the language model's ability to perform downstream tasks with little to no task-specific training.

Model architecture   GPT-3 uses the same model architecture as GPT-2, with one exception: the attention mechanisms in the transformer layers alternated between dense and locally banded sparse patterns. The sparse banded pattern was used in the Sparse Transformer [50] by only computing attention between a sparse selection of query-key pairs.

To study the effect of parameter count in-context learning, Brown et al. trained eight models of different sizes. The smallest model, "GPT-3 Small" had 125 million parameters, 12 Transformer decoder layers, model dimension of 768, 12 attention heads, each attention head had dimension of 64 ($d_k = d_v = 64$), processed tokens in batches of 500,000,

---

[1]Note that this changed in 2021 with the introduction of the ByT5 language model [280].

and used learning rate 6e-4. The largest model, "GPT-3 175B" or just "GPT-3", had 175 billion parameters, 96 Transformer decoder layers, model dimension of 12288, 96 attention heads, head dimension of 128 ($d_k = d_v = 128$), processed tokens in batches of 3.2 million, and used learning rate 0.6e-4. GPT-3 had over 1000 times as many parameters as GPT-3 small. All models were trained on 300 billion tokens and used a context window of 2048 tokens. Note that the position-wise feedforward network had $d_{ff} = 4d_{model}$. Larger models using larger batch sizes used smaller learning rates.

Performance   Several sizes of GPT-3 models were evaluated for zero-, one-, and few-shot learning, which Brown et al. describe as different types of in-context learning. With the few-shot type of learning, GPT-3 gives the model as many examples of the desired task that will fit into the context window (10–100 examples). One-shot learning then provides one example and a task description, while zero-shot provides no examples, only a task description. There is no gradient updating or fine-tuning. The model is assessed on 12 NLP datasets.

Results showed that as the number of model parameters increases, the model needs fewer demonstrations to learn how to perform a task (and hence to reach a given accuracy target). When few-shot is used, model performance increases more quickly with model size, suggesting larger models are better at in-context learning.

Evaluation and conditioning the model   For few-shot, K examples were randomly drawn from the training set (or dev set if there was no labeled training set) to be used as conditioning, separated by 1–2 newlines. K varied from 0 to the size of the context window. Some examples just have a description of the task used as conditioning. For multiple-choice tasks, K examples of context with the correct choice were used as conditioning and one additional example of context only was the item to be completed. As with GPT-2, the language model likelihood score for each possible completion was scored. Binary classification was usually treated as a multiple-choice question, where the possible answers were meaningful words, like "positive" or "negative". In some cases, this task was formatted the way it is for the T5 model. Fill-in-the-blank tasks were completed using beam search. See the seminal paper for examples from every dataset used to evaluate GPT-3.

Each of the sizes of GPT-3 models were also tested on several other tasks using zero-, one-, or few-shot conditioning: unscrambling words, SAT analogies, arithmetic, using unusual words in a sentence after seeing the word defined, generate news article text, and correcting English grammar.

6.2 COMPUTER VISION

The most obvious application of transformers to image processing is image recognition (AKA image classification). Prior to transformers, the highest quality in image recognition came from convolutional neural networks (CNNs) [150]. There are a few pure transformer models applied to image recognition that are competitive with state-of-the-art CNN models. In this section, we focus on the Vision Transformer (ViT) [78], which was introduced to see how effective pure transformer models could be for computer vision.

6.2.1 Vision Transformer

Given an image with resolution $H \times W$ and C channels, the image can be represented by $\mathbf{x} \in \mathbb{R}^{H \times W \times C}$. ViT starts by breaking the two-dimensional image into a sequence of N image patches, $\mathbf{x}_p \in \mathbb{R}^{N \times (P^2 \cdot C)}$, with resolution $P \times P$, where $N = HW/P^2$. The sequence of image patches is like the token sequence in the standard transformer [254].

Before sending the patch sequence through the embedding layer, a learnable embedding analogous to the $[CLS]$ token in BERT, $\mathbf{x}_{cls}$ is prepended onto each patch vector. So $\mathbf{x}_p \rightarrow [\mathbf{x}_{cls}; \mathbf{x}_p]$. Using the embedding layer, $\mathbf{E} \in \mathbb{R}^{(P^2 \cdot C) \times D}$, and one-dimensional positional encodings, $\mathbf{E}_{pos} \in \mathbb{R}^{(N+1) \times D}$, we compute the input to the Transformer. D is the Transformer hidden size.

$$\mathbf{z}_0 = [\mathbf{x}_{cls}; \mathbf{x}_p^{(1)}\mathbf{E}; \cdots ; \mathbf{x}_p^{(N)}\mathbf{E}] + \mathbf{E}_{pos} \qquad (6.3)$$

From here, $\mathbf{z}_0$ is passed into a mostly standard transformer encoder architecture with L encoder layers:

$$\mathbf{z}'_l = MultiHeadAttn(LayerNorm(\mathbf{z}_{l-1}) + \mathbf{z}_{l-1} \qquad (6.4)$$

$$\mathbf{z}_l = FeedFwd(LayerNorm(\mathbf{z}_l) + \mathbf{z}'_l \qquad (6.5)$$

$$\mathbf{y} = LayerNorm(\mathbf{z}_L^0), \qquad (6.6)$$

where $l = 1, \ldots, L$ and $\mathbf{z}_L^0$ is the classification embedding for the final encoder layer. Also, the feed-forward layer has two fully-connected layers followed by a GELU activation function. One of the ways in which ViT differs from the standard transformer is that in ViT the $LayerNorm$ operation is applied to the output of the previous layer before the residual connection takes place. In the standard transformer [254], the residual connection was added prior to $LayerNorm$.

Through a series of experiments with ViT, [78] demonstrates that the inductive biases introduced by CNNs are useful for small datasets, but not for larger ones. With larger datasets the model can learn the relevant correlations on its own, as has been shown for various Transformers. ViT also shows that the spatial relationship between patches (distance inside the image) is learned by the positional encodings. Patches that are close to each other end up with similar positional encodings. The two-dimensional spatial correlations are also learned by the positional encodings, i.e., patches in the same row or column have similar positional encodings. The experiments also demonstrated that hard-coding the two-dimensional structure of the image patches into the positional encodings does not improve quality. This is likely because building inductive biases into a model as versatile as a transformer prevents it from learning on its own what is or is not important.

Lastly, the Vision Transformer investigates a modification to the self-attention mechanism, axial attention [126, 114]. Axial attention, where attention is between patches in the same row or the same column. ViT actually creates axial transformer blocks, where there is a row attention mechanism followed by a column attention mechanism.

6.3 AUTOMATIC SPEECH RECOGNITION

Automatic speech recognition (ASR), which is when a system automatically converts a speech audio signal into text, presents a unique challenge that is not present in computer vision and NLP tasks. Speech signals are sequences of continuous values, and not discrete ones like those seen in images or text. This means you can't do pre-training in the same way as you would for computer vision or NLP. For example, in NLP you have a discrete words or subword units, defined in the input signal itself. Similarly, in computer vision, you have image subunits in the input signal, pixels. There are no built-in subunits in a speech signal. This makes pre-training hard, masked or unmasked. This section covers three of the ways in which transformers have been applied to ASR.

6.3.1 Wav2vec 2.0

The first step in wav2vec 2.0 [16] uses a convolutional feature encoder (it's a CNN) to convert the input speech audio, $\mathbf{X}$, into a sequence of representations, $(\mathbf{z}_1, \ldots, \mathbf{z}_T$. The length of the sequence, T, is the number of time steps in the audio. Some spans of in the sequence of speech representations are then masked.

The encodings are able to be learned because the speech is decomposed into discrete speech units akin to the WordPiece tokens used as inputs into a text Transformer. The speech units are a finite set of discrete units of the audio sequence and are shorter than phonemes (they're 25 ms in length). The latent speech encodings are analogous to the embeddings learned in the initial embedding layer in a text transformer. These masked encodings are passed into a transformer to build contextualized representations. A contrastive loss function [219, 250] lets the wav2vec 2.0 transformer learn the relative importance of the speech units.

Note that the discrete speech units also enable cross-lingual training, where the model learns which units are only used for a particular language and which units are used across multiple languages.

Training process As we have seen throughout this book, transformers can use pre-training on a large corpus to learn a wide variety of features of natural language, and then fine-tuning for a given set of tasks. This is what happens with wav2vec 2.0, except it combines unsupervised and self-supervised pre-training, only needing a relatively small amount of labeled data for fine-tuning.

6.3.2 Speech2Text2

Speech2Text2 [258] is another powerful application of the unsupervised pre-training of transformers to ASR, where a decoder block is added on top of a wav2vec 2.0 encoder. After pre-training, the model is fine-tuned with a CTC loss. The decoder is only trained during fine-tuning, it is not pre-trained.

Because Speech2Text2 uses a decoder, it can also be used to combine machine translation and ASR, i.e., the audio could be in English and the transcription could be in French. Wang et al. have also fine-tuned Speech2Text for this task, achieving a new state-of-the-art on some language pairs.

6.3.3 HuBERT: Hidden Units BERT

To deal with the no predefined speech units problem, Hsu et al. introduce HuBERT (Hidden Units BERT) [120]. HuBERT uses clustering to generate noisy speech subunits that can then be treated like subwords that can undergo BERT-like pre-training.

HuBERT uses the noisy labels as a sequence of input tokens that can be masked for BERT pre-training. So, just like BERT learns representations of the unmasked text so that it may correctly predict the masked tokens, HuBERT learns representations of the unmasked, noisy speech subunits so that it may correctly predict the masked speech units.

In HuBERT, the raw speech signal is put through a CNN encoder to produce, the encoded speech signal $X = [x_1, \ldots, x_T]$ of length T, much like in wav2vec 2.0. A set of indices in the encoded speech signal X is then masked. This masked sequence is used as the input to the BERT-like transformer. HuBERT also performs masking in the same way as wav2vec 2.0.

HuBERT uses k-means on MFCC features [279] of the raw speech signal to find nontrivial discrete hidden units [290]. It calls these $[z_1, \ldots, z_T]$, where $z_t \in [C]$ is a categorical variable of C classes. These z_t are used as the output "tokens" that the BERT pre-training needs to accurately predict. Hsu et al. also experiment with using an ensemble of clustering models in place of a single k-means, followed by product quantization [99].

After pre-training, HuBERT uses the standard connectionist temporal classification (CTC) loss to fine-tune the model using labeled audio data. Note that the CNN feature encoder is frozen during the fine-tuning.

6.4 MULTIMODAL AND MULTITASKING TRANSFORMER

After proving to be very effective in many NLP tasks, transformers have shown their effectiveness even in combined tasks involving various modalities like image, text, and videos. Especially around tasks combining image and text, many transformer architectures have been proposed extending the base BERT model to incorporate visual input along with language inputs [173, 123]. In this section, we will cover a couple of architectures that are more generic and adopted.

6.4.1 Vision-and-Language BERT (VilBERT)

Vision-and-Language BERT (VilBERT) is a joint model for learning task-agnostic representations for image and text [173]. The image is first converted into a stream of a sequence of regions mapped to feature vectors using an object detection network. The text follows the normal flow of tokens mapped to positional and word embeddings as a stream of sequences. As shown in Fig. 6.1, VilBERT uses the standard transformer block (TRM) and a co-attention transformer block (Co-TRM) that provides sparse interactions between the two modalities. The Co-TRM module computes query, key, and value matrices similar to the standard transformer block for visual and linguistic representations at any intermediate layer. However, the keys and values from each modality are provided as an input to the other modality's multi-headed attention block. Thus, the multi-headed attention block of Co-TRM produces attention-pooled features for each modality conditioned on the other and enabling joint learning. The architecture allows multiple layers of TRM and Co-TRM for refinement and is task-dependent. The output is task-dependent and can be as simple as a multi-layer perceptron (MLP) followed by a soft-max layer to compute a score giving similarity between the image and the text. There can be multiple outputs corresponding to multiple tasks, all learned together in parallel.

The training of VilBERT happens through various stages similar to inception network training. First, the text and image are trained independently. The BERT model is trained end-to-end on a large corpus for two tasks: masked language modeling (MLM) and next sentence prediction (NSP). The Faster R-CNN-based pre-trained object detection network extracts bounding boxes and their visual features from images and processes them through the network. Next, the Conceptual Captions

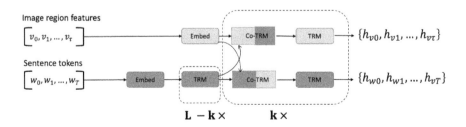

Figure 6.1 VilBERT processing text and image for learning joint representation for multi-modal tasks.

dataset comprising numerous examples of images and their captions is used for joint learning tasks such as mapping regions in the images to the text and masked word prediction from images. Finally, the model is trained for solving specific tasks involving visual and text modalities such as Visual Question-Answering (VQA), Visual Commonsense Reasoning (VCR), Image Retrieval and Phase Grounding. The research shows VilBERT achieves state-of-the-art results in all four tasks compared to existing task-specific models.

6.4.2   Unified Transformer (UniT)

In their work *Transformer is All You Need: Multimodal Multitask Learning with a Unified Transformer* [123], Hu and Singh propose a Unified Transformer (UniT) that can jointly learn and perform seven tasks across the modalities of text and images.

As shown in Fig. 6.2, for each modality, there is an encoder network, and the output of the encoder network is concatenated to give a joint representation. The combined encoder output flows through the decoder network with a multi-head cross-attention block for a task-specific input embedding outputting the results to each task-specific head such as object class detection, visual question answering, sentiment classifier, etc.

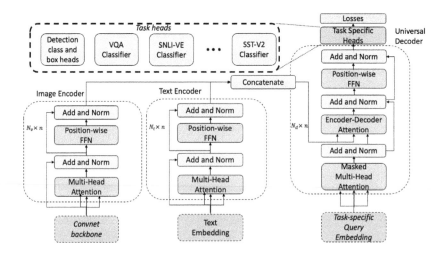

Figure 6.2 UniT processing text and image for learning joint representation for multi-modal tasks.

For training vision-only and visual-language-specific tasks, the image is first processed by a convolutional neural network block followed by a transformer encoder to get the hidden visual representations. In addition, given that different visual-related tasks such as object detection and VQA might require task-specific information, a task embedding vector is added into the transformer encoder. The text encoder uses pre-trained BERT with text embeddings and task-specific embedding vector similar to the image encoder. The decoder is domain agnostic taking the concatenated inputs from the modalities flowing into the multi-head cross-attention block and task-specific queries flowing into the input multi-head attention of the decoder transformer. The training happens on multiple tasks jointly, where a random task and a dataset to fill a batch of samples are chosen at each training iteration. UniT model shows comparable and robust performance on seven tasks across eight datasets to well-established previous work on each domain, keeping the parameters similar.

6.5 VIDEO PROCESSING WITH TIMESFORMER

There are several ways that transformers can be applied to videos. This section will discuss one such application, video classification/action recognition.

TimeSformer [29] is the answer to the question of whether it's possible to do performant video classification or action recognition with self-attention instead of convolutions. TimeSformer uses a modified attention mechanism and uses the Vision Transformer's method of breaking an image into a sequence of patches as its starting point.

6.5.1 Patch Embeddings

TimeSformer breaks a video clip into a sequence of image patches similar to how the Vision Transformer in section 6.2.1 breaks a two-dimensional image into a sequence of image patches. The input to the model is a video with F RGB frames at resolution $H \times W$. It can be represented by a four-dimensional matrix $\mathbf{X} \in \mathbb{R}^{H \times W \times 3 \times F}$. Each frame ($\mathbb{R}^{H \times W \times 3}$) in the input is then decomposed into N non-overlapping patches of size $P \times P$, where $N = HW/P^2$. Each patch is turned into a vector $\mathbf{x}_{(p,t)} \in \mathbb{R}^{3P^2}$, where $p = 1, \ldots, N$ is the patch index and $t = 1, \ldots, F$ is the time/frame index.

The next step is to generate an embedding vector, $\mathbf{z}_{(p,t)}^{(0)} \in \mathbb{R}^D$, for each patch, where D is the Transformer's hidden size:

$$\mathbf{z}_{(p,t)}^{(0)} = \mathbf{x}_{(p,t)}\mathbf{E} + \mathbf{e}_{(p,t)}^{pos}, \tag{6.7}$$

where $\mathbf{e}_{(p,t)}^{pos} \in \mathbb{R}^D$ is a positional encoding that includes the spatial location and frame index, $\mathbf{E}$ is a learned embedding layer, and D is a hidden dimension (similar to d_{model} in the standard transformer). Note that the superscript (0) in $\mathbf{z}_{(p,t)}^{(0)}$ represents that this is for the first TimeSformer layer, which has index 0. Just like in the Vision Transformer, TimeSformer prepends a learned embedding onto $\mathbf{z}_{(p,t)}^{(0)}$ that corresponds to BERT's special classification token, $\mathbf{z}_{(0,0)}^{(0)}$.

6.5.2 Self-Attention

In TimeSformer, the self-attention mechanism is *nearly* identical to every other transformer. In most transformers, the inputs to the multi-head attention are the query, key, and value matrices. Similar to 5.24, each is the result of transforming the input embedding into a different vector space. Each vector space is parameterized by the matrices $\mathbf{W}_Q$, $\mathbf{W}_K$, and $\mathbf{W}_Q$, respectively. The W matrices are used to rotate the input embeddings into the query, key, and value spaces. Thus, the query, key, and value vectors for a single patch in TimeSformer layer l are

$$\mathbf{q}_{(p,t)}^{(l,h)} = LayerNorm\left(\mathbf{z}_{(p,t)}^{(l-1)}\right)\mathbf{W}_Q^{(l,h)} \in \mathbb{R}^{D/H} \tag{6.8}$$

$$\mathbf{k}_{(p,t)}^{(l,h)} = LayerNorm\left(\mathbf{z}_{(p,t)}^{(l-1)}\right)\mathbf{W}_K^{(l,h)} \in \mathbb{R}^{D/H} \tag{6.9}$$

$$\mathbf{v}_{(p,t)}^{(l,h)} = LayerNorm\left(\mathbf{z}_{(p,t)}^{(l-1)}\right)\mathbf{W}_V^{(l,h)} \in \mathbb{R}^{D/H} \tag{6.10}$$

H is the number of attention heads, l is the layer index, and h is the attention head index. D/H is similar to the key/value dimension used in the vanilla Transformer. Note that TimeSformer gives query, key, and value the same dimension and that each $\mathbf{W}$ matrix is $\in \mathbb{R}^{D/H \times D}$. Note that the previous layer's output is put through the *LayerNorm* operation before query, key, and value computation; this is just like in the Vision Transformer, as shown in section 6.6.

6.5.2.1 Spatiotemporal self-attention

TimeSformer uses scaled dot-product attention, as seen in section 5.23. Using the query, key, and value vectors defined above, we can compute the attention weights between patch (p, t) and patch (p', t') in layer l:

$$a^{(l,h)}_{(p,t),(p',t')} = \text{softmax}\left(\mathbf{q}^{(l,h)}_{(p,t)} \cdot \mathbf{k}^{(l,h)}_{(p',t')}{}^T\right) \tag{6.11}$$

$$= \frac{\exp\left(\mathbf{q}^{(l,h)}_{(p,t)} \cdot \mathbf{k}^{(l,h)}_{(p',t')}{}^T\right)}{\sum_{(u,r)\in S_{(p,t)}} \exp\left(\mathbf{q}^{(l,h)}_{(p,t)} \cdot \mathbf{k}^{(l,h)}_{(u,r)}{}^T\right)} \tag{6.12}$$

where $S_{(p,t)}$ is the set of patches that patch (p, t) can attend to. Note that since $\mathbf{z}^{(l)}_{(p,t)}$ contains the classification embedding at $(0, 0)$, the query, key, and value include the classification token term: $\mathbf{q}_{(p,t)} = [\mathbf{q}_{(0,0)}; \mathbf{q}_{(p,t)}]$. The square root factor in section 6.12 has been omitted for brevity.

The $NF + 1$ weights for patch (p, t) can be grouped into a single vector

$$\mathbf{a}^{(l,h)}_{(p,t)} = \text{softmax}\left(\mathbf{q}^{(l,h)}_{(p,t)} \cdot \left[\mathbf{k}^{(l,h)}_{(0,0)}{}^T ; \mathbf{k}^{(l,h)}_{(p',t')}{}^T\right]\right) \tag{6.13}$$

By looking at the relative position of patch (p, t) and patch (p', t'), one sees that there are two types of attention in section 6.12. The case where (p, t) is only allowed to attend to patches in the same frame, i.e., $t' = t$, is spatial attention. This reduces the number of dot products that need to be computed from $NF + 1$ to $N + 1$. The case where (p, t) is only allowed to attend to patches in different frames, but at the same position $(p' = p)$, then we have temporal attention. This reduces the number of dot products that need to be computed from $NF + 1$ to $F + 1$. Both of the above simplifications amount to an attention mask and would need to be added to $S_{(p,t)}$ when computing the normalization factor of the softmax operation. The remainder of the multihead self-attention calculation proceeds as expected in a transformer.

6.5.2.2 Spatiotemporal attention blocks

The paper [29] considers four ways of restricting $S_{(p,t)}$: only spatial attention, divided space-time attention, sparse local and global attention, and axial attention.

Divided space-time attention is having separate spatial and temporal attention mechanisms; a temporal block, followed by a spatial block.

The output embedding of the multi-head temporal attention, $\mathbf{z}'^{(l)}_{(p,t)}$, is computed and then fed into the multi-head spatial attention block as input. In this scheme the temporal and spatial blocks each have their own separate query, key, and value spaces. Because the blocks are in sequence, there are $F + 1 + N + 1 = N + F + 2$ query-key comparisons per patch (p, t). Note that the ordering of the attention blocks was found via experiments. Sparse local and global attention is the combination of local space-time attention, where locality is defined as the neighboring $F \times H/2 \times W/2$ patches, and global attention with stride of 2 in temporal and spatial dimensions. As defined, sparse local and global attention is a coarse-grained approximation to the full spatiotemporal attention. Lastly, the axial attention is similar to that in the Vision Transformer, where there is spatial attention between patches in within a frame that are in the same row or column; there is also temporal attention between patches at the same location in different frames.

As spatial resolution increases and the videos get longer, divided space-time attention scales better than the joint space-time attention because the spatial and temporal components are separated in the divided case. Note that, for a single patch, the spatial and temporal attention are both linear. Spatial is $O(N)$ and temporal is $O(F)$, so the divided scales as $O(N + F)$. The joint attention is $O(N \cdot F)$.

The paper finds that in many cases, spatial attention is more important than temporal attention. But, there are cases where the temporal attention is very important. Another finding is that the divided space-time attention is able to learn more than the full, joint space-time attention because the divided case treats them as two separate attention mechanisms, and thus it has twice the parameters and can learn more, in principal. Because of this, the recommended attention method is divided space-time attention.

6.6   GRAPH TRANSFORMERS

Can transformers be applied to graph datasets? When a transformer uses a full attention mechanism, meaning it has no hard-coded sparsity, it treats an input sequence as a fully-connected graph. This is true for text, images, videos, etc. We saw this for text data with Big Bird in section 5.2.2.4, for images with Vision Transformer in section 6.2.1, and with video for TimeSformer in section 6.5. Fully-connected attention lets the model learn the relative importance of each connection. For graph datasets, however, any given node could have so many links that using fully-connected attention would be computationally intractable, since full attention already has quadratic complexity for simple sequences. This is the purpose of the Graph Transformer introduced in [80]. It addresses the complexity of self-attention by letting a node attend to other nodes in its local neighborhood.

6.6.1 Positional Encodings in a Graph

As discussed in section 5.2.1, scaled-dot product attention mechanisms have quadratic complexity in both time and memory. Since graphs can have a very large number of nodes, to make graph transformers computationally feasible, there must be local sparsity in the attention for any node. The problem with this is that *general* graphs have no notion of distance between nodes, making it non-trivial to use positional encodings to provide a measure of distance or locality, as is common in Transformers. As described in [80], this problem is solved by using Laplacian positional encodings [81], which are generated via a spectral embedding into Euclidean space.

6.6.1.1 Laplacian positional encodings

Laplacian positional encodings for a graph with n nodes are computed from the graph's adjacency and degree matrices:

$$\boldsymbol{\Delta} \; = \; \mathbb{I} - \mathbf{D}^{-1/2}\mathbf{A}\mathbf{D}^{-1/2} \tag{6.14}$$

$$= \; \mathbf{U}^T \boldsymbol{\Lambda} \mathbf{U}, \tag{6.15}$$

where $\mathbf{A}$ is the adjacency matrix, $\mathbf{D}$ is the degree matrix, $\boldsymbol{\Lambda}$ is the eigenvalue matrix (diagonal), and $\mathbf{U}$ is the eigenvector matrix.

The positional encodings for node i $\boldsymbol{\lambda}_i$ are constructed by taking the k smallest non-trivial eigenvectors, each of which is normalized, with a -1 factor randomly assigned to each.

6.6.2 Graph Transformer Input

We can describe a graph $\mathcal{G}$ as a collection of nodes and edges between the nodes. Each node i has features $\alpha_i \in \mathbb{R}^{d_n \times 1}$, where d_n is the number of node features. Each edge between nodes i and j has features $\beta_{ij} \in \mathbb{R}^{d_e \times 1}$, where d_e is the number of edge features. A graph Transformer's input layer has two embedding layers, one to embed the nodes and one to embed the edges. Both embedding layers produce $d-$dimensional embeddings, resulting in node embeddings for node i, $\tilde{\mathbf{h}}_i^{(0)}$ and edge embeddings $\tilde{\mathbf{e}}_{ij}^{(0)}$ between nodes i and j:

$$\tilde{\mathbf{h}}_i^{(0)} = \mathbf{A}^{(0)}\boldsymbol{\alpha}_i + \mathbf{a}^{(0)} \tag{6.16}$$

$$\tilde{\mathbf{e}}_{ij}^{(0)} = \mathbf{B}^{(0)}\boldsymbol{\beta}_{ij} + \mathbf{b}^{(0)}, \tag{6.17}$$

where $\mathbf{A}^{(0)} \in \mathbb{R}^{d \times d_n}$ and $\mathbf{B}^{(0)} \in \mathbb{R}^{d \times d_n}$ are the node and edge embedding matrices, respectively, and $\mathbf{a}^{(0)}$ and $\mathbf{b}^{(0)}$ are bias terms for the nodes and edges, respectively. The superscript (0) denotes that this is the input layer.

The Laplacian positional encodings $\boldsymbol{\lambda}_i$ also get embedded into a $d-$dimensional space with an additional learnable embedding layer $\mathbf{C}^{(0)} \in \mathbb{R}^{d \times k}$, to generate Laplacian positional embeddings $\boldsymbol{\lambda}_i^{(0)}$:

$$\boldsymbol{\lambda}_i^{(0)} = \mathbf{C}^{(0)}\boldsymbol{\lambda}_i + \mathbf{c}^{(0)} \tag{6.18}$$

$$\mathbf{h}_i^{(0)} = \tilde{\mathbf{h}}_i^{(0)} + \boldsymbol{\lambda}_i^{(0)} \tag{6.19}$$

Note that $\mathbf{c}^{(0)} \in \mathbb{R}^d$ is a bias term for the Laplacian positional embedding, $\mathbf{h}^{(0)}$ is the full node embedding, and Laplacian positional embeddings are only computed for the input layer and are not used inside Transformer layers.

6.6.2.1 Graphs without edge attributes

There are two ways to structure a graph Transformer, depending on whether the graph has edge attributes or not. When there are no edge attributes, the output of the multi-head attention mechanism in layer l is:

$$\tilde{\mathbf{h}}_i^{(l+1)} = [\mathbf{Attn}(1, l, i); \dots; \mathbf{Attn}(H, l, i)]\, \mathbf{O}^{(l)} \tag{6.20}$$

$$\mathbf{Attn}(m, l, i) = \sum_{j \in S_i} w_{ij}^{(m,l)} \mathbf{W}_v^{(m,l)} \mathbf{h}_j^{(l)} \tag{6.21}$$

$$w_{ij}^{(m,l)} = \operatorname*{softmax}_j \left(\frac{\mathbf{W}_q^{(m,l)}\mathbf{h}_i^{(l)} \cdot \mathbf{W}_k^{(m,l)}\mathbf{h}_j^{(l)}}{\sqrt{d_k}} \right) \tag{6.22}$$

where S_i is the set of key positions that query i attends to, m indexes the attention head, $\mathbf{W}_q^{(m,l)}$, $\mathbf{W}_k^{(m,l)}$, $\mathbf{W}_v^{(m,l)} \in \mathbb{R}^{d_k \times d}$, d_k is the key-value dimension, and $\mathbf{O}^{(l)} \in \mathbb{R}^{d \times d}$. Note that the exponents in the softmax calculation above are clamped to $[-5, 5]$ for numerical stability. Also

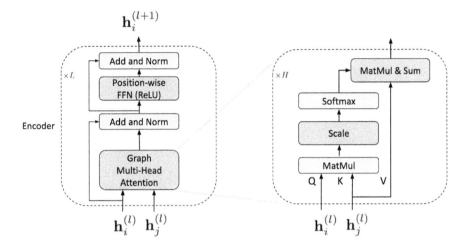

Figure 6.3 Diagram of the Graph Transformer encoder, without edge attributes. The encoder structure is shown on the left. The multi-head attention mechanism is shown on the right. is As described in section 6.6.1.1, Laplacian embeddings are only applied to the input layer, $l = 0$.

note that the definition of the weights matrices that are multiplied by the node embeddings to create the query, key, and value matrices are the transpose of the definition used elsewhere in this book.

$\tilde{\mathbf{h}}_i^{(l+1)}$ is passed into the remainder of the transformer layer as follows, resulting in the output of the transformer layer, $\mathbf{h}_i^{(l+1)}$:

$$\mathbf{h}_i^{(l+1)} = Norm(\mathbf{h}'^{(l+1)}_i + \mathbf{h}''^{(l+1)}_i) \tag{6.23}$$

$$\mathbf{h}'^{(l+1)}_i = Norm(\mathbf{h}_i^{(l)} + \tilde{\mathbf{h}}_i^{(l+1)}) \tag{6.24}$$

$$\mathbf{h}''^{(l+1)}_i = \mathbf{W}_2^{(l)} ReLU\left(\mathbf{W}_1^{(l)}\mathbf{h}'^{(l+1)}_i\right) \tag{6.25}$$

where $\mathbf{W}_1^{(l)} \in \mathbb{R}^{2d \times d}$, $\mathbf{W}_2^{(l)} \in \mathbb{R}^{d \times 2d}$, and $Norm$ can be layer normalization or batch normalization. The structure of the Graph Transformer described in (6.23)–(6.25) is shown in Fig. 6.3.

6.6.2.2 Graphs with edge attributes

For graphs that have attributes on the edges, (6.21)–(6.25) are modified and expanded to account for the edge embeddings. The node embeddings are updated in mostly the way. The only change is that the attention weights that go into the softmax operation now have a contribution from the edge embeddings:

$$\tilde{\mathbf{h}}_i^{(l+1)} = [\mathbf{Attn}(1,l,i);\dots;\mathbf{Attn}(H,l,i)]\,\mathbf{O}^{(l)} \qquad (6.26)$$

$$\tilde{\mathbf{e}}_{ij}^{(l+1)} = \left[\tilde{w}_{ij}^{(1,l)};\dots,\tilde{w}_{ij}^{(H,l)}\right]\mathbf{O}_{edge}^{(l)} \qquad (6.27)$$

$$\mathbf{Attn}(m,l,i) = \sum_{j \in S_i} w_{ij}^{(m,l)}\mathbf{V}^{(m,l)}\mathbf{h}_j^{(l)} \qquad (6.28)$$

$$w_{ij}^{(m,l)} = \operatorname*{softmax}_j\left(\tilde{w}_{ij}^{(m,l)}\right) \qquad (6.29)$$

$$\tilde{w}_{ij}^{(m,l)} = \left(\frac{\mathbf{W}_q^{(m,l)}\mathbf{h}_i^{(l)} \cdot \mathbf{W}_k^{(m,l)}\mathbf{h}_j^{(l)}}{\sqrt{d_k}}\right) \cdot \mathbf{W}_E^{(m,l)}\mathbf{e}_{ij}^{(l)}, \quad (6.30)$$

where, again, S_i is the set of key positions that query i attends to, m indexes the attention head, $\mathbf{W}_q^{(m,l)}$, $\mathbf{W}_k^{(m,l)}$, $\mathbf{W}_v^{(m,l)}$, $\mathbf{W}_E^{(m,l)} \in \mathbb{R}^{d_k \times d}$, d_k is the key-value dimension. The $\mathbf{W}_E^{(m,l)}$ are the weights for a value layer for the edges; it transforms the edge embeddings analogous to how $\mathbf{W}_v^{(m,l)}$ transforms the node embeddings.

Note that while there is a single multi-head attention mechanism when there are edge attributes, that there is a separate linear layer for combining the final attention for nodes and the final attention for edges. This can be seen from the existence of $\mathbf{O}^{(l)}$, $\mathbf{O}_{edge}^{(l)} \in \mathbb{R}^{d \times d}$. As in the case without edge attributes, the exponents in the softmax calculation above are clamped to $[-5, 5]$ for numerical stability.

$\tilde{\mathbf{h}}_i^{(l+1)}$ is passed into the remainder of the Transformer layer as follows, resulting in two outputs for the Transformer layer, $\mathbf{h}_i^{(l+1)}$ for nodes (as shown in (6.31)) and $\mathbf{e}_{ij}^{(l+1)}$ for edges:

$$\mathbf{h}_i^{(l+1)} = Norm(\mathbf{h'}_i^{(l+1)} + \mathbf{h''}_i^{(l+1)}) \qquad (6.31)$$

$$\mathbf{h'}_i^{(l+1)} = Norm(\mathbf{h}_i^{(l)} + \tilde{\mathbf{h}}_i^{(l+1)}) \qquad (6.32)$$

$$\mathbf{h''}_i^{(l+1)} = \mathbf{W}_{n,2}^{(l)}\,\mathrm{ReLU}\left(\mathbf{W}_{n,1}^{(l)}\mathbf{h'}_i^{(l+1)}\right) \qquad (6.33)$$

$$\mathbf{e}_{ij}^{(l+1)} = Norm(\mathbf{e'}_{ij}^{(l+1)} + \mathbf{e''}_{ij}^{(l+1)}) \qquad (6.34)$$

$$\mathbf{e'}_{ij}^{(l+1)} = Norm(\mathbf{e}_{ij}^{(l)} + \tilde{\mathbf{e}}_{ij}^{(l+1)}) \qquad (6.35)$$

$$\mathbf{e''}_{ij}^{(l+1)} = \mathbf{W}_{e,2}^{(l)}\,\mathrm{ReLU}\left(\mathbf{W}_{e,1}^{(l)}\mathbf{e'}_{ij}^{(l+1)}\right) \qquad (6.36)$$

where $\mathbf{W}_{n,1}^{(l)}$, $\mathbf{W}_{e,1}^{(l)} \in \mathbb{R}^{2d \times d}$, $\mathbf{W}_{n,2}^{(l)}$, $\mathbf{W}_{e,2}^{(l)} \in \mathbb{R}^{d \times 2d}$, and $Norm$ can be layer normalization or batch normalization. Subscripts n and e are for nodes and edges, respectively. This is shown schematically in Fig. 6.4.

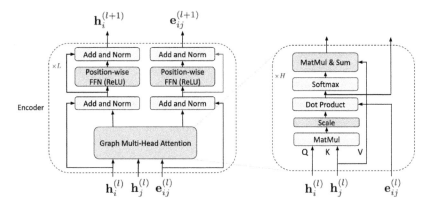

Figure 6.4 Diagram of the Graph Transformer encoder, with edge attributes. The encoder structure is shown on the left. The multi-head attention mechanism is shown on the right. As described in section 6.6.1.1, Laplacian embeddings are only applied to the input layer, $l = 0$.

6.7 REINFORCEMENT LEARNING

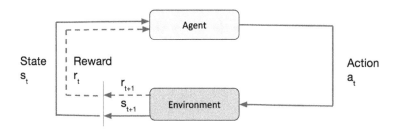

Figure 6.5 Depiction of the interaction between the agent and environment in reinforcement learning. At time t, the state observed by the agent is s_t. The agent then selects an action a_t. In the next time step, $t + 1$, the environment updates it state to s_{t+1} and issues a reward to the agent, r_{t+1}. After this, the cycle can repeat.

Reinforcement Learning (RL) is a machine learning method that uses rewards to train an autonomous agent that can choose its next action so that it gets the best cumulative reward, given its current state.

To understand the process of reinforcement learning, we can start with a finite Markov decision process [239], which is a formal way of looking at a sequence of decisions that an agent which interacts with an environment can take. The agent and the environment interact at a sequence of time steps $t = 0, \ldots, T$. At each t, the agent gets the environment's state $s_t \in \mathcal{S}$ and then chooses an action $a_t \in \mathcal{A}(s)$. At time $t + 1$, the agent receives a reward from the environment $r_{t+1} \in \mathbb{R}$ and the environment's state is updated to s_{t+1}. This simple idea is illustrated in Fig. 6.5. Note that generally speaking, the reward will be a function of the state and action, $r_t = R(s_t, a_t)$. As time progresses, a sequence of states, actions, and rewards accumulates: $(s_0, a_0, r_1, s_1, a_1, r_2, s_2, a_2, r_3, \ldots)$. This sequence can be called a trajectory.

In practice, r_t and s_t are random variables with probability distributions. The probability of moving to state s' and earning reward r, given that action a was taken in state s is given by

$$p(s', r|s, a) = Prob(s_t = s', r_t = r|s_{t-1} = s, a_{t-1} = a)$$
$$\sum_{s' \in \mathcal{S}} \sum_{r \in \mathcal{R}} p(s', r|s, a) = 1, \; \forall s \in \mathcal{S}, \; a \in \mathcal{A}(s) \tag{6.37}$$

The transition probabilities p fully characterize the dynamics of the environment and the agent does not know the set of rewards or the transition probabilities.

The task of RL is to learn the probability that the agent chooses action a while in state s. This probability distribution is called a policy.

6.7.1 Decision Transformer

Decision Transformer [41] is the result of an attempt to replace reinforcement learning (RL) methods with a transformer that models the sequence of states, actions, and rewards that is used to train an autonomous agent. This application is far from the language modeling tasks to which most transformers are applied.

There is one important difference between the finite Markov decision process outlined above and the process used for Decision Transformer. Decision Transformer is applied to a type of RL called offline RL. In offline RL, instead of having the agent interact with an environment and be given a state update after taking an action and getting the reward, there is a fixed dataset that contains trajectories drawn from arbitrary policies. This is a harder way for the agent to learn.

For offline RL, the trajectories in the dataset are of the form

$$(\hat{R}_1, s_1, a_1, \hat{R}_2, s_2, a_2, \ldots, \hat{R}_T, s_T, a_T) \tag{6.38}$$

where $\hat{R}_t = \sum_{t'=t}^{T} r_{t'}$ is the "return-to-go", which is the amount of reward that needs to be generated to get to the end of the trajectory from t.

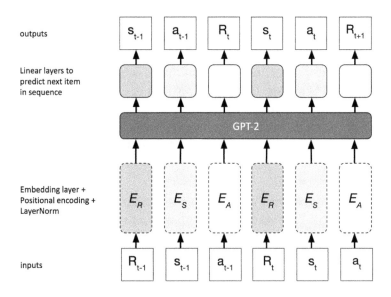

Figure 6.6 Decision Transformer architecture for offline RL. The first two time steps are shown. E_R, E_S, and E_A represent the combined embedding layer positional encoding, and layer norm for the returns-to-go, states, and actions, respectively. The layer after GPT-2 contains three linear submodules for predicting the next element of the sequence. Next state, action, and return-to-go are predicted using different submodules.

These fixed trajectories are used for autoregressive training. The previous K steps are passed to the Decision Transformer. Each step contains three "tokens": the state, action, and return-to-go. Each type of token has its own linear embedding layer, which is followed up by a Layer-Norm. There are also learned positional embeddings added to each type of token embeddings that are different that in the standard transformer because each time step has three tokens instead of one. The embeddings are then passed to a GPT-2 model, for autoregressive training. Note that for image inputs, the embedding layer is a convolutional encoder, as commonly used in computer vision. A diagram of the Decision Transformer architecture is shown in Fig. 6.6.

Since the input tokens are a sequence of rewards-to-go, states, and actions, the multi-head self-attention mechanism computes attention between rewards, states, and actions. This includes the cross-attention between the input tokens and the partially generated output tokens, which are only actions. Chen et al. surmise that the attention mechanism is what makes Decision Transformer able to learn the relationship between states, actions, and rewards. Chen et al. also believe that Decision Transformer may be useful for online RL methods, where it could be used to generate diverse behavior. Decision Transformer achieves state-of-the-art on various RL benchmarks.

6.8 CASE STUDY: AUTOMATIC SPEECH RECOGNITION

6.8.1 Goal

In this chapter, we looked at several applications of the transformer architecture. In this case study, we compare the transcription quality of Wav2vec 2.0 [16] to Speech2Text2 [258], and HuBERT [120], each of which is transformer-based and was discussed earlier in this chapter. We'll measure transcription quality with the word error rate and character error rate metrics.

6.8.2 Data, Tools, and Libraries

```
pip install -U transformers datasets librosa jiwer torchaudio
    sentencepiece
```

Listing 6.1 Python environment setup

We'll use Huggingface Transformers to load pre-trained models and Huggingface Datasets to load an automatic speech recognition (ASR) dataset, TIMIT [93]. After loading the necessary libraries in the environment, as shown in Listing 6.1, we can load the dataset

```
from datasets import load_dataset

timit = load_dataset("timit_asr", split="test")
```

Listing 6.2 Load dataset

6.8.3 Experiments, Results, and Analysis

6.8.3.1 Preprocessing speech data

```
import librosa
```

```
def process_data(batch):
    batch["speech"], batch["sampling_rate"] =
        librosa.load(batch["file"], sr=16000)
    return batch

timit = timit.map(process_data,
                remove_columns=['file', 'audio',
                'phonetic_detail', 'word_detail',
                'dialect_region', 'sentence_type',
                'speaker_id', 'id'])
```

Listing 6.3 Preprocess speech

6.8.3.2 Evaluation

There are three types of errors we can make during transcription:

- substitution: swapping a correct word or character for an incorrect one

- deletion: removing a correct word or character

- insertion: inserting a word or character

We can compute the word error rate and character error rate metrics by summing the three kinds of errors and dividing by the number of words (or characters):

$$WER = \frac{S+D+I}{N} \tag{6.39}$$

$$CER = \frac{S+D+I}{N} \tag{6.40}$$

where S is the number of substitutions, D is the number of deletions, I is the number of insertions, and N is the number of words (or characters, for CER) in the transcript. The Huggingface datasets library has both metrics built-in, so we will use those instead of writing our own.

```
from datasets import load_metric

wer = load_metric("wer")
cer = load_metric("cer")
```

Listing 6.4 Load WER and CER metric

Now we load each model and then transcribe and compute quality metrics.

Wav2vec 2.0 After running the listings up to and including Listing 6.5, we find that Wav2vec 2.0 achieves a WER of 0.09291 (9.29%) and a CER of 0.02212 (2.2%) on the TIMIT test set.

```python
import torch
from transformers import Wav2Vec2Processor, Wav2Vec2ForCTC

device = torch.device("cuda" if torch.cuda.is_available() else
    "cpu")
processor = Wav2Vec2Processor.from_pretrained
            ("facebook/wav2vec2-large-960h")
model =
    Wav2Vec2ForCTC.from_pretrained("facebook/wav2vec2-large-960h")
    .to(device)

def remove_punc(text):
    text = text.replace('.', '')
    text = text.replace(',', '')
    text = text.replace('?', '')
    text = text.replace(';', '')
    text = text.replace('!', '')
    return text

def wav2vec2_predict(batch):
    features = processor(
        batch["speech"],
        sampling_rate=batch["sampling_rate"][0],
        padding=True,
        return_tensors="pt")

    input_values = features["input_values"].to(device)

    with torch.no_grad():
        logits = model(input_values).logits

    predicted_ids = torch.argmax(logits, dim=-1)
    transcription = processor.batch_decode(predicted_ids)
    batch["transcription"] = transcription
    # Wav2vec 2's base model doesn't produce punctuation and
        uppercases text
    batch["target"] = [remove_punc(x.upper()) for x in
        batch["text"]]
    return batch
```

```
BATCH_SIZE = 16
result = timit.map(wav2vec2_predict,
                   batched=True,
                   batch_size=BATCH_SIZE,
                   remove_columns=["speech", "sampling_rate"])

print("WER: ", wer.compute(predictions=result["transcription"],
                           references=result["target"]))
print("CER: ", cer.compute(predictions=result["transcription"],
                           references=result["target"]))
```

Listing 6.5 Transcribe and evaluate with Wav2vec 2.0

Speech2Text2 [258] is a transformer decoder model that can be used with *any* speech encoder, such as Wav2Vec2 or HuBERT [120]. We'll use a Speech2Text2 model of comparable size to the Wav2vec2 model used in Listing 6.5.

```
from transformers import Speech2TextProcessor,
    Speech2TextForConditionalGeneration

s2t_processor = Speech2TextProcessor.from_pretrained
                ("facebook/s2t-large-librispeech-asr")
s2t_model = Speech2TextForConditionalGeneration.from_pretrained
                ("facebook/s2t-large-librispeech-asr").to(device)

def remove_punc(text):
    text = text.lower()
    text = text.replace('.', '')
    text = text.replace(',', '')
    text = text.replace('?', '')
    text = text.replace(';', '')
    text = text.replace('!', '')
    return text

def s2t_predict(batch):
    features = s2t_processor(
        batch["speech"],
        sampling_rate=batch["sampling_rate"][0],
        padding=True,
        return_tensors="pt")

    input_features = features["input_features"].to(device)
    # including the attention mask is important for this model
    # if it is omitted, then the model may generate
    #   transcription that is noticably longer than the target
    attention_mask = features["attention_mask"].to(device)
```

```
with torch.no_grad():
    generated_ids =
        s2t_model.generate(input_ids=input_features,
                            attention_mask=attention_mask)

batch["transcription"] =
    s2t_processor.batch_decode(generated_ids,
                               skip_special_tokens=True)
# Speech2Text2 model doesn't produce punctuation and
#   lowercases text
batch["target"] = [remove_punc(x) for x in batch["text"]]
return batch


BATCH_SIZE = 16
result = timit.map(s2t_predict,
                   batched=True,
                   batch_size=BATCH_SIZE,
                   remove_columns=["speech", "sampling_rate"])

print("WER: ", wer.compute(predictions=result["transcription"],
                           references=result["target"]))
print("CER: ", cer.compute(predictions=result["transcription"],
                           references=result["target"]))
```

Listing 6.6 Transcribe and evaluate with Speech2Text2

In Listing 6.6, you'll notice that we are explicitly passing the attention mask to the model. This turns out to be important for Speech2Text2. If the attention mask is omitted, then the model may generate a transcription that is longer than the target. With a GPU with speed comparable to a K80, the listing should run in about 4 minutes. The Speech2Text2 model achieves a WER of 0.10283 (10.28%) and a CER of 0.03624 (3.62%) on the TIMIT test set.

HuBERT [120], short for Hidden-Unit BERT, is a transformer-based self-supervised speech representation learning model that is able to learn an acoustic model and a language model directly from labeled audio data.

```
from transformers import Wav2Vec2Processor, HubertForCTC

hb_processor = Wav2Vec2Processor.from_pretrained
                    ("facebook/hubert-large-ls960-ft")
```

```python
hb_model = HubertForCTC.from_pretrained
                ("facebook/hubert-large-ls960-ft").to(device)

def remove_punc(text):
    text = text.upper()
    text = text.replace('.', '')
    text = text.replace(',', '')
    text = text.replace('?', '')
    text = text.replace(';', '')
    text = text.replace('!', '')
    return text

def hb_predict(batch):
    features = hb_processor(
        batch["speech"],
        sampling_rate=batch["sampling_rate"][0],
        padding=True,
        return_tensors="pt")

    input_values = features["input_values"].to(device)
    with torch.no_grad():
        logits = model(input_values).logits

    predicted_ids = torch.argmax(logits, dim=-1)
    transcription = processor.batch_decode(predicted_ids)
    batch["transcription"] = transcription
    # HuBERT doesn't produce punctuation and uppercases text
    batch["target"] = [remove_punc(x) for x in batch["text"]]
    return batch


BATCH_SIZE = 16
result = timit.map(hb_predict,
                batched=True,
                batch_size=BATCH_SIZE,
                remove_columns=["speech", "sampling_rate"])

print("WER: ", wer.compute(predictions=result["transcription"],
                references=result["target"]))
print("CER: ", cer.compute(predictions=result["transcription"],
                references=result["target"]))
```

Listing 6.7 Transcribe and evaluate with HuBERT

TABLE 6.1 WER and CER metrics on the TIMIT test set for Wav2vec 2.0, Speech2Text2, and HuBERT. Best score is in boldface

Model	WER	CER
Wav2vec 2.0	**0.09291**	**0.02212**
Speech2Text2	0.10283	0.03624
HuBERT	0.11544	0.02872

HuBERT achieves a WER of 0.11544 (11.54%) and a CER of 0.2872 (2.87%) on the TIMIT test set. For comparison, the WER and CER scores are gathered into Table 6.1, which shows Wav2vec 2.0 performs the best on TIMIT test, with Speech2Text2 in second place; HuBERT is in third.

## CHAPTER 7

Interpretability and Explainability Techniques for Transformers

IN critical applications in domains like healthcare, legislation, law enforcement, or financial, in addition to the predictions, there is a need to understand the models from an explainability standpoint. Unfortunately, one can categorize most state-of-the-art transformer models and techniques covered in this book as a "black box" that can significantly impede adoption. Therefore, there is a paramount need for building explainability around these complex state-of-the-art models from both an understanding and diagnosis perspective. As proposed by Xie et al., we will cover the traits of the models that address explainability, related areas that impact explainability, the taxonomy of explainable methods applied to transformer-based and attention-based systems, and finally, a detailed case study in the electronic health record systems using transformers with different explainable techniques to get practical insights [275].

7.1 TRAITS OF EXPLAINABLE SYSTEMS

One of the decisive goals of an explainable system is that it allows the system's end-users to understand the relationship between the input and the output. Thus, traits can be defined as the properties of the system

DOI: 10.1201/9781003170082-7

that a user can evaluate and measure. As proposed by Xie et al., the four necessary traits are:

1. **Confidence.** When the end-user (decision-maker) can align the transformer-based model's processing with their thought process based on the input and the output, the confidence in the system increases. Saliency maps of attention on image or text highlights the parts of the input that are important from the model perspective for decision-making (classification, recognition, question-answering, etc.), with the output mimicking how trained humans associate a focus-based mechanism as a form of explanation [195, 127, 254, 106, 154].

2. **Safety.** When deployed in applications that directly or indirectly impact human life, the transformer-based models should be deemed safe. One can qualify safety in terms of the (i) consistent and deterministic behavior, i.e., given the same input, the output remains the same every time, (ii) robust and reliable under standard and exceptional conditions, and (iii) the ability to guard against choices that negatively impact society in general [191].

3. **Trust.** Dependable models are the ones that do not need validation. It has been shown that models with high confidence in prediction do not guarantee trustworthiness [95, 191, 189, 291]. Xie et al. consider two significant trustworthiness criteria: (i) satisfactory testing and (ii) experience. Satisfactory testing is the ability of the model to approximate performance similar to its training. Quantitatively, when model performance metrics such as accuracy or precision are similar on training and unseen test data, the trust increases. Experience is a more qualitative assessment where one judges the system to be sufficient to perform the task without inspection. Data and concept drift in real-world deployments can further decrease the trust in the system. There have been many studies in recent times that explore safety from a model prediction viewpoint [134, 22, 252, 5].

4. **Ethics.** If the model does not violate any ethical principles set by the end-user, it can be considered ethical in its decision-making process. Developing frameworks and guidelines for ethics-based AI is growing as a field in and of itself [268, 59, 26, 20].

7.2 RELATED AREAS THAT IMPACT EXPLAINABILITY

Xie et al. identify four areas that are closely aligned with explainability and are related to the traits defined in the previous section.

- **Learning Mechanism**: The ability to provide insights into the model training process helps to increase the confidence and trust in the model. The process that leads to the learned state of the model can be further explored by: understanding the evolution of different layers from learning concepts or statistical patterns from the perspective of filters, weights, and activation [301, 294]. Study of convergence of different layers based on inputs and weights, and generalization properties of networks from memorization and statistical mechanics viewpoint [206].

- **Model Debugging**: Akin to software debugging, model debugging corresponds to the inspection of the model architecture, data processing through the networks, and the errors introduced during the training and runtime process [140]. A common research approach is to build auxiliary models that act as a diagnostic and inspection probe [2]. The proposal of ModelTracker by Amershi et al. allows visual interactions from mislabeled data, missing features identification, insights into insufficiency of training data for label learning, the impact of outliers, feature space visualization, model summary from performance, etc., a model-agnostic approach in debugging [4]. Neural stethoscopes by Fuchs et al. are another general-purpose framework that analyzes the learning process by quantifying the importance of influential factors by promoting and suppressing information [90].

- **Adversarial Attacks and Defense**: Adversarial examples are artificially engineered inputs to feed into the models and judge their ability to discriminate. Constructing adversarial examples needs an understanding of input spaces and the boundaries between classes in classification problems. Adversarial attacks and defense are two different ways to explore the models from an explainability and diagnostic perspective [291, 295]. Black-box and white-box attacks are two main types of adversarial attacks that generate examples to deceive the model [233, 86, 76]. Recent research shows that adding imperceptible noise by perturbing inputs reveals model vulnerabilities [178]. Adversarial defense is about making the model robust against adversarial examples. Two common methods of adversarial defense are (i) adversarial training, in which the training dataset is augmented with adversarial examples to introduce robustness, and (ii) perturbation removal, in which the model identifies adversarial examples and rejects them [95, 218].

- **Fairness and Bias**: One of the key goals for many models deployed in critical areas impacting humans is to be "fair" and unbiased in its decision-making process. Though an evolving field, fairness implies (i) group fairness, also called demographic parity or statistical parity, focusing on race, gender, sexual orientation, etc. [34], and (ii) individual fairness, focusing on individuals with similar features and characteristics generating similar model output [82]. Different techniques to address fairness can be classified as (i) pre-processing methods, removing sensitive features from the data, (ii) in-process methods, where fairness constraints are added, and (iii) post-processing methods to adjust the model predictions after training [36, 139, 96, 30].

7.3 EXPLAINABLE METHODS TAXONOMY

There are many surveys on explainable AI where different strategies have generated many taxonomies for categorizing explainability techniques. The Xie et al. taxonomy, based on foundational explainability methods, restricted only to generic or specific transformer-based models, is discussed in this section and as shown in Fig. 7.1.

7.3.1 Visualization Methods

Visualization methods reveal an explanation by highlighting the influence between the inputs and the outputs in a black-box model as shown in Fig. 7.2. A common way to visualize and explain is through saliency maps, highlighting the most salient inputs that maximally influence model behavior. Xie et al. further break visualization methods into backpropagation-based and perturbation-based visualizations.

7.3.1.1 *Backpropagation-based*

Using the gradient signals passed from output to input during training to understand the saliency of input data is the typical procedure in this group.

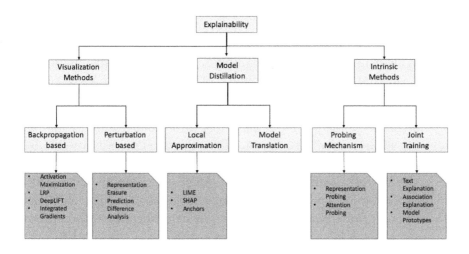

Figure 7.1 Explainable methods taxonomy.

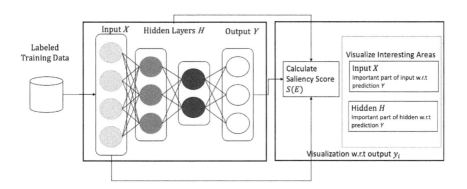

Figure 7.2 Visualization methods. Vary based on different saliency techniques $S(E)$ applied to inputs and hidden layers with respect to the output.

- **Activation maximization**: In their seminal work, Erhan et al. introduce a generic way to visualize the important features of any layer of a network by noting that the activation a_j^i, corresponding to the activation of unit i and layer j, can be maximized by keeping parameters θ fixed and optimizing the input $\mathbf{x}$ [85]. The general principle is to optimize the input $\mathbf{x}$ by computing the gradient of $a_j^i(\mathbf{x}, \theta)$ and updating the input $\mathbf{x}$ in the direction of the gradient.

- **Layer-wise Relevance Propagation (LRP)**: The LRP-based technique measures the relevance of each input feature to the output of the network [14, 73, 147, 188]. The most generic type of LRP is the Deep Taylor Decomposition based on the assumption that f, the network, is differentiable and can be approximated by a Taylor expansion of f at some root $\hat{\mathbf{x}}$ for which $f(\hat{\mathbf{x}}) = 0$. The choice for the root point is such that for it to be insignificantly different from the input $\mathbf{x}$ for which f generates a different prediction [187].

$$f(\mathbf{x}) = f(\hat{\mathbf{x}}) + \nabla_{\hat{\mathbf{x}}} f \cdot (\mathbf{x} - \hat{\mathbf{x}}) + \epsilon \qquad (7.1)$$

$$f(\mathbf{x}) = \sum_i^N \frac{\partial f}{\partial x_i}(\hat{x}_i) \cdot (x_i - \hat{x}_i) + \epsilon \qquad (7.2)$$

where ϵ sums up all second order and higher terms in the Taylor expansion. The relevance score for the inputs can be derived from the above equation as

$$r_i = \frac{\partial f}{\partial x_i}(\hat{x}_i) \cdot (x_i - \hat{x}_i) \qquad (7.3)$$

For a deep network with multiple layers, the Deep Taylor Decomposition assumes decomposition of the relevance scores, starting from the output to the input through the intermediate layers. The relevance score of node i at layer l, connected to M nodes at layer $l + 1$ is assumed to be decomposable and given by:

$$r_i^l = \sum_j^M r_{i,j}^l \qquad (7.4)$$

- **Deep Learning Important FeaTures (DeepLIFT)**: Shrikumar et al. proposed Deep Learning Important FeaTures

(DeepLIFT) where the relevance scores are assigned to the input features based on the difference between the input $\mathbf{x}$ and a "reference" input $\mathbf{x}'$, where $\mathbf{x}'$ is problem specific [228]. The choice of the reference input $\mathbf{x}'$ is domain specific. For example, in MNIST classification, input with all zeros representing the common background can be one of the choices for the reference input.

$\Delta t = f(\mathbf{x}) - f(\mathbf{x}')$ is the difference in neuron output between input $\mathbf{x}$ and a reference input $\mathbf{x}'$. The relevance score $R_{\Delta x_i \Delta t}$ assigned for the input feature x_i with N neurons necessary to compute t is given by:

$$\Delta t = \sum_{i=1}^{N} R_{\Delta x_i \Delta t} \tag{7.5}$$

Shrikumar et al. provide different ways to calculate the weighting between the influence Δx_i had on Δt using *Linear* rule, *Rescale* rule and *RevealCancel* rule. Defining a multiplier $m_{\Delta \mathbf{x} \Delta t}$ which measures the relevance of $\Delta \mathbf{x}$ with respect to Δt, averaged by $\Delta \mathbf{x}$ as:

$$m_{\Delta \mathbf{x} \Delta t} = \frac{R_{\Delta \mathbf{x} \Delta t}}{\Delta \mathbf{x}} \tag{7.6}$$

Layer by layer computation of relevance scores using chain rule is adopted in the DeepLIFT paper. Arkhangelskaia and Dutta apply DeepLIFT on the BERT model predictions and test the outcomes to monitor shifts in the attention values for input for the question-answering application [8].

- **Integrated Gradients (IG).** Integrated gradients by Sundarajan et al. is an explanation technique by computing relevance for a network f based on two axioms: sensitivity and implementation variance [236]. The sensitivity axiom: for an input $\mathbf{x}$ which differs from some baseline input $\mathbf{x}'$ along feature x_i and $f(\mathbf{x}) \neq f(\mathbf{x}')$ then x_i should have a non-zero relevance. The implementation invariance: for two networks f_1 and f_2 when outputs are equal for all possible inputs, the relevance score for every input feature x_i should be identical over f_1 and f_2.

  If f is the deep network with input $\mathbf{x}$ and a baseline input $\mathbf{x}'$ where the outputs are $[0, 1]$, the relevance of feature x_i of the input $\mathbf{x}$ over f is taken as integral of gradients through the path from $\mathbf{x}'$ to $\mathbf{x}$ and is given by:

$$IG_i(\mathbf{x}) = (x_i - x_i') \int_0^1 \frac{\partial f(\mathbf{x}' + \alpha(\mathbf{x}) - \mathbf{x}')}{\partial x_i} \tag{7.7}$$

where α is smoothly distributed in the range $[0, 1]$ and is associated with the path from $\mathbf{x}'$ to $\mathbf{x}$. The above equation can be approximated using Riemann summation using appropriate number of steps as described in the paper.

7.3.1.2 Perturbation-based

Altering the input and computing the feature relevance by comparing the difference in the output between the original and altered input is the core of all perturbation-based methods.

- **Representation Erasure**: Li et al. propose a generic technique for an explanation by examining the effect of erasing the input representation to see how such changes affect the output [157]. By analyzing the impact, one can identify essential representations that significantly contribute to the models' decisions. The erasure can be performed on various levels of representation, such as the input word-vector dimensions, input words or group of words, and intermediate hidden units. The straightforward technique is to compute the difference in log-likelihood on the labels when representations are erased. A more sophisticated method uses the reinforcement learning model to find the minimal set of words that must be erased to change the model's decision.

- **Meaningful Perturbation**: Fong and Vedaldi propose a meta-predictor using the perturbation technique to give local explanations based on the sensitive areas in the input that predicted the output [89]. The authors propose three classes of perturbations to generate visual explanations for image classification: (i) constant, replacing a region in the image with a constant value, (ii) noise, adding small noise to the region, and (iii) blur, blurring the region. For example, an explanation for a black-box image classifier (f) that predicts dog will be given by

$$D(\mathbf{x}, f) = \{\mathbf{x} \in \mathbf{X}_d \Leftrightarrow f(\mathbf{x}) = 1\} \qquad (7.8)$$

where $f(\mathbf{x}) = 1$ prediction of dog in the image and $\mathbf{X}_d$ is all images that the classifier predicts as dog. For a new image $\mathbf{x}^0$, the explanation technique creates perturbation in the input using the techniques described above to find locally sensitive areas that result in $f(\mathbf{x}^0)$ per the explanation rules.

- **Prediction Difference Analysis**: Zintgraf et al. propose a method based on Robnik-Sikonja and Kononenko research, to measure the influence based on altering input information for probabilistic-based classifiers [210, 304]. It evaluates the effect of an input feature x_i with respect to class c by determining the difference between $p(c|\mathbf{x}_{-i}$ and $p(c|\mathbf{x})$ using the marginal probability

$$p(c|\mathbf{x}_{-i}) = \sum_{x_i} p(x_i|\mathbf{x}_{-i})p(c|\mathbf{x}_{-i}, x_i) \tag{7.9}$$

where $mathbfx$ corresponds to all input features and $\mathbf{x}_{-i}$ corresponds to all features except x_i. The importance of the feature x_i is measured using:

$$\text{Diff}_i(c|\mathbf{x}) = \log_2\left(\text{odds}(c|\mathbf{x})\right) - \log_2\left(\text{odds}(c|\mathbf{x}_{-i})\right) \tag{7.10}$$

7.3.2 Model Distillation

Xie et al. refer to the model distillation category as a post-training method where the encoded knowledge in the model is distilled into a representation agreeable for an explanation by a user, as shown in Fig. 7.3. Xie et al. further divides this category into two subcategories: local approximation and model translation.

7.3.2.1 Local approximation

All local approximation methods hypothesize that learning local boundaries in a manifold is much simpler than learning a global discriminating model over an entire space [15]. For example, a simple linear classifier

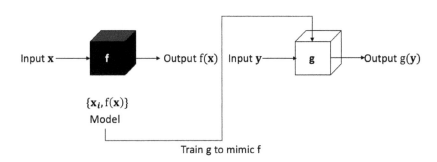

Figure 7.3 Model distillation.

can discriminate a subset of the data over a dense region in a manifold and offers a simple explanation for instances in that area. We will discuss few popular techniques that can be employed in model agnostic way.

- **Local Interpretable Model-agnostic Explanations (LIME):**
  Ribeiro et al. developed one of the most popular local approximation methods called Local Interpretable Model-agnostic Explanations (LIME) [208]. LIME generates new sample instances by perturbing any given instance of interest in its manifold proximity, measures the model outputs for each sample, and fitting a local linear interpretable model to the new samples. Thus by covering most instances and predictions from the global model, many local easily interpretable models like linearly weighted classifier/regressor or decision trees are built. Let us represent the entire deep learning model through function f, data instance of interest x, an explanation model h selected from a class $\mathcal{H}$ of interpretable models such as linear, logistic, or decision tree, the problem of identifying a local explainable model is then equivalent to optimizing for the objective $\zeta(x)$:

$$\zeta(x) = \arg\min_{h \in \mathcal{H}} \mathcal{L}\left(f, h, \pi_x(z)\right) + \Omega(h) \tag{7.11}$$

  where π_x is a kernel function that weighs a sample z based on its distance to the instance of interest x, $\mathcal{L}$ is a loss function and Ω is a complexity penalty such as the tree depth in decision tree. The loss function $\mathcal{L}$ provides a metric of how close the explanation model approximates the real model f in the locality of instance x.

- **SHapley Additive exPlanations (SHAP):** Shapley values have foundations in game theory, particularly cooperative game theory. One can view each feature as a player in a game, and the goal is to distribute payouts fairly among players who form a coalition based on their contribution to the total payout. The marginal contribution of each feature averaged across the set of all possible coalitions of features gives the Shapley values.

  Let us represent the entire deep learning model through function f, input with d features $\mathbf{x} = \{x_1, x_2, \ldots, x_d\}$, the Shapley value ϕ_j for the j-th feature is given by

$$\phi_j(f) = \frac{|S|!(d - |S| - 1)!}{d!} \left[f\left(S \cup \{x_j\}\right) - f\left(S\right)\right] \tag{7.12}$$

- **Anchors**: Anchors overcome limitations of many local explanation methods that use linear approximations for defining local behaviors. For many real-world domains, the linear approximation may lead to inaccurate decisions. Anchors are a high-precision explanation technique for generating local explanations by inferring a set of if-then rules in the feature space [209]. These rules serve as "anchors" for a set of features making it more robust against changes and on unseen data.

If x represents the instance for explanation, A represents a set of predicates, i.e., the resulting rule or anchor, such that $A(x) = 1$, f represents the black-box model, D represent a known distribution of perturbations, z is a sample drawn from the conditional distribution when rule A applies $D(z|A)$, and τ is the given precision threshold, then the anchor definition is given by:

$$\mathbb{E}_{D(z|A)}\left[\mathbb{1}_{f(x)=f(z)}\right] \geq \tau, \ A(x) = 1 \tag{7.13}$$

In general, finding anchors is infeasible in a continuous space, and by introducing a parameter δ, the definition can be changed in terms of probability to meet this precision threshold for some arbitrarily small δ as given by:

$$\Pr\left[\rho(A) \geq \tau\right] \geq 1 - \delta \tag{7.14}$$

Since there may be several anchors that meet this criterion, preference is given to the anchors with the highest coverage $cov(A)$, defined as

$$cov(A) = \mathbb{E}_{D(z)}\left[A(z)\right] \tag{7.15}$$

If A' is the set of anchors that satisfy (7.14), then anchor generation then becomes a combinatorial optimization problem given by:

$$\max_{A \in A'} cov(A) \tag{7.16}$$

In practice, various heuristics-based approaches are used. For example, a greedy search technique such as a bottom-up approach where you start with an empty rule set and generate a set of candidate rules by iteratively extending an anchor by one additional feature predicate creates this rule set in a greedy way. Beam-search can be used to improve upon this greedy search method by maintaining a candidate set of rules during the iterative search process.

7.3.2.2 *Model translation*

Model translation involves training an alternative "smaller" model on the entire dataset as input and outputs coming from the black-box model as the training data. Thus, this captures the global behavior in an explainable way as compared and contrasted with the local approximation techniques described above. The choice of the alternative model can be based on model size, ease of deployment, and explainable algorithm (e.g., decision tree, rule-based classifier, graphs, etc.) [112, 288, 21, 118]. The Tan et al. proposal to build a generic additive explainable model by decomposing the black-box model into explainable models such as splines or bagged trees and then build additive models using them is one such technique [240].

7.3.3 Intrinsic Methods

Intrinsic methods use the model architecture as is, and explanations are provided using the representations, for example, weights of hidden layers or the attention weights [207]. Intrinsic methods can be further classified into (i) probing mechanism-based and (ii) joint training-based.

7.3.3.1 *Probing mechanism*

Over the last few years, the idea of inserting a simple layer (e.g., one layer neural classifier) on top of either the attention heads or any intermediate layers of a deep learning model already trained on a primary task to validate "information" (auxiliary tasks) as a way to diagnose or explain has been an emerging trend. For example, on a BERT model trained for sentiment classification, one can insert a probe classifier on top of the intermediate layers in the trained model to measure the ability to identify linguistic information. The probe classifier can be used to validate information at the syntactic level, such as verbs, nouns, etc., and semantic level, such as recognizing entity, relations, entailment, etc., useful in the overall primary task of sentiment classification. A dataset with original sentences used for sentiment classification and labels identifying verbs, nouns, entities, etc., is created. The probe classifier to measure the performance of any layer then undergoes training and testing on the new auxiliary tasks by freezing the information at those layer(s), thus giving the quantitative measure of the layer in identifying or explaining [23].

Representation Probing In one of the earliest works, Hupkes et al. proposed the concept of probing using "diagnostic classifiers" to unveil how recurrent and recursive networks process hierarchical structures using arithmetic language tasks with exact syntax and semantics and a limited vocabulary [128]. Furthermore, it showed how neural architectures process languages with hierarchical compositional semantics and probe a black-box neural architecture for NLP tasks.

Conneau et al. introduced probing tasks to comprehensively score different neural architectures on different tasks to understand and quantify the linguistic properties of the sentence embeddings learned on the encoders [62]. They created probing tasks categorized as surface information, syntactic information, and semantic information. Surface information probing tasks answers questions; for example, "do the sentence embeddings preserve the sentence lengths?", using a classification dataset with sentence length as labels. Syntactic information probing tasks investigates syntax-based properties, for example, "are the embeddings sensitive to word order?", using a classification dataset with bigrams shifted as positives and non-shifted as negatives. Finally, semantic information probing tasks investigate semantics-based attributes retained in the embeddings, for example, "can the embeddings understand tenses?", using a tense classification dataset where VBP/VBZ forms are labeled as present and VBD as past tense. The comprehensive experiments in this work with different architectures and downstream tasks provided great insights into model architectures and their ability to preserve different linguistic properties.

Tenney et al. introduced "edge probing" to understand the hidden representation in deep learning architectures such as ELMO, GPT and BERT [245]. It investigates the role of the word in each position to encode structural, syntactic, semantic, and even long-range phenomena by freezing the layers and using a neural classifier to train and test on various tasks such as part-of-speech tagging (POS), constituent labeling, dependency labeling, named entity labeling, semantic role labeling (SRL), coreference, semantic proto-role and relation Classification. They show that contextualized embeddings improve over their non-contextualized equivalents, mostly on syntactic tasks compared to semantic tasks.

Tenney et al., in their work, further found that a model like BERT can rediscover linguistic information similar to a traditional NLP pipeline in an interpretable and localizable way [244]. They discovered the sequence: POS tagging, parsing, NER, semantic roles, coreference are part of the overall BERT model. They introduce two complementary metrics: scalar mixing weights and cumulative scoring. Scalar mixing weights is a training corpus-dependent metric highlighting layers that are most relevant for the probing classifier in the whole BERT model. Cumulative scoring is an evaluation set-dependent metric estimating how much higher a score one can obtain on a probing task with the introduction of each layer.

Hewitt and Liang, in their work, devise a control task strategy as a measure to address the probing confounder problem [110]. Probing confounder problem can be defined as—given the main neural architecture that needs to be explained, the probing classifier such as MLP or logistic regression and the supervised auxiliary task, how do we assign the credit for performance such as test accuracy to either of the three? They devise control tasks that can be easily learned by a probing diagnostic classifier but not encoded in the representations (actual neural model or layers). Evaluating the performance (testing accuracy) difference between the control tasks and auxiliary tasks with different probing classifier choices as a selectivity measure can easily assign the credit of learning to either the representation or the probing classifier. The work also answers questions such as "how does the probe design affect probing task performance?" and "can the probes pick spurious signals?".

Attention Probing   Probing either by adding an attention layer on top of an existing neural architecture or using existing attention weights from a layer of deep learning, mapping it to the inputs as "attention maps" to explore the relationship between the two is soon developing as an effective explanation technique.

Rocktäschel et al. proposed a neural word-by-word attention mechanism in a sequence-to-sequence network for reasoning over entailments of pairs of words and phrases [211]. Visualizations of word-by-word attention between the premise and hypothesis show that irrelevant parts of the premise, such as words capturing little meaning, are correctly neglected for entailment. The premise and hypothesis connected via deeper semantics show proper relevancy through the attention weights.

Xu et al. use an attention mechanism for automatic image captioning tasks [278]. The work shows that the attention mechanism not only achieves state-of-the-art results but highlights salient objects in the image while generating the corresponding words in the output sequence, thus useful for explanations.

Yang et al. employ a hierarchical attention mechanism for document classification [286]. The two levels of attention mechanisms, one at the word level and another at the sentence level, enable the model to attend differentially to content when building the document representation. Visualization of the attention layers demonstrates that the model selects informative words and sentences for classification.

Jesse Vig introduced a tool "BertViz" for visualizing attention in the Transformer at all levels, viz. at the whole model level, the attention-head level, and the individual neuron level [255]. The model view provides a single high-level view of the entire model across all the layers and heads for a given input. The model view helps in visualizing how attention patterns evolve in the attention heads across all layers. The attention-head view visualizes the attention patterns produced by one or more attention heads in a given layer and can help detect biases such as gender bias. The neuron view visualizes the individual neurons in the query and key vectors and their interaction producing attention, thus giving a detailed view of how the patterns are formed.

7.3.3.2 Joint training

In a joint training-based approach, the explanation task is associated with the actual learning task so that the model learns the explanation and the actual task jointly. The explanation task can be generating explanations in a natural language format or associating inputs with human-understandable concepts, or learning prototypes for the data that can be used as an explanation.

Creating user (expert or layman) friendly explanations at the prediction time by augmenting the deep learning architecture with a text explanation generation component and learning the explanations along with the original task is an evolving explainability approach [109, 293, 166, 111, 37]. Most approaches need explanations as part of training data along with the labeled data for the main task, which makes this approach prohibitively costly.

Associating input features (words or image components) or latent features with concepts or objects as a method of explanation either by associating saliency maps with inputs or latent activations with semantic concepts using regularization terms or changes to models is another method in this category [3, 77, 131, 153].

Many computer vision-based architectures, especially in classification problems, learn prototypes from the training process that can be then used to associate with new unseen instances as an explanation [159, 40].

7.4 ATTENTION AND EXPLANATION

As discussed in the previous section, one of the emerging patterns, especially in NLP, is to associate the magnitude of the attention weights with the inputs and use it to interpret the model behavior. Next, we discuss few papers and the research that impacts how one views attention mechanisms and their contribution towards explainability.

7.4.1 Attention is Not an Explanation

In this paper, Jain and Wallace try to ask fundamental questions on attention and their interpretations [132]. For example, when we create an attention map as shown in Fig. 7.4 that correlates attention weights directly to the input tokens or weights, the impact of many transformations or computations such as intermediate hidden states, query vectors, attention techniques is not taken into account. The paper poses two crucial questions—(i) do the attention heat maps reveal the importance of words/tokens? (ii) does the attention mechanism provide us with transparency, i.e., how did the model reach the prediction?

These abstract questions can be mapped to the following hypotheses for verification:

1. Attention weights should correlate with feature importance measures that have the semantics associated with them (e.g., gradient-based measures and leave-one-out)

2. Had we attended to different inputs, would the predictions be different?

Different NLP tasks such as text classification, question answering (QA), and Natural Language Inference (NLI) using contextualized BiLSTM and non-contextualized feedforward network with a standard attention mechanism is used for analyses.

7.4.1.1 Attention weights and feature importance

For the first hypothesis, the words from inputs are ranked on attention weights and on feature importance scores (gradients and leave-one-out),

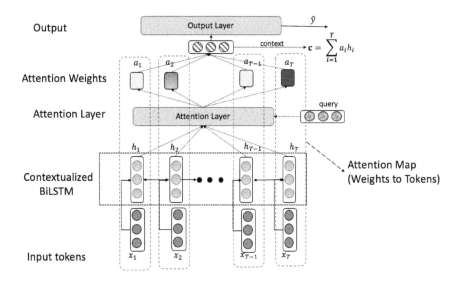

Figure 7.4 Attention probing with contextualized bidirectional LSTM as the neural model and an attention layer.

and the Kendal tau measure is used to measure correlation. The semantics associated with the feature importance scores, the experiment measures the output changes by perturbing individual words with the same attention and context.

The algorithm follows a straightforward process, first encode the input to get the hidden states $(\mathbf{h} \leftarrow \text{Enc}(\mathbf{x}))$, compute the attention$(\hat{a} \leftarrow \text{softmax}(\phi(\mathbf{h}, \mathbf{Q})))$ and the output $(\hat{y} \leftarrow \text{Dec}(\mathbf{h}, \mathbf{Q}))$.

For the gradient-based method, the gradient is computed with respect to each of the input to get the gradient score and the correlation score:

$$g_t \leftarrow |\sum_{w=1}^{|V|} 1[\mathbf{x}_{tw} = 1]\frac{\partial y}{\partial \mathbf{x}_{tw}}|, \forall t \in [1, T] \tag{7.17}$$

$$\tau_g \leftarrow \text{Kendall}\tau(\alpha, g) \tag{7.18}$$

For the leave-one-out method, one word is removed at a time, and Total Variation Distance (TVD) is used as a measure to compute the change in the distributions of output and the correlation score:

$$\Delta\hat{y}_t \leftarrow \text{TVD}(\hat{y}(\mathbf{x}_{-t}), \hat{y}(\mathbf{x})), \forall t \in [1, t] \tag{7.19}$$

*The experiments show a consistently low correlation between the atten-
tion weights and feature importance scores across all the datasets, especially for contextualized encoders.*

7.4.1.2 Counterfactual experiments

To validate the second hypothesis, the authors put forth two empirical
questions

1. How much does the output change if the attention scores are randomly permutated?

2. Can we find maximally different attention that does not change
   the output more than a predefined threshold epsilon?

Attention Permutation
Algorithm 2 captures the experiment to characterize the model behavior
when attention weights are shuffled

$\mathbf{h} \leftarrow \text{Enc}(\mathbf{x})$, $\hat{\alpha} \leftarrow \text{softmax}(\phi(\mathbf{h}, \mathbf{Q}))$
$\hat{y} \leftarrow \text{Dec}(\mathbf{h}, \hat{\alpha})$
for $p \leftarrow 1$ *to* 100 **do**
$\quad \alpha^p \leftarrow \text{Permute}(\hat{\alpha})$
$\quad \hat{y}^p \leftarrow \text{Dec}(\mathbf{h}, \hat{\alpha})$
$\quad \Delta\hat{y}^p \leftarrow \text{TVD}[\hat{y}^p, \hat{y}]$
end
$\Delta\hat{y}^{med} \leftarrow \text{Median}_p(\Delta\hat{y}^p)$
Algorithm 1: Permuting attention weights.

*The results for this experiment are different for different datasets.
Some datasets highlight that the attention weights might infer explaining
an output by a small set of features, but where perturbing the attention
makes little difference to the prediction, while for other datasets, this was
not observed.*

Adversarial attention
The intuition for this experiment is to explore new attention weights
that differ as much as possible from the observed attention distribution and yet give the exact prediction. A ϵ value is specified to simplify
the optimization process that defines the slight change in the prediction. Once the ϵ value is given, the aim to find k adversarial distributions $\{\alpha^{(1)}, \cdots, \alpha^{(k)}\}$, such that each $\alpha^{(}i)$ maximizes the distance
from original $\hat{\alpha}$ but does not change the output by more than ϵ. The

Jensen-Shannon Divergence is used to measure the difference between the distributions. The optimization equation is given by:

$$\text{maximize}_{\alpha^{(1)},\cdots,\alpha^{(k)}} f(\{\alpha^{(i)}\}_{i=1}^k) \tag{7.20}$$

where $f(\{\alpha^{(i)}\}_{i=1}^k)$ is:

$$\sum_{i=1}^k \text{JSD}[\alpha^{(i)}, \hat{\alpha}] + \frac{1}{k(k-1)} \sum_{i<j}^k \text{JSD}[\alpha^{(i)}, \alpha^{(j)}] \tag{7.21}$$

The first part of the equation $\sum_{i=1}^k \text{JSD}[\alpha^{(i)}, \hat{\alpha}]$ finds maximally different attention from the observed $\hat{\alpha}$ and the second part $\frac{1}{k(k-1)} \sum_{i<j}^k \text{JSD}[\alpha^{(i)}, \alpha^{(j)}]$ is maximally different from each other. The adversarial attention finding algorithm can be summarized as:

$\mathbf{h} \leftarrow \text{Enc}(\mathbf{x}), \ \hat{\alpha} \leftarrow \text{softmax}(\phi(\mathbf{h}, \mathbf{Q}))$
$\hat{y} \leftarrow \text{Dec}(\mathbf{h}, \hat{\alpha})$
$\alpha^{(1)}, \cdots, \alpha^{(k)} \leftarrow \text{Optimize7.20 for } i \leftarrow 1 \text{ to } k \text{ do}$
$\quad \hat{y}^{(i)} \leftarrow \text{Dec}(\mathbf{h}, \hat{\alpha}^{(i)})$
$\quad \Delta\hat{y}^{(i)} \leftarrow \text{TVD}[\hat{y}, \hat{y}^{(i)}]$
$\quad \Delta\alpha^{(i)} \leftarrow \text{JSD}[\hat{\alpha}, \alpha^{(i)}]$
end
$\epsilon \max \text{JSD} \leftarrow \max_i 1[\Delta\hat{y}^{(i)} \le \epsilon]\Delta\alpha^{(i)}$
Algorithm 2: Finding adversarial attention weights.

Similar to the permutation attention weights experiments, the results for the adversarial attention experiments also varied based on the data.

The attention distribution does not uniquely characterize why a particular prediction was made by the model as you can find alternative attention heatmaps that give the same predictions.

The overall conclusion drawn from the research was—attention does not provide a consistent interpretation of why a model made a particular prediction.

7.4.2 Attention is Not Not an Explanation

Wiegreffe and Pinter contest the claims and assumptions made by Jain and Wallace in the research above and show through experiments the usefulness of attention mechanisms for explainability [269]. Wiegreffe and Pinter's main contention from Jain and Wallace's research is that their "explanation" study is ambiguous, correlation experiments are insufficient, and the adversarial weight experiments were vague and impractical.

Contextualizing explainability in AI literature and the NLP domain shows two forms of explanations—(i) plausible explanation and (ii) faithful explainability. The goal of plausible explanation is to provide human-understandable rationales for the model's behavior. The plausible explanation is subjective and requires human-in-the-loop to judge whether the explanation is justified and builds trust in the model. Faithful explainability is a more rigorous form of explanation and aligns more closely with the desired properties of transparency and interpretability and what the authors explore in their work. The goal of the technique is to quantify the correlation between the input (tokens/words) and the output (predictions) for a predictive task. One of the requisite for this form of explanation is that—model explanations are exclusive, i.e., a predictive model should exhibit one set of behavior for one reasoning process.

The authors lay the following three requirements for faithful explanations for attention mechanisms.

1. Attention mechanism should be a NECESSARY component for good model performance.

2. Attention distributions should be hard to manipulate, i.e., if any trained model can vary the distribution of attention weights and yet have similar predictions, they may not be suitable for the explanation. This directly corresponds to the exclusivity requisite for faithful explanations and will guide the search for adversarial models.

3. Attention distributions should work well in uncontextualized settings. Since the attention weights are typically learned on contextualized hidden layer outputs, to see the impact on input tokens, one needs to use uncontextualized settings to judge their usefulness.

7.4.2.1 Is attention necessary for all tasks?

The authors use the same three sets of tasks and six classification datasets using the BiLSTM model from the Jain and Wallace setting and create another model where the attention weights are uniform in distribution compared to the learned weights. Based on the F1 scores on all six classification datasets comparing the uniform and learned attention weights, the news datasets show no variations and hence are not used for the subsequent two analyses. The Stanford Sentiment Treebank

(SST) is a borderline case and shows a small difference as compared to the MIMIC (III) and IMDB dataset.

7.4.2.2 Searching for adversarial models

To find attention weight distributions that mimic the base model predictions, the authors propose a model-consistent training protocol for finding adversarial attention distributions through a combined parameterization that holds for all training examples. The two measures they employ for the adversarial training are Total Variation Distance (TVD) and Jensen-Shannon Divergence (JSD).

Total Variation Distance (TVD) is used for comparing the class predictions from two models and is given by:

$$\text{TVD}(\hat{y}_1, \hat{y}_2) = \frac{1}{2} \sum_{i=1}^{|y|} |\hat{y}_{1i} - \hat{y}_{2i}| \tag{7.22}$$

Jensen-Shannon Divergence (JSD) is used for comparing the two attention distributions and is given by:

$$\text{JSD}(\alpha_1, \alpha_2) = \frac{1}{2}\text{KL}[\alpha_1\|\bar{\alpha}] + \frac{1}{2}\text{KL}[\alpha_2\|\bar{\alpha}] \text{ where } \bar{\alpha} = \frac{\alpha_1 + \alpha_2}{2} \tag{7.23}$$

The adversarial training algorithm is first to train a base model(M_b). Then train an adversarial model (M_a) that minimizes the output prediction score from the base model yet maximizing the changes in the learned attention distribution from the base model using following instance-wide loss function:

$$\mathcal{L}(M_a, M_b) = \text{TVD}(\hat{y}_1^{(i)}, \hat{y}_2^{(i)}) - \lambda \text{KL}(\alpha_a^{(i)}\|\alpha_b^{(i)}) \tag{7.24}$$

where $\hat{y}^{(i)}$ and $\alpha(i)$ denote predictions and attention distributions for an instance i, and λ controls the trade-off between the prediction distance and attention distribution changes.

For the diabetes dataset (and the anemia and the IMDB), they find it challenging to find adversarial weights that produce divergent attention weights and not losing the predictive performance, thus supporting the use of attention for the faithful explanation. On the contrary, Stanford Sentiment Treebank (SST) dataset shows no use of attention weights for the faithful explanation.

7.4.2.3 Attention probing

To validate if the attention distributions work well in uncontextualized settings, the attention weights from the BiLSTM are imposed on an uncontextualized trained MLP layer with the bag of word-vector representation. Thus, high performance in the task implies that attention scores capture the relationship between the input and the output. Except for Stanford Sentiment Treebank (SST) dataset, every task and dataset shows the BiLSTM trained attention weights outperforming the MLP and the uniform weights, indicating the usefulness of attention weights.

In conclusion, the research has laid down three essential components for validating the usefulness of the attention mechanism and three methods to quantify it for faithful explanation. The usefulness of the attention mechanism is shown to be task dependent.

7.5 QUANTIFYING ATTENTION FLOW

As discussed in the previous two sections, correlating the attention weights to inputs for explanation in a simple BiLSTM with a single attention layer before the output itself is an open research topic. In transformers with self-attention, multiple attention heads, and many attention layers in the encoder, the problem becomes even more difficult. In their research, Abnar and Zuidema propose a couple of techniques to resolve this problem, viz., Attention Rollout and Attention Flow, both compute attention scores at each layer from that layer to the input tokens (i.e., token attention) for visualization and interpretation [1]!

7.5.1 Information Flow as DAG

The attention module in transformers at any layer has a residual connection from the input, so values (V) at any layer $l + 1$ is given by $V_{l+1} = V_l + W_{att}V_l$ where W_{att} is the attention matrix. The authors propose adding identity matrix I and calculating the raw attention updated by residual connections as:

$$A = 0.5 \cdot W_{att} + 0.5 \cdot I \cdot A \qquad (7.25)$$

This equation can be used to create an information flow graph for the Transformer model at any node or layer. The research proposes using a Directed Acyclic Graph (DAG) with input tokens, or the hidden embeddings as the graph nodes and raw attention weights as the edges.

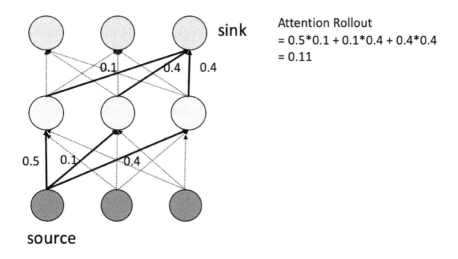

Attention Rollout
$= 0.5*0.1 + 0.1*0.4 + 0.4*0.4$
$= 0.11$

Figure 7.5 Example of attention rollout mechanism between two nodes.

7.5.2 Attention Rollout

Once the DAG has been constructed from the Transformer model, the attention rollout mechanism quantifies the impact of attention to input tokens by computing the proportion of the information that can propagate through each link recursively to all of the input tokens. The attention rollout mechanism for a given layer i and all the attention weights in the previous layers computes attention to input tokens by recursively multiplying the attention weights matrices, starting from the input layer up to layer i and can be written as:

$$\tilde{A}(l_i) = \begin{cases} A(l_i)\tilde{A}(l_{i-1}) \ if \ i > j \\ A(l_i) \ if \ i = j \end{cases} \tag{7.26}$$

Fig. 7.5 shows attention rollout computation between an input token (source) and the output using the recursive multiplication of weights.

7.5.3 Attention Flow

A flow network is a directed graph with a "capacity" affiliated with every edge in a graph as per the graph theory. A maximum flow algorithm finds a flow with the maximum possible value between any given source and the sink given the flow network. In this technique, when the graph network mapping to the flow network of the transformers happens, with

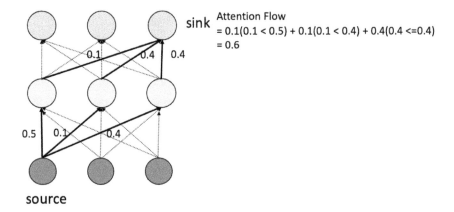

Figure 7.6 Example of attention flow mechanism between two nodes.

the edges as the attention weights; the maximum flow algorithm can compute the maximum attention flow from any node of any layer to the input nodes(tokens).

Fig. 7.6 shows attention flow computation between an input token (source) and the output using the capacity (minimum weights).

The research shows that the two methods give complementary viewpoints, and compared to draw attention, both yield higher correlations with importance scores of input tokens using gradient-based and the ablation method.

7.6 CASE STUDY: TEXT CLASSIFICATION WITH EXPLAIN-ABILITY

7.6.1 Goal

In the healthcare domain, the transparency and interpretability of machine learning models are imperative for their adoption. This section will go through a use case using explainability techniques on state-of-the-art transformers to illustrate the usefulness of explainability techniques. The goal is to compare a simple traditional interpretable machine learning algorithm like logistic regression to the state-of-the-art BERT and Clinical BERT to see the performance gain and application of post-hoc techniques to explain the black-box models.

7.6.2 Data, Tools, and Libraries

Healthcare data usage has lots of restrictions and constraints due to HIPAA privacy regulations. However, `MTSamples.com` collects transcribed medical reports with sample transcription reports for forty specialties and work types to overcome these limitations and help transcriptions be more accessible. Kaggle's medical transcriptions dataset and the classification task are based on this dataset. The medical-nlp project further transforms the data into four labels or specialities (Surgery, Medical Records, Internal Medicine, and Other) using the medical taxonomy. We will use the transformed dataset and classification task for the case study.

We use pandas for basic text processing and exploratory data analysis. Sklearn library is used for traditional NLP pipeline and logistic regression model. We employ the Huggingface implementation of BERT and Bio_ClinicalBERT as our transformer implementations. Captum library is used to perform input attribution via the saliency method. For understanding and visualizing how the BERT layers and heads work we use the exBERT visualization package.

7.6.3 Experiments, Results, and Analysis

7.6.3.1 Exploratory data analysis

We perform some basic EDA to understand the data from distribution and corpus wise.

Figs. 7.7 to 7.10 shows interesting outputs from word cloud, document length distribution, top words, and class distribution. The word cloud (Fig. 7.7) and top frequency words plot (Fig. 7.9) clearly show bias towards terms such as *diagnoses, injury, chronic,* etc., which form the base language for most medical transcriptions and records. The document length distribution plot (Fig. 7.8) shows a long-tailed distribution with greater than 25% documents falling beyond the maximum sequence length for BERT. Finally, the conversion of 40 classes to 4 categories (Fig. 7.10) shows almost a balanced distribution and becomes helpful in classifier comparisons as the impact of imbalance is now minimized.

7.6.3.2 Experiments

We use the 90–10% split of training and testing and further create a validation set of 10% for hyperparameter and learning curves. We will first compare the base BERT with BIO_ClinicalBERT both fine-tuned on the training data and evaluated on test data.

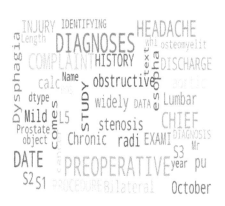

Figure 7.7 Word cloud.

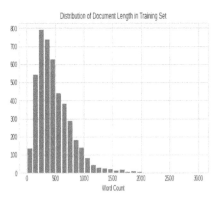

Figure 7.8 Document length distribution.

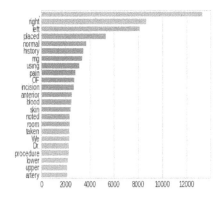

Figure 7.9 Top words.

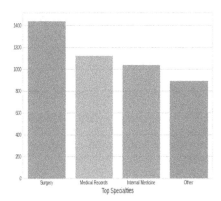

Figure 7.10 Class distribution.

Tables 7.1 and 7.2 show that the BIO_ClinicalBERT with its pretraining on a large corpus of medical records has a slight advantage over the base BERT for classification.

7.6.3.3 Error analysis and explainability

Next, we will try to perform error analysis using explainable techniques to get more insights. The error analysis on the 500 sized test data shows

1. The BIO_ClinincalBERT performs better than the base model on 51 instances.

TABLE 7.1 Fine-tuned base BERT on Test Data

Class/Metrics	Precision	Recall	F1
Surgery	0.792	0.768	0.779
Medical Records	0.612	0.510	0.556
Internal Medicine	0.588	0.642	0.614
Other	0.587	0.670	0.626
accuracy			0.67
macro avg	0.645	0.648	0.644
weighted avg	0.673	0.670	0.670

TABLE 7.2 Fine-tuned Bio_Clinical BERT on Test Data

Class/Metrics	Precision	Recall	F1
Surgery	0.796	0.788	0.792
Medical Records	0.605	0.676	0.639
Internal Medicine	0.690	0.633	0.660
Other	0.589	0.582	0.586
accuracy			0.694
macro avg	0.670	0.670	0.669
weighted avg	0.696	0.694	0.694

2. The BIO_ClinincalBERT performs worse than the base model on 39 instances.

3. Both models miss on 114 instances.

4. Both models predict correctly on 296 instances.

```
def do_attribution(text, tokenizer, model, device,
    class_idx=0):
        inputs = tokenizer(text, return_tensors='pt',
            truncation=True, max_length=512)
        tokens =
            tokenizer.convert_ids_to_tokens(inputs['input_ids'].
                squeeze().tolist())
        logits = model(inputs['input_ids'].to(device)).logits
        probas = logits.softmax(-1).squeeze(0)

        model.zero_grad()
```

```
attr_raw = sal.attribute(embed_text(text, tokenizer,
    model, device),
                        additional_forward_args=(model,
                            class_idx),
                        abs=False)
attr_sum = attr_raw.sum(-1).squeeze(0)
attr_norm = attr_sum / torch.norm(attr_sum)
record = viz.VisualizationDataRecord(
    attr_norm,
    pred_prob=probas.max(),
    pred_class=classes[probas.argmax().item()],
    true_class=classes[class_idx], # change if you
        aren't passing the true (labeled) class index
    attr_class=classes[class_idx],
    attr_score=attr_norm.sum(),
    raw_input=tokens,
    convergence_score=None
)
return record
```

Listing 7.1 Saliency explanations

The Listing 7.1 shows the saliency-based implementation for visualization of input attributions.

In Figs. 7.11 and 7.12, we can see the difference in explanations for each of the models on the same record—we are attributing each token for the correct class **Surgery**. The base BERT model gives an incorrect prediction for this example. At a glance, we can see that the most significant negative attributions for the base BERT model come from kidney-related terms (kidney, renal, etc.), possibly indicating that the base BERT model associates such terms with a class other than **Surgery**. The domain-adapted Bio_Clinical BERT has positive and negative attributions for *bladder* as well as positive explanations for the descriptions of the procedures (e.g., "placed in dorsal lithotomy position" and "prepped and draped in the standard fashion"). This may give us some insight into how the additional pre-training is helping Bio_Clinical BERT achieve a relatively better performance.

In the example as shown in Figs. 7.14 and 7.12, we can see that the BIO_ClinicalBERT correctly predicts **Medical Records** while the base BERT predicts **Internal Medicine**. Highlights on context words such as "past medical history", "present", "admitted", etc. in the BIO_ClinicalBERT saliency visualization further highlights reasons why *Medical Records* is the predicted class for the BIO_ClinicalBERT.

We can also visualize the self-attention weights to gain another view

Base Attributions

True Label	Predicted Label	Attribution Label	Attribution Score	Word Importance
Surgery	Internal Medicine (0.50)	Surgery	13.74	[CLS] pre ##oper ##native dia ##gno ##ses : . 1 . right renal mass . . . 2 . hem ##at ##furia . . post ##oper ##native dia ##gno ##ses : . 1 . right renal mass . . . 2 . right ur ##eter ##ope ##al ##fvic junction obstruction . . procedures performed : . 1 . cy ##sto ##ure ##th ##ros ##co ##py . . 2 . right retro ##grade p ##ye ##llogram . . 3 . right ur ##eter ##al p ##ye ##llos ##to ##py . . 4 . right renal bio ##psy . . 5 . right double - i 4 . 5 x 26 mm ur ##eter ##al ste ##nt placement . . an ##resthesia : . se ##ffdation : . specimen : . urine for cy ##ffology and culture sensitivity . right renal pe ##fivis urine for cy ##ntology . and right upper pole bio ##pps ##fies . . indication : . the patient is a 74 - year - old male who was initially seen in the office with hem ##fat ##furia . he was then brought to the hospital for other medical problems and found to still have hem ##fat ##furia . he has a cat scan with abnormal appearing right kidney and it was felt that he will benefit from cy ##sto ##scope evaluation . . procedure : . after consent was obtained , the patient was brought to the operating room and placed in the su ##fpine position . he was given iv se ##ffdation and placed in dorsal lit ##fhot ##fomy position . he was then prep ##fpod and draped in the standard fashion . a # 21 french cy ##sto ##scope was then passed through his ur ##feter on which patient was noted to have a h ##fyp ##fos ##fpad ##fias and passed through across the ends of the bladder . the patient was noted to have mildly enlarged prostate . however , it was non - ob ##fst ##fru ##fcting . . upon visual ##fization of the bladder , the patient was noted to have some tube ##frc ##fulation to the bladder . there were no masses or any other abnormalities noted other than the tube ##frc ##fulation . attention was then turned to the right ur ##feter ##al or ##fifice and an open - end of the cat ##fhet ##fer was then passed into the right ur ##feter ##al or ##fifice . a retro ##fgrade p ##fye ##fllogram was performed . upon visual ##fization , there was no visual ##fization of the upper collecting system on the right side . at this point , a guide ##fwire was then passed through the open - end of the ur ##feter ##al cat ##fhet ##fer and the cat ##fhet ##fer was removed . the bladder was drained and the cy ##fsto ##fscope was removed . the rigid ur ##feter ##fos ##fcope was then passed into the bladder and into the right ur ##feter ##al or ##fifice with the assistance of a second glide ##fwire . the ur ##feter ##fos ##fcope was [SEP]

Figure 7.11 Saliency-based visualization for a correct prediction for the base BERT.

Domain Adapted Attributions

True Label	Predicted Label	Attribution Label	Attribution Score	Word Importance
Surgery	Surgery (0.73)	Surgery	17.18	[CLS] pre ##oper ##ative di ##ag ##nose ##s : . 1 . right re ##nal mass . . 2 . hem ##at ##uria . . post ##oper ##ative di ##ag ##nose ##s : . 1 . right re ##nal mass . . 2 . right u ##fret ##ero ##poi ##vic junction o ##bs ##truction . . procedures performed . . 1 . c ##ys ##fiour ##eth ##ros ##copy . . 2 . right re ##tro ##grade p ##lye ##los ##copy . . 4 . right re ##fnal bio ##psy . . 5 . right double - j 4 . 5 x 26 mm u ##fret ##eral s ##fitpn ##t placement . . an ##fiest ##fihesia . . se ##fidation . . specimen : . urine for c ##fyt ##ology and culture sensitivity . right re ##fnal p ##fet ##fivis urine for c ##fyt ##ology . and right upper pole bio ##ps ##fies . . indication : . the patient is a 74 - year - old male who was initially seen in the office with hem ##fat ##furia . he was then brought to the hospital for other medical problems and found to still have hem ##fat ##furia . he has a cat scan with abnormal appearing right kidney and it was felt that he will benefit from c ##fys ##fos ##cope evauation . . procedure : . after consent was obtained . the patient was brought to the operating room and placed in the su ##fipine position . he was given i ##fv se ##fidation and placed in dorsal lit ##fhot ##fromy position . he was then pre ##fipped and draped in the standard fashion . a # 21 f ##french c ##fys ##fios ##cope was then passed through his u ##fret ##fier on which patient was noted to have a h ##fy ##fipo ##fisp ##fiadia ##fis and passed through across the ends of the bladder . the patient was noted to have mildly enlarged pro ##fistate : however . it was non - o ##fibs ##fitruct ##fling . . upon visual ##fiization of the bladder . the patient was noted to have some tube ##frc ##fiulation to the bladder . there were no masses or any other abnormal ##fities noted other than the tube ##frc ##fiulation . attention was then turned to the right u ##fret ##feral or ##fifilice and an open - end of the cat ##fhe ##fiter was then passed into the right u ##fret ##feral or ##fifilice . a re ##fitro ##figrade p ##lye ##filog ##fitram was performed . upon visual ##fiization , there was no visual ##fiization of the upper collecting system on the right side . at this point . a guide ##fiwire was then passed through the open - end of the u ##fret ##feral cat ##fhe ##fiter and the cat ##fhe ##fiter was removed . the bladder was drained and the c ##fys ##fios ##cope was removed . the rigid u ##fret ##fero ##fiscope was then passed into the bladder [SEP]

Figure 7.12 Saliency-based visualization for a correct prediction for the domain adapted BIO_ClinicalBERT.

Base Attributions

True Label	Predicted Label	Attribution Label	Attribution Score	Word Importance
Medical Records	Internal Medicine (0.48)	Medical Records	15.04	[CLS] admitting diagnosis : . ce ##re ##bro ##vas ##cular accident (cv ##a) . , history of present illness : . the patient is a 56 - year - old gentleman with a significant past medical history for nas ##rop ##thar ##hyn ##ge ##al cancer status post radiation therapy to his ph ##ary ##nx and neck in 1991 who presents to the emergency room after awakening at 2 : 30 a . m . this morning with trouble swallowing , trouble breathing , and left - sided numb ##ness and weakness . this occurred at 2 : 30 a . m . he s wife said that he had trouble speaking as well , but gradually the symptoms resolved but he was still complaining of a headache and at that point , he was brought to the emergency room . he arrived at the emergency room here via private ambulance at 6 : 30 a . m . in the morning . upon initial evaluation . he did have some left - sided weakness and was complaining of a headache . he underwent work ##up including a ct , which was negative and his symptoms slowly began to resolve . he was initially admitted . placed on pl ##avi ##x and as ##pi ##rin . however a few hours later . his symptoms returned and he had increasing weakness of his left arm and left leg as well as st ##lur ##rred speech . repeat ct scan again done reportedly was negative and he was subsequently the ##par ##ini ##zed and admitted . he also underwent an echo , car ##ot ##id ultrasound , and lab work in the emergency room . wife is at the bedside and denies he had any other symptoms previous to this . he denied any chest pain or pal ##pit ##ations . she does report that he is on a z - pak . got a co ##ntr ##son ##re shot and some deco ##nge ##stan ##rt from dr . abc on saturday because of congestion and that had gotten better . all ##er ##rgies : . he has no known drug all ##er ##rgies . current medications : . 1 . multi ##vita ##min . . 2 . ib ##up ##ro ##ffen p . r . n . , past medical history : . 1 . nas ##rop ##thar ##hyn ##nge ##al cancer . occurred in 1991 . status post x ##rt of the nas ##rop ##thar ##hyn ##nge ##al area and his neck because of spread to the l ##nym ##rph nodes . . 2 . lu ##mba ##rr disk disease . . 3 . status post disk ##ect ##rtomy . . 4 . chronic neck pain secondary to x ##rrt . . 5 . history of tha ##lass ##emia . . 6 . chronic di ##zzziness since his x ##rrt in 1991 . . past surgical history : . lu ##mba ##rr disk ##ect ##rtomy , which is approximately 7 to 8 years ago . otherwise negative . [SEP]

Figure 7.13 Saliency-based visualization for an incorrect prediction for the base BERT.

Domain Adapted Attributions

True Label	Predicted Label	Attribution Label	Attribution Score
Medical Records	Medical Records (0.67)	Medical Records	15.44

Word importance

[CLS] admitting diagnosis : . c ##ere ##bro ##vas #cular accident (c ##va) . . history of present illness : . the patient is a 56 - year - old gentleman with a significant past medical history for na ##so ##pha ##ryn ##ge ##al cancer status post radiation therapy to his p ##har ##ynx and neck in 1991 who presents to the emergency room after awake ##ning at 2 : 30 a . m . this morning with trouble swallowing , trouble breathing , and left - sided numb ##ness and weakness . this occurred at 2 : 30 a . m . his wife said that he had trouble speaking as well , but gradually the symptoms resolved but he was still complaining of a headache and at that point , he was brought to the emergency room . he arrived at the emergency room here via private ambulance at 6 : 30 a . m . in the morning . upon initial evaluation , he did have some left - sided weakness and was complaining of a headache . he underwent work ##up including a c ##ft , which was negative and his symptoms slowly began to resolve . he was initially admitted , placed on p ##flav ##ix and as ##pi ##rin . however a few hours later , his symptoms returned and he had increasing weakness of his left arm and left leg as well as s ##lu ##rred speech . repeat c ##ft scan again done reportedly was negative and he was subsequently he ##par ##in ##zed and admitted . he also underwent an echo , car ##ot ##id ultra ##sound , and lab work in the emergency room . wife is at the bedside and denies he had any other symptoms previous to this . he denied any chest pain or p ##al ##pit ##ations . she does report that he is on a z - p ##ak , got a co ##ft ##ison ##e shot , and some de ##icon ##ges ##tant from d ##r . a ##fb ##fc on sat ##ur ##day because of congestion and that had gotten better . . all ##er ##gies . . he has no known drug all ##er ##gies . . current medications : . 1 . multi #vi ##tam ##in . . 2 . i ##bu ##p ##ro ##ffen p . r . n . . past medical history : . 1 . na ##so ##pha ##ryn ##ge ##al cancer . occurred in 1991 . status post x ##rt of the na ##so ##pha ##ryn ##ge ##al area and his neck because of spread to the l #lymph nodes . . 2 . l #lumba ##r disk disease . . 3 . status post disk ##ec ##tom ##y . . 4 . chronic neck pain secondary to x ##rt . . 5 . history of th ##rala ## isse ##mia . . 6 . chronic di ##izzi ##ness since his x ##rt in 1991 . . past surgical history : . l #lumba ##r disk [SEP]

Figure 7.14 Saliency-based visualization for an incorrect prediction for the domain adapted BIO_ClinincalBERT.

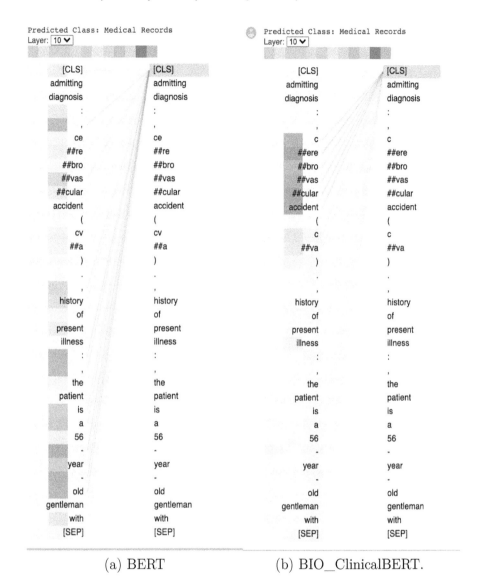

(a) BERT (b) BIO_ClinicalBERT.

Figure 7.15 Sample example visualized at a layer by two different architectures: (a) BERT and (b) BIO_ClinicalBERT.

into the representations learned by the BERT models. The BertViz library provides an interactive front-end to explore these token weights. Unfortunately, BertViz does not scale well to long sequences, so we truncated the inputs to illustrate local attention effects for BERT and BIO_ClinicalBERT to highlight the relationship between the token weights and class token at a layer These are shown in Fig. 7.15.

Bibliography

[1] S. ABNAR AND W. ZUIDEMA, *Quantifying attention flow in transformers*, arXiv preprint arXiv:2005.00928, (2020).

[2] G. ALAIN AND Y. BENGIO, *Understanding intermediate layers using linear classifier probes*, arXiv preprint arXiv:1610.01644, (2016).

[3] D. ALVAREZ-MELIS AND T. S. JAAKKOLA, *Towards robust interpretability with self-explaining neural networks*, arXiv preprint arXiv:1806.07538, (2018).

[4] S. AMERSHI, M. CHICKERING, S. M. DRUCKER, B. LEE, P. SIMARD, AND J. SUH, *Modeltracker: Redesigning performance analysis tools for machine learning*, in Proceedings of the 33rd Annual ACM Conference on Human Factors in Computing Systems, 2015, pp. 337–346.

[5] D. AMODEI, C. OLAH, J. STEINHARDT, P. CHRISTIANO, J. SCHULMAN, AND D. MANÉ, *Concrete problems in ai safety*, arXiv preprint arXiv:1606.06565, (2016).

[6] A. ANDONI, P. INDYK, T. LAARHOVEN, I. P. RAZENSHTEYN, AND L. SCHMIDT, *Practical and optimal lsh for angular distance*, in NIPS, 2015.

[7] D. ARACI, *Finbert: Financial sentiment analysis with pre-trained language models*, ArXiv, abs/1908.10063 (2019).

[8] E. ARKHANGELSKAIA AND S. DUTTA, *Whatcha lookin'at? deeplifting bert's attention in question answering*, arXiv preprint arXiv:1910.06431, (2019).

[9] M. ARTETXE, S. RUDER, AND D. YOGATAMA, *On the cross-lingual transferability of monolingual representations*, in Proceedings of the 58th Annual Meeting of the Association for

Computational Linguistics, Online, July 2020, Association for Computational Linguistics, pp. 4623–4637.

[10] M. ARTETXE, S. RUDER, AND D. YOGATAMA, *On the cross-lingual transferability of monolingual representations*, in Proceedings of the 58th Annual Meeting of the Association for Computational Linguistics, ACL 2020, Online, July 5-10, 2020, D. Jurafsky, J. Chai, N. Schluter, and J. R. Tetreault, eds., Association for Computational Linguistics, 2020, pp. 4623–4637.

[11] M. ARTETXE AND H. SCHWENK, *Massively multilingual sentence embeddings for zero-shot cross-lingual transfer and beyond*, Trans. Assoc. Comput. Linguistics, 7 (2019), pp. 597–610.

[12] P. AZUNRE, *Transfer Learning for Natural Language Processing*, Manning, 2021.

[13] L. J. BA, J. R. KIROS, AND G. E. HINTON, *Layer normalization*, CoRR, abs/1607.06450 (2016).

[14] S. BACH, A. BINDER, G. MONTAVON, F. KLAUSCHEN, K.-R. MÜLLER, AND W. SAMEK, *On pixel-wise explanations for non-linear classifier decisions by layer-wise relevance propagation*, PloS one, 10 (2015), p. e0130140.

[15] D. BAEHRENS, T. SCHROETER, S. HARMELING, M. KAWANABE, K. HANSEN, AND K.-R. MÜLLER, *How to explain individual classification decisions*, The Journal of Machine Learning Research, 11 (2010), pp. 1803–1831.

[16] A. BAEVSKI, H. ZHOU, A. RAHMAN MOHAMED, AND M. AULI, *wav2vec 2.0: A framework for self-supervised learning of speech representations*, ArXiv, abs/2006.11477 (2020).

[17] D. BAHDANAU, K. CHO, AND Y. BENGIO, *Neural machine translation by jointly learning to align and translate*, CoRR, abs/1409.0473 (2014).

[18] A. BAPNA, N. ARIVAZHAGAN, AND O. FIRAT, *Controlling computation versus quality for neural sequence models*, ArXiv, abs/2002.07106 (2020).

[19] A. BAPNA, M. CHEN, O. FIRAT, Y. CAO, AND Y. WU, *Training deeper neural machine translation models with transparent attention*, in EMNLP, 2018.

[20] S. BAROCAS AND D. BOYD, *Engaging the ethics of data science in practice*, Communications of the ACM, 60 (2017), pp. 23–25.

[21] O. BASTANI, C. KIM, AND H. BASTANI, *Interpreting black-box models via model extraction*, arXiv preprint arXiv:1705.08504, (2017).

[22] K. BAUM, M. A. KÖHL, AND E. SCHMIDT, *Two challenges for ci trustworthiness and how to address them*, in Proceedings of the 1st Workshop on Explainable Computational Intelligence (XCI 2017), 2017.

[23] Y. BELINKOV, *Probing classifiers: Promises, shortcomings, and alternatives*, arXiv preprint arXiv:2102.12452, (2021).

[24] I. BELTAGY, K. LO, AND A. COHAN, *Scibert: A pretrained language model for scientific text*, in EMNLP, 2019.

[25] I. BELTAGY, M. E. PETERS, AND A. COHAN, *Longformer: The long-document transformer*, ArXiv, abs/2004.05150 (2020).

[26] E. M. BENDER, D. HOVY, AND A. SCHOFIELD, *Integrating ethics into the nlp curriculum*, in Proceedings of the 58th Annual Meeting of the Association for Computational Linguistics: Tutorial Abstracts, 2020, pp. 6–9.

[27] Y. BENGIO, P. LAMBLIN, D. POPOVICI, AND H. LAROCHELLE, *Greedy layer-wise training of deep networks*, in Proceedings of the 19th International Conference on Neural Information Processing Systems, NIPS'06, MIT Press, 2006, pp. 153–160.

[28] Y. BENGIO AND Y. LECUN, *Scaling learning algorithms towards AI*, MIT Press, 2007.

[29] G. BERTASIUS, H. WANG, AND L. TORRESANI, *Is space-time attention all you need for video understanding?*, in ICML, 2021.

[30] A. BEUTEL, J. CHEN, Z. ZHAO, AND E. H. CHI, *Data decisions and theoretical implications when adversarially learning fair representations*, arXiv preprint arXiv:1707.00075, (2017).

[31] S. R. BOWMAN, L. VILNIS, O. VINYALS, A. DAI, R. JOZE-FOWICZ, AND S. BENGIO, *Generating sentences from a continuous space*, in Proceedings of The 20th SIGNLL Conference on Computational Natural Language Learning, Berlin, Germany, August 2016, Association for Computational Linguistics, pp. 10–21.

[32] T. B. BROWN, B. MANN, N. RYDER, M. SUBBIAH, J. KAPLAN, P. DHARIWAL, A. NEELAKANTAN, P. SHYAM, G. SASTRY, A. ASKELL, S. AGARWAL, A. HERBERT-VOSS, G. KRUEGER, T. HENIGHAN, R. CHILD, A. RAMESH, D. M. ZIEGLER, J. WU, C. WINTER, C. HESSE, M. CHEN, E. SIGLER, M. LITWIN, S. GRAY, B. CHESS, J. CLARK, C. BERNER, S. MCCANDLISH, A. RADFORD, I. SUTSKEVER, AND D. AMODEI, *Language models are few-shot learners*, ArXiv, abs/2005.14165 (2020).

[33] J. CAGE, *Python Transformers By Huggingface Hands On: 101 practical implementation hands-on of ALBERT/ViT/BigBird and other latest models with huggingface transformers*, 2021.

[34] T. CALDERS, F. KAMIRAN, AND M. PECHENIZKIY, *Building classifiers with independency constraints*, in 2009 IEEE International Conference on Data Mining Workshops, IEEE, 2009, pp. 13–18.

[35] R. A. CALIXN, *Deep Learning Algorithms: Transformers, gans, encoders, rnns, cnns, and more*, 2020.

[36] F. P. CALMON, D. WEI, B. VINZAMURI, K. N. RAMAMURTHY, AND K. R. VARSHNEY, *Optimized pre-processing for discrimination prevention*, in Proceedings of the 31st International Conference on Neural Information Processing Systems, 2017, pp. 3995–4004.

[37] O.-M. CAMBURU, T. ROCKTÄSCHEL, T. LUKASIEWICZ, AND P. BLUNSOM, *e-snli: Natural language inference with natural language explanations*, arXiv preprint arXiv:1812.01193, (2018).

[38] D. M. CER, M. T. DIAB, E. AGIRRE, I. LOPEZ-GAZPIO, AND L. SPECIA, *Semeval-2017 task 1: Semantic textual similarity multilingual and crosslingual focused evaluation*, in SemEval@ACL, 2017.

[39] M. CHARIKAR, *Similarity estimation techniques from rounding algorithms*, in STOC '02, 2002.

[40] C. CHEN, O. LI, C. TAO, A. J. BARNETT, J. SU, AND C. RUDIN, *This looks like that: deep learning for interpretable image recognition*, arXiv preprint arXiv:1806.10574, (2018).

[41] L. CHEN, K. LU, A. RAJESWARAN, K. LEE, A. GROVER, M. LASKIN, P. ABBEEL, A. SRINIVAS, AND I. MORDATCH, *Decision transformer: Reinforcement learning via sequence modeling*, ArXiv, abs/2106.01345 (2021).

[42] S. F. CHEN, D. BEEFERMAN, AND R. ROSENFELD, *Evaluation metrics for language models*, (1998).

[43] Z. CHEN, H. ZHANG, X. ZHANG, AND L. ZHAO, *Quora question pairs*, 2017.

[44] E. A. CHI, J. HEWITT, AND C. D. MANNING, *Finding universal grammatical relations in multilingual BERT*, in Proceedings of the 58th Annual Meeting of the Association for Computational Linguistics, ACL 2020, Online, July 5–10, 2020, D. Jurafsky, J. Chai, N. Schluter, and J. R. Tetreault, eds., Association for Computational Linguistics, 2020, pp. 5564–5577.

[45] Z. CHI, L. DONG, F. WEI, X. MAO, AND H. HUANG, *Can monolingual pretrained models help cross-lingual classification?*, in Proceedings of the 1st Conference of the Asia-Pacific Chapter of the Association for Computational Linguistics and the 10th International Joint Conference on Natural Language Processing, AACL/IJCNLP 2020, Suzhou, China, December 4–7, 2020, K. Wong, K. Knight, and H. Wu, eds., Association for Computational Linguistics, 2020, pp. 12–17.

[46] Z. CHI, L. DONG, F. WEI, W. WANG, X. MAO, AND H. HUANG, *Cross-lingual natural language generation via pretraining*, in The Thirty-Fourth AAAI Conference on Artificial Intelligence, AAAI 2020, The Thirty-Second Innovative Applications of Artificial Intelligence Conference, IAAI 2020, The Tenth AAAI Symposium on Educational Advances in Artificial Intelligence, EAAI 2020, New York, NY, USA, February 7–12, 2020, AAAI Press, 2020, pp. 7570–7577.

[47] Z. CHI, L. DONG, F. WEI, N. YANG, S. SINGHAL, W. WANG, X. SONG, X. MAO, H. HUANG, AND M. ZHOU, *Infoxlm: An information-theoretic framework for cross-lingual language model pre-training*, in Proceedings of the 2021 Conference of the North American Chapter of the Association for Computational Linguistics: Human Language Technologies, NAACL-HLT 2021, Online, June 6–11, 2021, K. Toutanova, A. Rumshisky, L. Zettlemoyer, D. Hakkani-Tür, I. Beltagy, S. Bethard, R. Cotterell, T. Chakraborty, and Y. Zhou, eds., Association for Computational Linguistics, 2021, pp. 3576–3588.

[48] Z. CHI, L. DONG, F. WEI, N. YANG, S. SINGHAL, W. WANG, X. SONG, X.-L. MAO, H. HUANG, AND M. ZHOU, *InfoXLM: An information-theoretic framework for cross-lingual language model pre-training*, in Proceedings of the 2021 Conference of the North American Chapter of the Association for Computational Linguistics: Human Language Technologies, Online, June 2021, Association for Computational Linguistics, pp. 3576–3588.

[49] M. CHIDAMBARAM, Y. YANG, D. M. CER, S. YUAN, Y.-H. SUNG, B. STROPE, AND R. KURZWEIL, *Learning cross-lingual sentence representations via a multi-task dual-encoder model*, in RepL4NLP@ACL, 2019.

[50] R. CHILD, S. GRAY, A. RADFORD, AND I. SUTSKEVER, *Generating long sequences with sparse transformers*, ArXiv, abs/1904.10509 (2019).

[51] K. CHO, B. VAN MERRIËNBOER, C. GULCEHRE, D. BAHDANAU, F. BOUGARES, H. SCHWENK, AND Y. BENGIO, *Learning phrase representations using RNN encoder–decoder for statistical machine translation*, in Proceedings of the 2014 Conference on Empirical Methods in Natural Language Processing (EMNLP), Doha, Qatar, October 2014, Association for Computational Linguistics, pp. 1724–1734.

[52] R. CHOENNI AND E. SHUTOVA, *What does it mean to be language-agnostic? probing multilingual sentence encoders for typological properties*, arXiv preprint arXiv:2009.12862, (2020).

[53] K. CHOROMANSKI, V. LIKHOSHERSTOV, D. DOHAN, X. SONG, A. GANE, T. SARLÓS, P. HAWKINS, J. DAVIS, A. MOHIUDDIN,

L. KAISER, D. BELANGER, L. J. COLWELL, AND A. WELLER, *Rethinking attention with performers*, ArXiv, abs/2009.14794 (2021).

[54] H. W. CHUNG, T. FEVRY, H. TSAI, M. JOHNSON, AND S. RUDER, *Rethinking embedding coupling in pre-trained language models*, in International Conference on Learning Representations, 2021.

[55] H. W. CHUNG, D. GARRETTE, K. C. TAN, AND J. RIESA, *Improving multilingual models with language-clustered vocabularies*, in Proceedings of the 2020 Conference on Empirical Methods in Natural Language Processing, EMNLP 2020, Online, November 16–20, 2020, B. Webber, T. Cohn, Y. He, and Y. Liu, eds., Association for Computational Linguistics, 2020, pp. 4536–4546.

[56] J. H. CLARK, E. CHOI, M. COLLINS, D. GARRETTE, T. KWIATKOWSKI, V. NIKOLAEV, AND J. PALOMAKI, *Tydi qa: A benchmark for information-seeking question answering in typologically diverse languages*, Transactions of the Association for Computational Linguistics, (2020).

[57] K. CLARK, U. KHANDELWAL, O. LEVY, AND C. D. MANNING, *What does bert look at? an analysis of bert's attention*, ArXiv, abs/1906.04341 (2019).

[58] K. CLARK, M.-T. LUONG, Q. V. LE, AND C. D. MANNING, *Electra: Pre-training text encoders as discriminators rather than generators*, ArXiv, abs/2003.10555 (2020).

[59] M. COECKELBERGH, *AI ethics*, MIT Press, 2020.

[60] R. COLLOBERT AND J. WESTON, *A unified architecture for natural language processing: Deep neural networks with multitask learning*, in Proceedings of the 25th International Conference on Machine Learning, ACM, 2008, pp. 160–167.

[61] A. CONNEAU, K. KHANDELWAL, N. GOYAL, V. CHAUDHARY, G. WENZEK, F. GUZMÁN, E. GRAVE, M. OTT, L. ZETTLEMOYER, AND V. STOYANOV, *Unsupervised cross-lingual representation learning at scale*, in Proceedings of the 58th Annual Meeting of the Association for Computational Linguistics, ACL 2020, Online, July 5–10, 2020, D. Jurafsky, J. Chai, N. Schluter, and J. R.

Tetreault, eds., Association for Computational Linguistics, 2020, pp. 8440–8451.

[62] A. CONNEAU, G. KRUSZEWSKI, G. LAMPLE, L. BARRAULT, AND M. BARONI, *What you can cram into a single vector: Probing sentence embeddings for linguistic properties*, arXiv preprint arXiv:1805.01070, (2018).

[63] A. CONNEAU AND G. LAMPLE, *Cross-lingual language model pretraining*, in Advances in Neural Information Processing Systems 32: Annual Conference on Neural Information Processing Systems 2019, NeurIPS 2019, 8–14 December 2019, Vancouver, BC, Canada, H. M. Wallach, H. Larochelle, A. Beygelzimer, F. d'Alché-Buc, E. B. Fox, and R. Garnett, eds., 2019, pp. 7057–7067.

[64] A. CONNEAU, R. RINOTT, G. LAMPLE, A. WILLIAMS, S. R. BOWMAN, H. SCHWENK, AND V. STOYANOV, *Xnli: Evaluating cross-lingual sentence representations*, in Proceedings of the 2018 Conference on Empirical Methods in Natural Language Processing, Association for Computational Linguistics, 2018.

[65] J.-B. CORDONNIER, A. LOUKAS, AND M. JAGGI, *Multi-head attention: Collaborate instead of concatenate*, ArXiv, abs/2006.16362 (2020).

[66] Z. DAI, G. LAI, Y. YANG, AND Q. V. LE, *Funnel-transformer: Filtering out sequential redundancy for efficient language processing*, ArXiv, abs/2006.03236 (2020).

[67] Z. DAI, Z. YANG, Y. YANG, J. CARBONELL, Q. V. LE, AND R. SALAKHUTDINOV, *Transformer-xl: Attentive language models beyond a fixed-length context*, in ACL, 2019.

[68] W. DE VRIES, A. VAN CRANENBURGH, AND M. NISSIM, *What's so special about bert's layers? A closer look at the NLP pipeline in monolingual and multilingual models*, in Proceedings of the 2020 Conference on Empirical Methods in Natural Language Processing: Findings, EMNLP 2020, Online Event, 16–20 November 2020, T. Cohn, Y. He, and Y. Liu, eds., vol. EMNLP 2020 of Findings of ACL, Association for Computational Linguistics, 2020, pp. 4339–4350.

[69] M. DEHGHANI, S. GOUWS, O. VINYALS, J. USZKOREIT, AND L. KAISER, *Universal transformers*, ArXiv, abs/1807.03819 (2019).

[70] J. DENG, W. DONG, R. SOCHER, L.-J. LI, K. LI, AND L. FEI-FEI, *ImageNet: A Large-Scale Hierarchical Image Database*, in CVPR09, 2009.

[71] J. DEVLIN, M.-W. CHANG, K. LEE, AND K. TOUTANOVA, *Bert: Pre-training of deep bidirectional transformers for language understanding*, in NAACL-HLT, 2019.

[72] J. DEVLIN, M.-W. CHANG, K. LEE, AND K. TOUTANOVA, *BERT: Pre-training of deep bidirectional transformers for language understanding*, in Proceedings of the 2019 Conference of the North American Chapter of the Association for Computational Linguistics: Human Language Technologies, Volume 1 (Long and Short Papers), Minneapolis, Minnesota, June 2019, Association for Computational Linguistics, pp. 4171–4186.

[73] Y. DING, Y. LIU, H. LUAN, AND M. SUN, *Visualizing and understanding neural machine translation*, in Proceedings of the 55th Annual Meeting of the Association for Computational Linguistics (Volume 1: Long Papers), 2017, pp. 1150–1159.

[74] S. DODDAPANENI, G. RAMESH, A. KUNCHUKUTTAN, P. KUMAR, AND M. M. KHAPRA, *A primer on pretrained multilingual language models*, CoRR, abs/2107.00676 (2021).

[75] W. B. DOLAN AND C. BROCKETT, *Automatically constructing a corpus of sentential paraphrases*, in IJCNLP, 2005.

[76] Y. DONG, F. LIAO, T. PANG, H. SU, J. ZHU, X. HU, AND J. LI, *Boosting adversarial attacks with momentum*, in Proceedings of the IEEE Conference on Computer Vision and Pattern Recognition, 2018, pp. 9185–9193.

[77] Y. DONG, H. SU, J. ZHU, AND B. ZHANG, *Improving interpretability of deep neural networks with semantic information*, in Proceedings of the IEEE Conference on Computer Vision and Pattern Recognition, 2017, pp. 4306–4314.

[78] A. DOSOVITSKIY, L. BEYER, A. KOLESNIKOV, D. WEISSENBORN, X. ZHAI, T. UNTERTHINER, M. DEHGHANI, M. MINDERER, G. HEIGOLD, S. GELLY, J. USZKOREIT, AND N. HOULSBY, *An image is worth 16x16 words: Transformers for image recognition at scale*, ArXiv, abs/2010.11929 (2021).

[79] P. DUFTER AND H. SCHÜTZE, *Identifying elements essential for BERT's multilinguality*, in Proceedings of the 2020 Conference on Empirical Methods in Natural Language Processing (EMNLP), Online, November 2020, Association for Computational Linguistics, pp. 4423–4437.

[80] V. P. DWIVEDI AND X. BRESSON, *A generalization of transformer networks to graphs*, ArXiv, abs/2012.09699 (2020).

[81] V. P. DWIVEDI, C. K. JOSHI, T. LAURENT, Y. BENGIO, AND X. BRESSON, *Benchmarking graph neural networks*, ArXiv, abs/2003.00982 (2020).

[82] C. DWORK, N. IMMORLICA, A. T. KALAI, AND M. LEISERSON, *Decoupled classifiers for group-fair and efficient machine learning*, in Conference on Fairness, Accountability and Transparency, PMLR, 2018, pp. 119–133.

[83] C. ECKART AND G. M. YOUNG, *The approximation of one matrix by another of lower rank*, Psychometrika, 1 (1936), pp. 211–218.

[84] P. ERDÖS, *On random graphs, i*, 1959.

[85] D. ERHAN, Y. BENGIO, A. COURVILLE, AND P. VINCENT, *Visualizing higher-layer features of a deep network*, University of Montreal, 1341 (2009), p. 1.

[86] K. EYKHOLT, I. EVTIMOV, E. FERNANDES, B. LI, A. RAHMATI, C. XIAO, A. PRAKASH, T. KOHNO, AND D. SONG, *Robust physical-world attacks on deep learning visual classification*, in Proceedings of the IEEE Conference on Computer Vision and Pattern Recognition, 2018, pp. 1625–1634.

[87] W. FEDUS, B. ZOPH, AND N. SHAZEER, *Switch transformers: Scaling to trillion parameter models with simple and efficient sparsity*, arXiv preprint arXiv:2101.03961, (2021).

[88] F. FENG, Y. YANG, D. CER, N. ARIVAZHAGAN, AND W. WANG, *Language-agnostic BERT sentence embedding*, CoRR, abs/2007.01852 (2020).

[89] R. C. FONG AND A. VEDALDI, *Interpretable explanations of black boxes by meaningful perturbation*, in Proceedings of the IEEE International Conference on Computer Vision, 2017, pp. 3429–3437.

[90] F. B. FUCHS, O. GROTH, A. R. KOSIOREK, A. BEWLEY, M. WULFMEIER, A. VEDALDI, AND I. POSNER, *Neural stethoscopes: Unifying analytic, auxiliary and adversarial network probing.*, (2018).

[91] K. FUKUSHIMA, *Neural network model for a mechanism of pattern recognition unaffected by shift in position—Neocognitron*, Trans. IECE, J62-A(10) (1979), pp. 658–665.

[92] P. GAGE, *A new algorithm for data compression*, The C Users Journal archive, 12 (1994), pp. 23–38.

[93] E. A. GAROFOLO, JOHN S., *Timit acoustic-phonetic continuous speech corpus*, 1993.

[94] A. N. GOMEZ, M. REN, R. URTASUN, AND R. B. GROSSE, *The reversible residual network: Backpropagation without storing activations*, in NIPS, 2017.

[95] I. J. GOODFELLOW, J. SHLENS, AND C. SZEGEDY, *Explaining and harnessing adversarial examples*, arXiv preprint arXiv:1412.6572, (2014).

[96] P. GORDALIZA, E. DEL BARRIO, G. FABRICE, AND J.-M. LOUBES, *Obtaining fairness using optimal transport theory*, in International Conference on Machine Learning, PMLR, 2019, pp. 2357–2365.

[97] A. GRAVES, *Generating sequences with recurrent neural networks.*, CoRR, abs/1308.0850 (2013).

[98] A. GRAVES, G. WAYNE, AND I. DANIHELKA, *Neural turing machines*, CoRR, abs/1410.5401 (2014).

[99] R. M. GRAY AND D. L. NEUHOFF, *Quantization*, IEEE Trans. Inf. Theory, 44 (1998), pp. 2325–2383.

[100] S. GRAY, A. RADFORD, AND D. P. KINGMA, *GPU kernels for block-sparse weights*, 2017.

[101] M. GROOTENDORST, *Bertopic: Leveraging bert and c-tf-idf to create easily interpretable topics.*, 2020.

[102] M. GUO, Y. ZHANG, AND T. LIU, *Gaussian transformer: A lightweight approach for natural language inference*, in AAAI, 2019.

[103] Q. GUO, X. QIU, P. LIU, X. XUE, AND Z. ZHANG, *Multi-scale self-attention for text classification*, in AAAI, 2020.

[104] K. HE, H. FAN, Y. WU, S. XIE, AND R. GIRSHICK, *Momentum contrast for unsupervised visual representation learning*, 2020.

[105] K. HE, X. ZHANG, S. REN, AND J. SUN, *Deep residual learning for image recognition*, 2016 IEEE Conference on Computer Vision and Pattern Recognition (CVPR), (2016), pp. 770–778.

[106] R. HE, W. S. LEE, H. T. NG, AND D. DAHLMEIER, *Effective attention modeling for aspect-level sentiment classification*, in Proceedings of the 27th International Conference on Computational Linguistics, 2018, pp. 1121–1131.

[107] R. HE, A. RAVULA, B. KANAGAL, AND J. AINSLIE, *Realformer: Transformer likes residual attention*, in FINDINGS, 2021.

[108] D. O. HEBB, *The organization of behavior: A neuropsychological theory*, Wiley, 1949.

[109] L. A. HENDRICKS, Z. AKATA, M. ROHRBACH, J. DONAHUE, B. SCHIELE, AND T. DARRELL, *Generating visual explanations*, in European conference on computer vision, Springer, 2016, pp. 3–19.

[110] J. HEWITT AND P. LIANG, *Designing and interpreting probes with control tasks*, arXiv preprint arXiv:1909.03368, (2019).

[111] M. HIND, D. WEI, M. CAMPBELL, N. C. CODELLA, A. DHURANDHAR, A. MOJSILOVIĆ, K. NATESAN RAMAMURTHY, AND K. R. VARSHNEY, *Ted: Teaching ai to explain its decisions*, in Proceedings of the 2019 AAAI/ACM Conference on AI, Ethics, and Society, 2019, pp. 123–129.

[112] G. HINTON, O. VINYALS, AND J. DEAN, *Distilling the knowledge in a neural network*, arXiv preprint arXiv:1503.02531, (2015).

[113] G. E. HINTON, S. OSINDERO, AND Y.-W. TEH, *A fast learning algorithm for deep belief nets*, Neural Comput., 18 (2006), pp. 1527–1554.

[114] J. HO, N. KALCHBRENNER, D. WEISSENBORN, AND T. SALIMANS, *Axial attention in multidimensional transformers*, ArXiv, abs/1912.12180 (2019).

[115] S. HOCHREITER, *The vanishing gradient problem during learning recurrent neural nets and problem solutions*, International Journal of Uncertainty, Fuzziness and Knowledge-Based Systems, 6 (1998), pp. 107–116.

[116] S. HOCHREITER AND J. SCHMIDHUBER, *Long short-term memory*, Neural Comput., 9 (1997), pp. 1735–1780.

[117] J. J. HOPFIELD, *Neural networks and physical systems with emergent collective computational abilities*, Proceedings of the National Academy of Sciences of the United States of America, 79 (1982), pp. 2554–2558.

[118] B.-J. HOU AND Z.-H. ZHOU, *Learning with interpretable structure from rnn*, arXiv preprint arXiv:1810.10708, (2018).

[119] J. HOWARD AND S. RUDER, *Universal language model fine-tuning for text classification*, in ACL, 2018.

[120] W.-N. HSU, B. BOLTE, Y.-H. H. TSAI, K. LAKHOTIA, R. SALAKHUTDINOV, AND A. MOHAMED, *Hubert: Self-supervised speech representation learning by masked prediction of hidden units*, ArXiv, abs/2106.07447 (2021).

[121] J. HU, M. JOHNSON, O. FIRAT, A. SIDDHANT, AND G. NEUBIG, *Explicit alignment objectives for multilingual bidirectional encoders*, 2021.

[122] J. HU, S. RUDER, A. SIDDHANT, G. NEUBIG, O. FIRAT, AND M. JOHNSON, *XTREME: A massively multilingual multi-task benchmark for evaluating cross-lingual generalisation*, in Proceedings of the 37th International Conference on Machine Learning,

ICML 2020, 13–18 July 2020, Virtual Event, vol. 119 of Proceedings of Machine Learning Research, PMLR, 2020, pp. 4411–4421.

[123] R. HU AND A. SINGH, *Transformer is all you need: Multimodal multitask learning with a unified transformer*, ArXiv, abs/2102.10772 (2021).

[124] C.-Z. A. HUANG, A. VASWANI, J. USZKOREIT, N. M. SHAZEER, C. HAWTHORNE, A. M. DAI, M. HOFFMAN, AND D. ECK, *An improved relative self-attention mechanism for transformer with application to music generation*, ArXiv, abs/1809.04281 (2018).

[125] H. HUANG, Y. LIANG, N. DUAN, M. GONG, L. SHOU, D. JIANG, AND M. ZHOU, *Unicoder: A universal language encoder by pre-training with multiple cross-lingual tasks*, in Proceedings of the 2019 Conference on Empirical Methods in Natural Language Processing and the 9th International Joint Conference on Natural Language Processing, EMNLP-IJCNLP 2019, Hong Kong, China, November 3–7, 2019, K. Inui, J. Jiang, V. Ng, and X. Wan, eds., Association for Computational Linguistics, 2019, pp. 2485–2494.

[126] Z. HUANG, X. WANG, L. HUANG, C. HUANG, Y. WEI, H. SHI, AND W. LIU, *Ccnet: Criss-cross attention for semantic segmentation*, 2019 IEEE/CVF International Conference on Computer Vision (ICCV), (2019), pp. 603–612.

[127] D. A. HUDSON AND C. D. MANNING, *Compositional attention networks for machine reasoning*, arXiv preprint arXiv:1803.03067, (2018).

[128] D. HUPKES, S. VELDHOEN, AND W. ZUIDEMA, *Visualisation and'diagnostic classifiers' reveal how recurrent and recursive neural networks process hierarchical structure*, Journal of Artificial Intelligence Research, 61 (2018), pp. 907–926.

[129] P. INDYK AND R. MOTWANI, *Approximate nearest neighbors: towards removing the curse of dimensionality*, in STOC '98, 1998.

[130] S. IOFFE AND C. SZEGEDY, *Batch normalization: Accelerating deep network training by reducing internal covariate shift.*, CoRR, abs/1502.03167 (2015).

[131] R. IYER, Y. LI, H. LI, M. LEWIS, R. SUNDAR, AND K. SYCARA, *Transparency and explanation in deep reinforcement learning neural networks*, in Proceedings of the 2018 AAAI/ACM Conference on AI, Ethics, and Society, 2018, pp. 144–150.

[132] S. JAIN AND B. C. WALLACE, *Attention is not explanation*, arXiv preprint arXiv:1902.10186, (2019).

[133] W. JAMES AND F. H. BURKHARDT, *The principles of psychology, the works of William James*, Transactions of the Charles S. Peirce Society, 19 (1983).

[134] H. JIANG, B. KIM, M. Y. GUAN, AND M. R. GUPTA, *To trust or not to trust a classifier.*, in NeurIPS, 2018, pp. 5546–5557.

[135] K. K, Z. WANG, S. MAYHEW, AND D. ROTH, *Cross-lingual ability of multilingual BERT: an empirical study*, in 8th International Conference on Learning Representations, ICLR 2020, Addis Ababa, Ethiopia, April 26–30, 2020, OpenReview.net, 2020.

[136] L. KAISER AND I. SUTSKEVER, *Neural GPUs learn algorithms*, arXiv: Learning, (2016).

[137] D. KAKWANI, A. KUNCHUKUTTAN, S. GOLLA, G. N.C., A. BHATTACHARYYA, M. M. KHAPRA, AND P. KUMAR, *IndicNLPSuite: Monolingual Corpora, Evaluation Benchmarks and Pre-trained Multilingual Language Models for Indian Languages*, in Findings of EMNLP, 2020.

[138] K. S. KALYAN, A. RAJASEKHARAN, AND S. SANGEETHA, *AMMUS : A survey of transformer-based pretrained models in natural language processing*, CoRR, abs/2108.05542 (2021).

[139] F. KAMIRAN AND T. CALDERS, *Data preprocessing techniques for classification without discrimination*, Knowledge and Information Systems, 33 (2012), pp. 1–33.

[140] D. KANG, D. RAGHAVAN, P. BAILIS, AND M. ZAHARIA, *Model assertions for debugging machine learning*, in NeurIPS MLSys Workshop, 2018.

[141] S. KHANUJA, D. BANSAL, S. MEHTANI, S. KHOSLA, A. DEY, B. GOPALAN, D. K. MARGAM, P. AGGARWAL, R. T. NAGIPOGU, S. DAVE, S. GUPTA, S. C. B. GALI, V. SUBRAMANIAN,

AND P. TALUKDAR, *Muril: Multilingual representations for Indian languages*, 2021.

[142] N. KITAEV, L. KAISER, AND A. LEVSKAYA, *Reformer: The efficient transformer*, ArXiv, abs/2001.04451 (2020).

[143] G. KOBAYASHI, T. KURIBAYASHI, S. YOKOI, AND K. INUI, *Attention is not only a weight: Analyzing transformers with vector norms*, in EMNLP, 2020.

[144] T. KUDO AND J. RICHARDSON, *SentencePiece: A simple and language independent subword tokenizer and detokenizer for neural text processing*, in Proceedings of the 2018 Conference on Empirical Methods in Natural Language Processing: System Demonstrations, Brussels, Belgium, November 2018, Association for Computational Linguistics, pp. 66–71.

[145] G. LAI, Q. XIE, H. LIU, Y. YANG, AND E. H. HOVY, *Race: Large-scale reading comprehension dataset from examinations*, in EMNLP, 2017.

[146] G. LAMPLE AND A. CONNEAU, *Cross-lingual language model pretraining*, Advances in Neural Information Processing Systems (NeurIPS), (2019).

[147] S. LAPUSCHKIN, A. BINDER, G. MONTAVON, K.-R. MULLER, AND W. SAMEK, *Analyzing classifiers: Fisher vectors and deep neural networks*, in Proceedings of the IEEE Conference on Computer Vision and Pattern Recognition, 2016, pp. 2912–2920.

[148] A. LAUSCHER, V. RAVISHANKAR, I. VULIC, AND G. GLAVAS, *From zero to hero: On the limitations of zero-shot cross-lingual transfer with multilingual transformers*, CoRR, abs/2005.00633 (2020).

[149] Y. LECUN, *Une procédure d'apprentissage pour réseau a seuil asymmetrique (a learning scheme for asymmetric threshold networks)*, in Proceedings of Cognitiva 85, 1985, pp. 599–604.

[150] Y. LECUN, B. BOSER, J. S. DENKER, D. HENDERSON, R. E. HOWARD, W. HUBBARD, AND L. D. JACKEL, *Backpropagation applied to handwritten zip code recognition*, Neural Computation, 1 (1989), pp. 541–551.

[151] J. LEE, Y. LEE, J. KIM, A. R. KOSIOREK, S. CHOI, AND Y. TEH, *Set transformer: A framework for attention-based permutation-invariant neural networks*, in ICML, 2019.

[152] J. LEE, W. YOON, S. KIM, D. KIM, S. KIM, C. H. SO, AND J. KANG, *Biobert: a pre-trained biomedical language representation model for biomedical text mining*, Bioinformatics, 36 (2020), pp. 1234–1240.

[153] T. LEI, R. BARZILAY, AND T. JAAKKOLA, *Rationalizing neural predictions*, arXiv preprint arXiv:1606.04155, (2016).

[154] G. LETARTE, F. PARADIS, P. GIGUÈRE, AND F. LAVIOLETTE, *Importance of self-attention for sentiment analysis*, in Proceedings of the 2018 EMNLP Workshop BlackboxNLP: Analyzing and Interpreting Neural Networks for NLP, 2018, pp. 267–275.

[155] M. LEWIS, Y. LIU, N. GOYAL, M. GHAZVININEJAD, A. MOHAMED, O. LEVY, V. STOYANOV, AND L. ZETTLEMOYER, *BART: Denoising sequence-to-sequence pre-training for natural language generation, translation, and comprehension*, in Proceedings of the 58th Annual Meeting of the Association for Computational Linguistics, Online, July 2020, Association for Computational Linguistics, pp. 7871–7880.

[156] P. S. H. LEWIS, B. OGUZ, R. RINOTT, S. RIEDEL, AND H. SCHWENK, *MLQA: evaluating cross-lingual extractive question answering*, in Proceedings of the 58th Annual Meeting of the Association for Computational Linguistics, ACL 2020, Online, July 5–10, 2020, D. Jurafsky, J. Chai, N. Schluter, and J. R. Tetreault, eds., Association for Computational Linguistics, 2020, pp. 7315–7330.

[157] J. LI, W. MONROE, AND D. JURAFSKY, *Understanding neural networks through representation erasure*, arXiv preprint arXiv:1612.08220, (2016).

[158] J. LI, Z. TU, B. YANG, M. R. LYU, AND T. ZHANG, *Multi-head attention with disagreement regularization*, ArXiv, abs/1810.10183 (2018).

[159] O. LI, H. LIU, C. CHEN, AND C. RUDIN, *Deep learning for case-based reasoning through prototypes: A neural network that explains*

its predictions, in Proceedings of the AAAI Conference on Artificial Intelligence, vol. 32, 2018.

[160] Y. LIANG, N. DUAN, Y. GONG, N. WU, F. GUO, W. QI, M. GONG, L. SHOU, D. JIANG, G. CAO, X. FAN, R. ZHANG, R. AGRAWAL, E. CUI, S. WEI, T. BHARTI, Y. QIAO, J. CHEN, W. WU, S. LIU, F. YANG, D. CAMPOS, R. MAJUMDER, AND M. ZHOU, *XGLUE: A new benchmark dataset for cross-lingual pre-training, understanding and generation*, in Proceedings of the 2020 Conference on Empirical Methods in Natural Language Processing, EMNLP 2020, Online, November 16–20, 2020, B. Webber, T. Cohn, Y. He, and Y. Liu, eds., Association for Computational Linguistics, 2020, pp. 6008–6018.

[161] J. LIBOVICKÝ, R. ROSA, AND A. FRASER, *How language-neutral is multilingual bert?*, arXiv preprint arXiv:1911.03310, (2019).

[162] T. LIMISIEWICZ, D. MARECEK, AND R. ROSA, *Universal dependencies according to BERT: both more specific and more general*, in Proceedings of the 2020 Conference on Empirical Methods in Natural Language Processing: Findings, EMNLP 2020, Online Event, 16–20 November 2020, T. Cohn, Y. He, and Y. Liu, eds., vol. EMNLP 2020 of Findings of ACL, Association for Computational Linguistics, 2020, pp. 2710–2722.

[163] T. LIN, Y. WANG, X. LIU, AND X. QIU, *A survey of transformers*, ArXiv, abs/2106.04554 (2021).

[164] S. LINNAINMAA, *The representation of the cumulative rounding error of an algorithm as a Taylor expansion of the local rounding errors*, Master's thesis, Univ. Helsinki, 1970.

[165] C. LIU, T. HSU, Y. CHUANG, AND H. LEE, *A study of cross-lingual ability and language-specific information in multilingual BERT*, CoRR, abs/2004.09205 (2020).

[166] H. LIU, Q. YIN, AND W. Y. WANG, *Towards explainable nlp: A generative explanation framework for text classification*, arXiv preprint arXiv:1811.00196, (2018).

[167] P. J. LIU, M. SALEH, E. POT, B. GOODRICH, R. SEPASSI, L. KAISER, AND N. M. SHAZEER, *Generating Wikipedia by summarizing long sequences*, ArXiv, abs/1801.10198 (2018).

[168] Q. LIU, D. MCCARTHY, I. VULIĆ, AND A. KORHONEN, *Investigating cross-lingual alignment methods for contextualized embeddings with token-level evaluation*, in Proceedings of the 23rd Conference on Computational Natural Language Learning (CoNLL), Hong Kong, China, November 2019, Association for Computational Linguistics, pp. 33–43.

[169] Y. LIU, J. GU, N. GOYAL, X. LI, S. EDUNOV, M. GHAZVININEJAD, M. LEWIS, AND L. ZETTLEMOYER, *Multilingual denoising pre-training for neural machine translation*, Transactions of the Association for Computational Linguistics, 8 (2020), pp. 726–742.

[170] Y. LIU, M. OTT, N. GOYAL, J. DU, M. JOSHI, D. CHEN, O. LEVY, M. LEWIS, L. ZETTLEMOYER, AND V. STOYANOV, *Roberta: A robustly optimized bert pretraining approach*, ArXiv, abs/1907.11692 (2019).

[171] Z. LIU, G. I. WINATA, A. MADOTTO, AND P. FUNG, *Exploring fine-tuning techniques for pre-trained cross-lingual models via continual learning*, CoRR, abs/2004.14218 (2020).

[172] I. LOSHCHILOV AND F. HUTTER, *Decoupled weight decay regularization*, arXiv preprint arXiv:1711.05101, (2017).

[173] J. LU, D. BATRA, D. PARIKH, AND S. LEE, *ViLBERT: Pretraining task-agnostic visiolinguistic representations for vision-and-language tasks*, arXiv preprint arXiv:1908.02265, (2019).

[174] Y. LU, Z. LI, D. HE, Z. SUN, B. DONG, T. QIN, L. WANG, AND T.-Y. LIU, *Understanding and improving transformer from a multi-particle dynamic system point of view*, ArXiv, abs/1906.02762 (2019).

[175] F. LUO, W. WANG, J. LIU, Y. LIU, B. BI, S. HUANG, F. HUANG, AND L. SI, *{VECO}: Variable encoder-decoder pretraining for cross-lingual understanding and generation*, 2021.

[176] M. LUONG, H. PHAM, AND C. D. MANNING, *Effective approaches to attention-based neural machine translation*, CoRR, abs/1508.04025 (2015).

[177] X. MA, X. KONG, S. WANG, C. ZHOU, J. MAY, H. MA, AND L. ZETTLEMOYER, *Luna: Linear unified nested attention*, ArXiv, abs/2106.01540 (2021).

[178] A. MADRY, A. MAKELOV, L. SCHMIDT, D. TSIPRAS, AND A. VLADU, *Towards deep learning models resistant to adversarial attacks*, arXiv preprint arXiv:1706.06083, (2017).

[179] W. S. MCCULLOCH AND W. PITTS, *Neurocomputing: Foundations of research*, MIT Press, 1988, ch. A Logical Calculus of the Ideas Immanent in Nervous Activity, pp. 15–27.

[180] S. MEHTA, M. GHAZVININEJAD, S. IYER, L. ZETTLEMOYER, AND H. HAJISHIRZI, *Delight: Deep and light-weight transformer*, in ICLR, 2021.

[181] S. MEHTA, R. KONCEL-KEDZIORSKI, M. RASTEGARI, AND H. HAJISHIRZI, *Pyramidal recurrent unit for language modeling*, in EMNLP, 2018.

[182] ——, *Define: Deep factorized input word embeddings for neural sequence modeling*, ArXiv, abs/1911.12385 (2020).

[183] T. MIKOLOV, K. CHEN, G. CORRADO, AND J. DEAN, *Efficient estimation of word representations in vector space*, CoRR, abs/1301.3781 (2013).

[184] T. MIKOLOV, M. KARAFIÁT, L. BURGET, J. CERNOCKÝ, AND S. KHUDANPUR, *Recurrent neural network based language model.*, in INTERSPEECH, T. Kobayashi, K. Hirose, and S. Nakamura, eds., ISCA, 2010, pp. 1045–1048.

[185] T. MIKOLOV, I. SUTSKEVER, K. CHEN, G. S. CORRADO, AND J. DEAN, *Distributed representations of words and phrases and their compositionality*, in Advances in Neural Information Processing Systems 26, C. J. C. Burges, L. Bottou, M. Welling, Z. Ghahramani, and K. Q. Weinberger, eds., Curran Associates, Inc., 2013, pp. 3111–3119.

[186] M. MINSKY AND S. A. PAPERT, *Perceptrons: An introduction to computational geometry*, MIT press, 2017.

[187] G. MONTAVON, S. LAPUSCHKIN, A. BINDER, W. SAMEK, AND K.-R. MÜLLER, *Explaining nonlinear classification decisions with deep Taylor decomposition*, Pattern Recognition, 65 (2017), pp. 211–222.

[188] G. MONTAVON, W. SAMEK, AND K.-R. MÜLLER, *Methods for interpreting and understanding deep neural networks*, Digital Signal Processing, 73 (2018), pp. 1–15.

[189] S.-M. MOOSAVI-DEZFOOLI, A. FAWZI, O. FAWZI, AND P. FROSSARD, *Universal adversarial perturbations*, in Proceedings of the IEEE Conference on Computer Vision and Pattern Recognition, 2017, pp. 1765–1773.

[190] N. MOSTAFAZADEH, M. ROTH, A. LOUIS, N. CHAMBERS, AND J. F. ALLEN, *LSDSem 2017 shared task: The story cloze test*, in LSDSem@EACL, 2017.

[191] A. NGUYEN, J. YOSINSKI, AND J. CLUNE, *Deep neural networks are easily fooled: High confidence predictions for unrecognizable images*, in Proceedings of the IEEE Conference on Computer Vision and Pattern Recognition, 2015, pp. 427–436.

[192] J. NIVRE, M. ABRAMS, Ž. AGIĆ, L. AHRENBERG, L. ANTONSEN, K. APLONOVA, M. J. ARANZABE, G. ARUTIE, M. ASAHARA, L. ATEYAH, M. ATTIA, AND ET. AL., *Universal dependencies 2.3*, 2018. LINDAT/CLARIAH-CZ digital library at the Institute of Formal and Applied Linguistics (ÚFAL), Faculty of Mathematics and Physics, Charles University.

[193] J. NIVRE, R. BLOKLAND, N. PARTANEN, AND M. RIESSLER, *Universal dependencies 2.2*, November 2018.

[194] X. OUYANG, S. WANG, C. PANG, Y. SUN, H. TIAN, H. WU, AND H. WANG, *ERNIE-M: Enhanced multilingual representation by aligning cross-lingual semantics with monolingual corpora*, 2021.

[195] D. H. PARK, L. A. HENDRICKS, Z. AKATA, A. ROHRBACH, B. SCHIELE, T. DARRELL, AND M. ROHRBACH, *Multimodal explanations: Justifying decisions and pointing to the evidence*, in Proceedings of the IEEE Conference on Computer Vision and Pattern Recognition, 2018, pp. 8779–8788.

[196] D. B. PARKER, *Learning-logic*, Tech. Rep. TR-47, Center for Comp. Research in Economics and Management Sci., MIT, 1985.

[197] M. PETERS, M. NEUMANN, M. IYYER, M. GARDNER, C. CLARK, K. LEE, AND L. ZETTLEMOYER, *Deep contextualized word representations*, in Proceedings of the 2018 Conference

of the North American Chapter of the Association for Computational Linguistics: Human Language Technologies, Volume 1 (Long Papers), New Orleans, Louisiana, June 2018, Association for Computational Linguistics, pp. 2227–2237.

[198] J. PHANG, I. CALIXTO, P. M. HTUT, Y. PRUKSACHATKUN, H. LIU, C. VANIA, K. KANN, AND S. R. BOWMAN, *English intermediate-task training improves zero-shot cross-lingual transfer too*, in Proceedings of the 1st Conference of the Asia-Pacific Chapter of the Association for Computational Linguistics and the 10th International Joint Conference on Natural Language Processing, AACL/IJCNLP 2020, Suzhou, China, December 4–7, 2020, K. Wong, K. Knight, and H. Wu, eds., Association for Computational Linguistics, 2020, pp. 557–575.

[199] T. PIRES, E. SCHLINGER, AND D. GARRETTE, *How multilingual is multilingual bert?*, in Proceedings of the 57th Conference of the Association for Computational Linguistics, ACL 2019, Florence, Italy, July 28–August 2, 2019, Volume 1: Long Papers, A. Korhonen, D. R. Traum, and L. Màrquez, eds., Association for Computational Linguistics, 2019, pp. 4996–5001.

[200] E. M. PONTI, G. GLAVAŠ, O. MAJEWSKA, Q. LIU, I. VULIĆ, AND A. KORHONEN, *XCOPA: A multilingual dataset for causal commonsense reasoning*, in Proceedings of the 2020 Conference on Empirical Methods in Natural Language Processing (EMNLP), 2020.

[201] O. PRESS, N. A. SMITH, AND O. LEVY, *Improving transformer models by reordering their sublayers*, in ACL, 2020.

[202] A. RADFORD AND K. NARASIMHAN, *Improving language understanding by generative pre-training*, 2018.

[203] A. RADFORD, J. WU, R. CHILD, D. LUAN, D. AMODEI, AND I. SUTSKEVER, *Language models are unsupervised multitask learners*, 2019.

[204] J. W. RAE, A. POTAPENKO, S. M. JAYAKUMAR, AND T. LILLICRAP, *Compressive transformers for long-range sequence modelling*, ArXiv, abs/1911.05507 (2020).

[205] C. RAFFEL, N. M. SHAZEER, A. ROBERTS, K. LEE, S. NARANG, M. MATENA, Y. ZHOU, W. LI, AND P. J. LIU, *Exploring the limits of transfer learning with a unified text-to-text transformer*, ArXiv, abs/1910.10683 (2020).

[206] M. RAGHU, J. GILMER, J. YOSINSKI, AND J. SOHL-DICKSTEIN, *SVCCA: Singular vector canonical correlation analysis for deep learning dynamics and interpretability*, arXiv preprint arXiv:1706.05806, (2017).

[207] G. RAS, M. VAN GERVEN, AND P. HASELAGER, *Explanation methods in deep learning: Users, values, concerns and challenges*, in Explainable and Interpretable Models in Computer Vision and Machine Learning, Springer, 2018, pp. 19–36.

[208] M. T. RIBEIRO, S. SINGH, AND C. GUESTRIN, *" why should i trust you?" explaining the predictions of any classifier*, in Proceedings of the 22nd ACM SIGKDD International Conference on Knowledge Discovery and Data Mining, 2016, pp. 1135–1144.

[209] ――――, *Anchors: High-precision model-agnostic explanations*, in Proceedings of the AAAI Conference on Artificial Intelligence, vol. 32, 2018.

[210] M. ROBNIK-ŠIKONJA AND I. KONONENKO, *Explaining classifications for individual instances*, IEEE Transactions on Knowledge and Data Engineering, 20 (2008), pp. 589–600.

[211] T. ROCKTÄSCHEL, E. GREFENSTETTE, K. M. HERMANN, T. KOČISKÝ, AND P. BLUNSOM, *Reasoning about entailment with neural attention*, arXiv preprint arXiv:1509.06664, (2015).

[212] F. ROSENBLATT, *The perceptron: A probabilistic model for information storage and organization in the brain*, Psychological Review, (1958), pp. 65–386.

[213] D. ROTHMAN, *Transformers for Natural Language Processing*, Packt, 2021.

[214] A. ROY, M. SAFFAR, A. VASWANI, AND D. GRANGIER, *Efficient content-based sparse attention with routing transformers*, Transactions of the Association for Computational Linguistics, 9 (2021), pp. 53–68.

[215] U. ROY, N. CONSTANT, R. AL-RFOU, A. BARUA, A. PHILLIPS, AND Y. YANG, *LAReQA: Language-agnostic answer retrieval from a multilingual pool*, in Proceedings of the 2020 Conference on Empirical Methods in Natural Language Processing (EMNLP), Online, November 2020, Association for Computational Linguistics, pp. 5919–5930.

[216] S. RUDER, N. CONSTANT, J. BOTHA, A. SIDDHANT, O. FIRAT, J. FU, P. LIU, J. HU, G. NEUBIG, AND M. JOHNSON, *XTREME-R: towards more challenging and nuanced multilingual evaluation*, CoRR, abs/2104.07412 (2021).

[217] D. E. RUMELHART, G. E. HINTON, AND R. J. WILLIAMS, *Neurocomputing: Foundations of research*, MIT Press, 1988, ch. Learning Representations by Back-propagating Errors, pp. 696–699.

[218] P. SAMANGOUEI, M. KABKAB, AND R. CHELLAPPA, *Defense-GAN: Protecting classifiers against adversarial attacks using generative models*, arXiv preprint arXiv:1805.06605, (2018).

[219] S. SCHNEIDER, A. BAEVSKI, R. COLLOBERT, AND M. AULI, *wav2vec: Unsupervised pre-training for speech recognition*, in INTERSPEECH, 2019.

[220] M. SCHUSTER AND K. NAKAJIMA, *Japanese and Korean voice search*, 2012 IEEE International Conference on Acoustics, Speech and Signal Processing (ICASSP), (2012), pp. 5149–5152.

[221] H. SCHWENK AND X. LI, *A corpus for multilingual document classification in eight languages*, in Proceedings of the Eleventh International Conference on Language Resources and Evaluation (LREC 2018), N. C. C. chair), K. Choukri, C. Cieri, T. Declerck, S. Goggi, K. Hasida, H. Isahara, B. Maegaard, J. Mariani, H. Mazo, A. Moreno, J. Odijk, S. Piperidis, and T. Tokunaga, eds., Paris, France, may 2018, European Language Resources Association (ELRA).

[222] R. SENNRICH, B. HADDOW, AND A. BIRCH, *Improving neural machine translation models with monolingual data*, 2016.

[223] R. SENNRICH, B. HADDOW, AND A. BIRCH, *Neural machine translation of rare words with subword units*, in Proceedings of the 54th Annual Meeting of the Association for Computational

Linguistics (Volume 1: Long Papers), Berlin, Germany, August 2016, Association for Computational Linguistics, pp. 1715–1725.

[224] P. SHAW, J. USZKOREIT, AND A. VASWANI, *Self-attention with relative position representations*, in NAACL-HLT, 2018.

[225] N. SHAZEER, A. MIRHOSEINI, K. MAZIARZ, A. DAVIS, Q. LE, G. HINTON, AND J. DEAN, *Outrageously large neural networks: The sparsely-gated mixture-of-experts layer*, arXiv preprint arXiv:1701.06538, (2017).

[226] N. M. SHAZEER, *Fast transformer decoding: One write-head is all you need*, ArXiv, abs/1911.02150 (2019).

[227] N. M. SHAZEER, Z. LAN, Y. CHENG, N. DING, AND L. HOU, *Talking-heads attention*, ArXiv, abs/2003.02436 (2020).

[228] A. SHRIKUMAR, P. GREENSIDE, AND A. KUNDAJE, *Learning important features through propagating activation differences*, in International Conference on Machine Learning, PMLR, 2017, pp. 3145–3153.

[229] J. SINGH, B. MCCANN, R. SOCHER, AND C. XIONG, *Bert is not an interlingua and the bias of tokenization*, in Proceedings of the 2nd Workshop on Deep Learning Approaches for Low-Resource NLP (DeepLo 2019), 2019, pp. 47–55.

[230] R. SOCHER, A. PERELYGIN, J. WU, J. CHUANG, C. D. MANNING, A. NG, AND C. POTTS, *Recursive deep models for semantic compositionality over a sentiment treebank*, in EMNLP, 2013.

[231] K. SONG, X. TAN, T. QIN, J. LU, AND T.-Y. LIU, *Mass: Masked sequence to sequence pre-training for language generation*, in ICML, 2019.

[232] J. SU, Y. LU, S. PAN, B. WEN, AND Y. LIU, *Roformer: Enhanced transformer with rotary position embedding*, ArXiv, abs/2104.09864 (2021).

[233] J. SU, D. V. VARGAS, AND K. SAKURAI, *One pixel attack for fooling deep neural networks*, IEEE Transactions on Evolutionary Computation, 23 (2019), pp. 828–841.

[234] S. SUBRAMANIAN, R. COLLOBERT, M. RANZATO, AND Y.-L. BOUREAU, *Multi-scale transformer language models*, ArXiv, abs/2005.00581 (2020).

[235] S. SUKHBAATAR, E. GRAVE, P. BOJANOWSKI, AND A. JOULIN, *Adaptive attention span in transformers*, in ACL, 2019.

[236] M. SUNDARARAJAN, A. TALY, AND Q. YAN, *Axiomatic attribution for deep networks*, in International Conference on Machine Learning, PMLR, 2017, pp. 3319–3328.

[237] I. SUTSKEVER, *Training recurrent neural networks*, Ph.D. Thesis from University of Toronto, Toronto, Ont., Canada, (2013).

[238] I. SUTSKEVER, O. VINYALS, AND Q. V. LE, *Sequence to sequence learning with neural networks*, in Advances in neural information processing systems, 2014, pp. 3104–3112.

[239] R. S. SUTTON AND A. G. BARTO, *Reinforcement learning: An introduction*, IEEE Transactions on Neural Networks, 16 (2005), pp. 285–286.

[240] S. TAN, R. CARUANA, G. HOOKER, P. KOCH, AND A. GORDO, *Learning global additive explanations for neural nets using model distillation*, arXiv preprint arXiv:1801.08640, (2018).

[241] Y. TAY, D. BAHRI, D. METZLER, D.-C. JUAN, Z. ZHAO, AND C. ZHENG, *Synthesizer: Rethinking self-attention in transformer models*, ArXiv, abs/2005.00743 (2021).

[242] Y. TAY, D. BAHRI, L. YANG, D. METZLER, AND D.-C. JUAN, *Sparse Sinkhorn attention*, in ICML, 2020.

[243] Y. TAY, M. DEHGHANI, D. BAHRI, AND D. METZLER, *Efficient transformers: A survey*, ArXiv, abs/2009.06732 (2020).

[244] I. TENNEY, D. DAS, AND E. PAVLICK, *BERT rediscovers the classical NLP pipeline*, in Proceedings of the 57th Annual Meeting of the Association for Computational Linguistics, July 2019, pp. 4593–4601.

[245] I. TENNEY, P. XIA, B. CHEN, A. WANG, A. POLIAK, R. T. MCCOY, N. KIM, B. VAN DURME, S. R. BOWMAN, D. DAS, ET AL., *What do you learn from context? probing for sentence*

structure in contextualized word representations, arXiv preprint arXiv:1905.06316, (2019).

[246] E. F. TJONG KIM SANG, *Introduction to the CoNLL-2002 shared task: Language-independent named entity recognition*, in COLING-02: The 6th Conference on Natural Language Learning 2002 (CoNLL-2002), 2002.

[247] E. F. TJONG KIM SANG AND F. DE MEULDER, *Introduction to the CoNLL-2003 shared task: Language-independent named entity recognition*, in Proceedings of the Seventh Conference on Natural Language Learning at HLT-NAACL 2003, 2003, pp. 142–147.

[248] J. L. UDAY KAMATH AND J. WHITAKER, *Deep Learning for NLP and Speech Recognition*, 2019.

[249] V. VALKOV, *Sentiment Analysis with BERT and Transformers by Hugging Face using PyTorch and Python.* `https://bit.ly/32Mb2mw`, 2020.

[250] A. VAN DEN OORD, Y. LI, AND O. VINYALS, *Representation learning with contrastive predictive coding*, ArXiv, abs/1807.03748 (2018).

[251] A. VAN DEN OORD, Y. LI, AND O. VINYALS, *Representation learning with contrastive predictive coding*, 2019.

[252] K. R. VARSHNEY AND H. ALEMZADEH, *On the safety of machine learning: Cyber-physical systems, decision sciences, and data products*, Big data, 5 (2017), pp. 246–255.

[253] A. VASWANI, N. SHAZEER, N. PARMAR, J. USZKOREIT, L. JONES, A. N. GOMEZ, L. KAISER, AND I. POLOSUKHIN, *Attention is all you need*, CoRR, abs/1706.03762 (2017).

[254] A. VASWANI, N. M. SHAZEER, N. PARMAR, J. USZKOREIT, L. JONES, A. N. GOMEZ, L. KAISER, AND I. POLOSUKHIN, *Attention is all you need*, ArXiv, abs/1706.03762 (2017).

[255] J. VIG, *A multiscale visualization of attention in the transformer model*, in Proceedings of the 57th Annual Meeting of the Association for Computational Linguistics: System Demonstrations, Florence, Italy, July 2019, Association for Computational Linguistics, pp. 37–42.

[256] A. VYAS, A. KATHAROPOULOS, AND F. FLEURET, *Fast transformers with clustered attention*, ArXiv, abs/2007.04825 (2020).

[257] A. WANG, A. SINGH, J. MICHAEL, F. HILL, O. LEVY, AND S. BOWMAN, *GLUE: A multi-task benchmark and analysis platform for natural language understanding*, in Proceedings of the 2018 EMNLP Workshop BlackboxNLP: Analyzing and Interpreting Neural Networks for NLP, Brussels, Belgium, November 2018, Association for Computational Linguistics, pp. 353–355.

[258] C. WANG, A. WU, J. M. PINO, A. BAEVSKI, M. AULI, AND A. CONNEAU, *Large-scale self- and semi-supervised learning for speech translation*, ArXiv, abs/2104.06678 (2021).

[259] S. WANG, B. Z. LI, M. KHABSA, H. FANG, AND H. MA, *Linformer: Self-attention with linear complexity*, ArXiv, abs/2006.04768 (2020).

[260] X. WANG, Y. JIANG, N. BACH, T. WANG, F. HUANG, AND K. TU, *Structure-level knowledge distillation for multilingual sequence labeling*, in Proceedings of the 58th Annual Meeting of the Association for Computational Linguistics, ACL 2020, Online, July 5–10, 2020, D. Jurafsky, J. Chai, N. Schluter, and J. R. Tetreault, eds., Association for Computational Linguistics, 2020, pp. 3317–3330.

[261] Y. WANG, W. CHE, J. GUO, Y. LIU, AND T. LIU, *Cross-lingual BERT transformation for zero-shot dependency parsing*, in Proceedings of the 2019 Conference on Empirical Methods in Natural Language Processing and the 9th International Joint Conference on Natural Language Processing, EMNLP-IJCNLP 2019, Hong Kong, China, November 3–7, 2019, K. Inui, J. Jiang, V. Ng, and X. Wan, eds., Association for Computational Linguistics, 2019, pp. 5720–5726.

[262] Z. WANG, Y. MA, Z. LIU, AND J. TANG, *R-transformer: Recurrent neural network enhanced transformer*, ArXiv, abs/1907.05572 (2019).

[263] Z. WANG, J. XIE, R. XU, Y. YANG, G. NEUBIG, AND J. G. CARBONELL, *Cross-lingual alignment vs joint training: A comparative study and A simple unified framework*, in 8th Interna-

tional Conference on Learning Representations, ICLR 2020, Addis Ababa, Ethiopia, April 26–30, 2020, OpenReview.net, 2020.

[264] A. WARSTADT, A. SINGH, AND S. R. BOWMAN, *Neural network acceptability judgments*, arXiv preprint arXiv:1805.12471, (2018).

[265] D. WATTS AND S. STROGATZ, *Collective dynamics of 'small-world' networks*, Nature, 393 (1998), pp. 440–442.

[266] X. WEI, R. WENG, Y. HU, L. XING, H. YU, AND W. LUO, *On learning universal representations across languages*, in 9th International Conference on Learning Representations, ICLR 2021, Virtual Event, Austria, May 3–7, 2021, OpenReview.net, 2021.

[267] P. J. WERBOS, *Beyond Regression: New Tools for Prediction and Analysis in the Behavioral Sciences*, PhD thesis, Harvard University, 1974.

[268] J. WHITTLESTONE, R. NYRUP, A. ALEXANDROVA, AND S. CAVE, *The role and limits of principles in ai ethics: towards a focus on tensions*, in Proceedings of the 2019 AAAI/ACM Conference on AI, Ethics, and Society, 2019, pp. 195–200.

[269] S. WIEGREFFE AND Y. PINTER, *Attention is not not explanation*, arXiv preprint arXiv:1908.04626, (2019).

[270] C. WU, F. WU, T. QI, AND Y. HUANG, *Hi-transformer: Hierarchical interactive transformer for efficient and effective long document modeling*, ArXiv, abs/2106.01040 (2021).

[271] S. WU AND M. DREDZE, *Beto, Bentz, Becas: The surprising cross-lingual effectiveness of BERT*, in Proceedings of the 2019 Conference on Empirical Methods in Natural Language Processing and the 9th International Joint Conference on Natural Language Processing, EMNLP-IJCNLP 2019, Hong Kong, China, November 3–7, 2019, K. Inui, J. Jiang, V. Ng, and X. Wan, eds., Association for Computational Linguistics, 2019, pp. 833–844.

[272] Y. WU, M. SCHUSTER, Z. CHEN, Q. V. LE, M. NOROUZI, W. MACHEREY, M. KRIKUN, Y. CAO, Q. GAO, K. MACHEREY, ET AL., *Google's neural machine translation system: Bridging the gap between human and machine translation*, arXiv preprint arXiv:1609.08144, (2016).

[273] Y. Wu, M. Schuster, Z. Chen, Q. V. Le, M. Norouzi, W. Macherey, M. Krikun, Y. Cao, Q. Gao, K. Macherey, J. Klingner, A. Shah, M. Johnson, X. Liu, L. Kaiser, S. Gouws, Y. Kato, T. Kudo, H. Kazawa, K. Stevens, G. Kurian, N. Patil, W. Wang, C. Young, J. Smith, J. Riesa, A. Rudnick, O. Vinyals, G. Corrado, M. Hughes, and J. Dean, *Google's neural machine translation system: Bridging the gap between human and machine translation*, CoRR, abs/1609.08144 (2016).

[274] Z. Wu, Z. Liu, J. Lin, Y. Lin, and S. Han, *Lite transformer with long-short range attention*, ArXiv, abs/2004.11886 (2020).

[275] N. Xie, G. Ras, M. van Gerven, and D. Doran, *Explainable deep learning: A field guide for the uninitiated*, arXiv preprint arXiv:2004.14545, (2020).

[276] J. Xin, R. Tang, J. Lee, Y. Yu, and J. J. Lin, *DeeBERT: Dynamic early exiting for accelerating bert inference*, in ACL, 2020.

[277] Y. Xiong, Z. Zeng, R. Chakraborty, M. Tan, G. M. Fung, Y. Li, and V. Singh, *Nyströmformer: A Nyström-based algorithm for approximating self-attention*, in AAAI, 2021.

[278] K. Xu, J. Ba, R. Kiros, K. Cho, A. Courville, R. Salakhudinov, R. Zemel, and Y. Bengio, *Show, attend and tell: Neural image caption generation with visual attention*, in International conference on machine learning, PMLR, 2015, pp. 2048–2057.

[279] M. Xu, L. yu Duan, J. Cai, L. Chia, C. Xu, and Q. Tian, *HMM-based Audio Keyword Generation*, in PCM, 2004.

[280] L. Xue, A. Barua, N. Constant, R. Al-Rfou, S. Narang, M. Kale, A. Roberts, and C. Raffel, *ByT5: Towards a token-free future with pre-trained byte-to-byte models*, ArXiv, abs/2105.13626 (2021).

[281] L. Xue, N. Constant, A. Roberts, M. Kale, R. Al-Rfou, A. Siddhant, A. Barua, and C. Raffel, *mT5: A massively multilingual pre-trained text-to-text transformer*, in NAACL, 2021.

[282] J. YANG, S. MA, D. ZHANG, S. WU, Z. LI, AND M. ZHOU, *Alternating language modeling for cross-lingual pre-training*, Proceedings of the AAAI Conference on Artificial Intelligence, 34 (2020), pp. 9386–9393.

[283] Y. YANG, G. H. ÁBREGO, S. YUAN, M. GUO, Q. SHEN, D. CER, Y. SUNG, B. STROPE, AND R. KURZWEIL, *Improving multilingual sentence embedding using bi-directional dual encoder with additive margin softmax*, CoRR, abs/1902.08564 (2019).

[284] Y. YANG, D. M. CER, A. AHMAD, M. GUO, J. LAW, N. CONSTANT, G. H. ÁBREGO, S. YUAN, C. TAR, Y.-H. SUNG, B. STROPE, AND R. KURZWEIL, *Multilingual universal sentence encoder for semantic retrieval*, in ACL, 2020.

[285] Y. YANG, Y. ZHANG, C. TAR, AND J. BALDRIDGE, *PAWS-X: A Cross-lingual Adversarial Dataset for Paraphrase Identification*, in Proc. of EMNLP, 2019.

[286] Z. YANG, D. YANG, C. DYER, X. HE, A. SMOLA, AND E. HOVY, *Hierarchical attention networks for document classification*, in Proceedings of the 2016 Conference of the North American Chapter of the Association for Computational Linguistics: Human Language Technologies, 2016, pp. 1480–1489.

[287] Q. YANG WU, Z. LAN, J. GU, AND Z. YU, *Memformer: The memory-augmented transformer*, ArXiv, abs/2010.06891 (2020).

[288] J. YIM, D. JOO, J. BAE, AND J. KIM, *A gift from knowledge distillation: Fast optimization, network minimization and transfer learning*, in Proceedings of the IEEE Conference on Computer Vision and Pattern Recognition, 2017, pp. 4133–4141.

[289] P. YIN, G. NEUBIG, W.-T. YIH, AND S. RIEDEL, *TaBERT: Pretraining for joint understanding of textual and tabular data*, in Proceedings of the 58th Annual Meeting of the Association for Computational Linguistics, Online, July 2020, Association for Computational Linguistics, pp. 8413–8426.

[290] C. YING LEE AND J. R. GLASS, *A nonparametric Bayesian approach to acoustic model discovery*, in ACL, 2012.

[291] X. YUAN, P. HE, Q. ZHU, AND X. LI, *Adversarial examples: Attacks and defenses for deep learning*, IEEE transactions on neural networks and learning systems, 30 (2019), pp. 2805–2824.

[292] M. ZAHEER, G. GURUGANESH, K. A. DUBEY, J. AINSLIE, C. ALBERTI, S. ONTAÑÓN, P. PHAM, A. RAVULA, Q. WANG, L. YANG, AND A. AHMED, *Big bird: Transformers for longer sequences*, ArXiv, abs/2007.14062 (2020).

[293] R. ZELLERS, Y. BISK, A. FARHADI, AND Y. CHOI, *From recognition to cognition: Visual commonsense reasoning*, in Proceedings of the IEEE/CVF Conference on Computer Vision and Pattern Recognition, 2019, pp. 6720–6731.

[294] Q. ZHANG, R. CAO, Y. N. WU, AND S.-C. ZHU, *Growing interpretable part graphs on ConvNets via multi-shot learning*, in Proceedings of the AAAI Conference on Artificial Intelligence, vol. 31, 2017.

[295] W. E. ZHANG, Q. Z. SHENG, A. A. F. ALHAZMI, AND C. LI, *Generating textual adversarial examples for deep learning models: A survey*, CoRR, abs/1901.06796, (2019).

[296] X. ZHANG, F. WEI, AND M. ZHOU, *Hibert: Document level pretraining of hierarchical bidirectional transformers for document summarization*, in ACL, 2019.

[297] X. ZHANG, J. J. ZHAO, AND Y. A. LECUN, *Character-level convolutional networks for text classification*, ArXiv, abs/1509.01626 (2015).

[298] W. ZHAO, S. EGER, J. BJERVA, AND I. AUGENSTEIN, *Inducing language-agnostic multilingual representations*, CoRR, abs/2008.09112 (2020).

[299] Y. ZHAO, L. DONG, Y. SHEN, Z. ZHANG, F. WEI, AND W. CHEN, *Memory-efficient differentiable transformer architecture search*, in FINDINGS, 2021.

[300] W. ZHENG, Z. CHEN, J. LU, AND J. ZHOU, *Hardness-aware deep metric learning*, in Proceedings of the IEEE/CVF Conference on Computer Vision and Pattern Recognition (CVPR), June 2019.

[301] B. ZHOU, A. KHOSLA, A. LAPEDRIZA, A. OLIVA, AND A. TORRALBA, *Object detectors emerge in deep scene cnns*, arXiv preprint arXiv:1412.6856, (2014).

[302] H. ZHOU, S. ZHANG, J. PENG, S. ZHANG, J. LI, H. XIONG, AND W. ZHANG, *Informer: Beyond efficient transformer for long sequence time-series forecasting*, in AAAI, 2021.

[303] Y. ZHU, R. KIROS, R. S. ZEMEL, R. SALAKHUTDINOV, R. URTASUN, A. TORRALBA, AND S. FIDLER, *Aligning books and movies: Towards story-like visual explanations by watching movies and reading books*, 2015 IEEE International Conference on Computer Vision (ICCV), (2015), pp. 19–27.

[304] L. M. ZINTGRAF, T. S. COHEN, T. ADEL, AND M. WELLING, *Visualizing deep neural network decisions: Prediction difference analysis*, arXiv preprint arXiv:1702.04595, (2017).

[305] P. ZWEIGENBAUM, S. SHAROFF, AND R. RAPP, *Overview of the second BUCC shared task: Spotting parallel sentences in comparable corpora*, in Proceedings of the 10th Workshop on Building and Using Comparable Corpora, Vancouver, Canada, August 2017, Association for Computational Linguistics, pp. 60–67.

Index

Milton Keynes UK
Ingram Content Group UK Ltd.
UKHW031532071024
449327UK00005B/100

9 780367 771652